Encoded In The Stars
The Science of Destiny and the Blueprint of the Soul

By: Deilen Michelle Villegas, Ph.D.

Copyright© 2026 by **Dr. Deilen Michelle Villegas, Ph.D., DNM, HHP**
All rights reserved.

No part of this book may be reproduced, stored in a retrieval system, or transmitted in any form or by any means—electronic, mechanical, photocopying, recording, or otherwise—without prior written permission from the author, except for brief quotations used in reviews or scholarly works.

This publication is intended for educational and informational purposes only. The author and publisher are not responsible for any adverse effects or consequences resulting from the use of any information contained in this book. Readers are encouraged to consult qualified professionals regarding personal health, psychological, or spiritual concerns.

For permissions, contact publisher:

Published by The Shamanic Goddess, LLC
Charlotte, North Carolina, United States
www.DrDeilenMVillegas.com | www.TheShamanicGoddess.com

Book Title: Encoded in the Stars: The Science of Destiny and the Blueprint of the Soul

Publisher: The Shamanic Goddess, LLC

Printed in the United States of America

First Edition – 2026

ISBN: 978-1-969550-05-8

All images, diagrams, and content are the intellectual property of the author unless otherwise noted. Quotations and references are credited to their original sources in accordance with fair use and academic citation standards.

Disclaimer

This book is a work of integrative research and reflective education that merges science, spirituality, psychology, and ancient wisdom. The information presented within **Encoded in the Stars: The Science of Destiny and the Blueprint of the Soul** is intended for **educational, inspirational, and self-development purposes only**.

The content of this book does **not constitute medical, psychological, financial, or legal advice**. Readers should not use the information provided as a substitute for professional diagnosis, treatment, or guidance from qualified health care practitioners, mental health professionals, or licensed advisors.

The author's intention is to bridge modern science and spiritual philosophy through an interdisciplinary approach that encourages self-awareness, holistic growth, and the pursuit of purpose. While references to scientific studies, metaphysical systems, and cultural traditions are included, the interpretations and correlations presented are based on both scholarly research and the author's professional and spiritual experience.

The author and publisher disclaim any liability for the misuse, misinterpretation, or application of the material presented. Each reader assumes full responsibility for their personal choices and experiences arising from engaging with this work.

By reading this book, you acknowledge that your life path, beliefs, and choices are uniquely your own, and that the journey of discovery and self-realization is a deeply individual process.

TABLE OF CONTENTS

Copyright

Disclaimer

Dedication

About the Author

Preface

INTRODUCTION: The Code of Existence

CHAPTER 1: The Universe Within You: The Science of Destiny

CHAPTER 2: The Celestial Blueprint: Understanding Natal Charts

CHAPTER 3: Time, Place, and Purpose: Astrocartography and Energy Portals

CHAPTER 4: The Mathematics of the Soul: Numerology and Life Path Numbers

CHAPTER 5: The Human Design Experiment

CHAPTER 6: Lineage, Karma, and Genetic Memory

CHAPTER 7: Activation Points: Destiny Through Experience

CHAPTER 8: Synchronicity and the Language of the Universe

CHAPTER 9: The Frequency of Fulfillment: Living Your Design

CHAPTER 10: The Return to Source: Purpose as Sacred Responsibility

BONUS CHAPTER: Medical Astrology: The

Body as Cosmic Intelligence

CONCLUSION: Remembering What You've Always Been

APPENDICES
- **Appendix A:** Glossary of Cosmic Sciences
- **Appendix B:** Recommended Tools & Platforms
- **Appendix C:** Scientific & Metaphysical Research Citations

Dedication

To the Seekers—
the ones who have questioned the "why" behind every storm,
the "how" behind every rebirth,
and the "when" behind every breakthrough.

To those who have walked through shadow and still looked up at the stars—
this book is for you.

May you come to remember that nothing about you is accidental.
Your existence was written in divine mathematics,
encoded in the vibration of time,
and awakened by the breath of your own becoming.

To the ancestors whose light continues to guide us—
thank you for writing our stories in the constellations,
for whispering wisdom through our blood,
and for reminding us that destiny is not found; it is remembered.

And to my children, Azrael, Xavier, and Isabel—
you are living proof that the universe speaks in legacy,
that every generation carries the keys to unlock a higher truth.
May you always follow your stars and trust the sacred blueprint within you.

About The Author

Dr. Deilen Michelle Villegas, Ph.D., DNM, HHP, BCETS, BCMHC

Dr. Deilen Michelle Villegas is a Board-Certified Holistic Health and Wellness Practitioner, Metaphysician, and Clinical Mental Health Counselor whose life's work bridges the realms of science, spirituality, and ancestral wisdom. As the Founder and CEO of *The Shamanic Goddess, LLC*, Dr. Villegas has devoted over eighteen years to the art and science of integrative healing—guiding individuals toward wholeness through a mind-body-spirit approach rooted in evidence, energy, and empowerment.

Her academic foundation is as vast as her spiritual insight. Holding a Ph.D. in Organizational Leadership, a Ph.D. in Metaphysical Science and Natural Medicine, an M.Sc. in Complementary & Integrative Medicine, and an M.A. in Clinical Mental Health Counseling, Dr. Villegas unites the precision of research with the intuition of ancient wisdom traditions. Her professional experience spans Internal Medicine, Pediatrics, Oncology, OB/GYN, and Behavioral Health—giving her a deep understanding of the human condition from both a clinical and energetic perspective.

A passionate educator and visionary, Dr. Villegas is known

for her transformative teachings on trauma recovery, nervous system regulation, holistic health, and metaphysical sciences. Through her writings, lectures, and community programs, she empowers readers and practitioners alike to see beyond symptoms—to perceive the sacred systems of consciousness, energy, and biology that compose the human experience.

In *Encoded in the Stars: The Science of Destiny and the Blueprint of the Soul*, Dr. Villegas continues her mission to demystify the intersection of quantum physics and spirituality, showing readers how their purpose, gifts, and challenges are interwoven with the fabric of the cosmos. Her work invites every soul to reclaim the truth that destiny is not written by chance—but intentionally encoded in the divine mathematics of creation.

When she's not writing, teaching, or serving her community, Dr. Villegas spends her time nurturing her family, creating herbal remedies, and mentoring the next generation of holistic practitioners. Her life is her message: that alignment with one's divine design is the highest form of healing—and the truest path to freedom.

Preface

The Remembering of What Was Always Written

There comes a moment in every soul's journey when curiosity becomes remembrance—when we begin to sense that our lives were never random, but deliberately designed through an intricate dance between matter and energy, spirit and science, destiny and free will.

I wrote *Encoded in the Stars: The Science of Destiny and the Blueprint of the Soul* as both a continuation and expansion of the work I began in *Awakened Science.* That first book unveiled the bridge between quantum physics and divinity—the sacred union of consciousness and creation. This one ventures deeper into the personal: into the moment *you* were written into existence.

From the exact alignment of planets at your birth, to the frequencies that shaped your DNA, to the ancestral codes carried in your bloodline—everything about you was intelligently woven together by the Universe's own design. You are a living equation of time, space, vibration, and purpose. And the moment you learn to decode your personal blueprint, life begins to unfold in clarity, not chaos.

We will journey through systems both ancient and modern:
Astrology, to interpret the language of the stars.
Astrocartography, to understand the sacred geography of your path.
Numerology, to uncover the vibrational mathematics of your soul.
Human Design, to reveal how your energy was meant to flow.
And Ancestral Lineage, to honor the karmic stories that prepared the way for your evolution.

This is not a book of fortune-telling or mysticism for entertainment. It is a text of remembrance, a manual for self-realization, and an invitation to align your biology, psychology, and spirituality with your divine coordinates. Through the lens of quantum science, epigenetics, and metaphysical law, you will see how your destiny is not controlled by the stars—but *reflected* in them.

As you read, take what resonates and allow it to awaken what you already know within. Each chapter is a key, each reflection an activation, and each realization a reminder that your purpose was never lost—it was only waiting to be remembered.

You are not here by coincidence. You are here because the Universe wrote you into existence on purpose.

Now, it's time to read the language of your own soul.

INTRODUCTION: THE CODE OF EXISTENCE

"The Universe is not outside of you. Look inside yourself; everything that you want, you already are." — Rumi

There are moments in life when the veil between logic and mystery grows thin—when what we have been taught to separate suddenly begins to merge. In those moments, we sense that science and spirit were never meant to compete, but to complete one another.

This is the essence of *The Code of Existence*: the revelation that everything in creation, from the birth of galaxies to the birth of you, is governed by divine order.

Destiny Not As Fate, But As Frequency

For centuries, humanity has wrestled with the concept of destiny. Many have viewed it as an unchangeable script—a cosmic decree sealed before birth. But destiny is not a fixed point written in stone; it is a living frequency, a vibration you are continuously tuning into through your choices, beliefs, and awareness.

In quantum physics, we understand that all matter, including thought and emotion, is energy vibrating at specific frequencies. These frequencies interact, harmonize, or resist one another based on resonance. In this same way, your soul carries a vibrational signature—a harmonic code that resonates with certain experiences, people, and opportunities that align with your evolution.

Your purpose is not something you stumble upon by accident;

it's something you *vibrate* into alignment with. Each moment of your life, every challenge and breakthrough, is designed to bring your energy back into coherence with the original frequency of your divine design.

Your Birth As A Divine Equation Of Time, Space, And Soul Intention

The moment you took your first breath, the entire cosmos conspired in mathematical precision. The alignment of the planets, the rotation of the Earth, the gravitational pull of the Moon, and the electromagnetic hum of the Sun—all formed a celestial fingerprint unique to you.

You were not born *under* the stars; you were born *with* them.
Your birth chart, in its sacred geometry, is the map of the universe reflected within your own consciousness—a mirror showing how your soul intended to express itself in physical form.

Astrology, Numerology, Astrocartography, Human Design, and Ancestral Coding are not systems of prediction, but of *recognition*. Each one reveals a layer of the energetic blueprint that defines your purpose, potential, and path of transformation.

They are languages through which the Universe speaks— inviting you to remember that your life is not random, but intelligently designed.

The Fusion Of Metaphysics And Modern Science

Modern science is slowly uncovering what the mystics have always known—that consciousness is not confined to the brain, but is the very field through which the universe expresses itself.

Quantum entanglement reveals that particles separated by light-years remain mysteriously connected, mirroring the spiritual truth that all things are interwoven in oneness.

The time-space continuum teaches that past, present, and future are not linear but simultaneous, echoing the ancient belief in reincarnation and karmic cycles.

Carl Jung's theory of synchronicity describes meaningful coincidences that defy logic but reveal divine order—a scientific glimpse into the language of destiny itself.

And **Rupert Sheldrake's morphic resonance** proposes that memory is not confined to biology, but exists as an energetic field that links species, generations, and souls—a modern echo of ancestral remembrance.

When we examine these discoveries through both lenses—metaphysical and scientific—we begin to see an elaborate web of profound coherence. The laws of energy, vibration, and consciousness are not separate from the laws of physics; they are extensions of the same truth, interpreted through different dimensions of understanding.

The Systems Of The Soul: An Overview

This book explores five major systems that decode the architecture of human purpose:

1. **Astrology** – The cosmic clock that records the energetic imprint of your birth.

2. **Numerology** – The mathematics of vibration, showing the frequency of your name, date of birth, and life path.

3. **Astrocartography** – The geography of your destiny, revealing how locations on Earth activate different aspects of your soul.

4. **Human Design** – The synthesis of ancient wisdom and modern science that defines your energy type,

strategy, and inner authority.

5. **Ancestral Coding** – The genetic and energetic imprints passed through your lineage, carrying both karmic lessons and spiritual gifts.

Together, these systems form a multidimensional map—one that connects the physical, mental, emotional, and spiritual layers of your being. Through them, you will uncover not only *who* you are, but *why* you are.

The Science Of Remembering

Each human being is a microcosm of the universe—a reflection of cosmic intelligence experiencing itself through form. The ancient Hermetic principle states, "As above, so below; as within, so without." When you remember this truth, you begin to recognize the divine pattern that animates every cell of your being and every event in your life.

You are not a victim of circumstance, nor a product of chance. You are consciousness encoded in matter, designed to evolve through experience and awareness. Every hardship, every victory, every crossroads—each one is an activation point guiding you back to resonance with your higher design.

Reflective Question

What if your birth wasn't random, but a pre-coded vibration of purpose waiting to be remembered?

CHAPTER 1

The Universe Within You: The Science of Destiny

The universe does not begin at the edge of the stars.
It begins within you.

Modern science is now confirming what ancient civilizations understood intuitively: the human being is not separate from the cosmos, but an expression of it. Your body is not merely a biological structure—it is a living, responsive field of energy, information, and consciousness, continuously interacting with the universe that surrounds it.

To understand destiny, we must first understand *interconnection*.

The Interconnected Web of Existence

Quantum physics has radically transformed our understanding of reality—not by adding complexity, but by revealing an underlying unity that was previously invisible to the human eye. At the quantum level, particles do not behave as isolated, self-contained objects. They exist as probabilities, relationships, and interactions within a vast, dynamic field. Reality, at its most fundamental layer, is relational.

One of the most profound confirmations of this truth is **quantum entanglement**—a phenomenon in which two or more particles become so deeply linked that the state of one instantaneously influences the state of another, regardless of distance. Whether separated by inches or galaxies, these particles behave as though they are part of the same system, responding as one.

This discovery did more than challenge classical physics; it dismantled one of humanity's most deeply held assumptions—the illusion of separation.

What quantum science reveals is that connection is not something that happens *after* matter forms. Connection is what allows matter to exist at all. Relationship precedes form. Interaction precedes individuality. Nothing comes into being alone.

When we apply this understanding beyond particles and into living systems, a profound realization emerges: **consciousness itself cannot be confined to a single body, brain, or moment in time**. Just as particles are embedded in quantum fields, human beings are embedded in vast informational and energetic networks that extend beyond physical boundaries.

You are not a closed system.

Your thoughts, emotions, biology, and experiences are constantly exchanging information with the environment—responding to planetary rhythms, electromagnetic fields, social dynamics, ancestral memory, and collective consciousness. Every breath you take participates in this exchange. Every decision you make sends ripples through the field.

This is what is meant by an *interconnected web of existence*—a living matrix in which information, memory, influence, and intention move freely across space and time. In this web, nothing is truly lost, and nothing happens in isolation. Experiences echo. Patterns repeat. Wisdom transmits. Trauma imprints. Healing reverberates.

From this perspective, destiny is no longer a solitary journey. It is a relational unfolding.

Your life is shaped not only by personal choice, but by resonance—by what you are energetically aligned with, consciously and unconsciously. You are drawn toward certain people, places, challenges, and opportunities not by chance, but by frequency. These encounters are not random interruptions; they are points of entanglement—moments where your personal field intersects with the larger intelligence of the universe.

This understanding reframes how we perceive struggle, synchronicity, and purpose. What appears as a coincidence becomes communication. What feels like repetition becomes instruction. What seems like a delay becomes recalibration.

Your life, therefore, is not unfolding *independently* of the universe—as though you were a separate observer moving through a neutral world.
It is unfolding *with* the universe—as a participant in an intelligent, responsive, and ever-evolving system.

You are not navigating existence alone.
You are being carried, shaped, and informed by the same web that formed the stars.

And when you learn to recognize this connection—not intellectually, but somatically and intuitively—you stop trying to force life into meaning. Meaning begins to reveal itself naturally, through alignment.

Because in an interconnected universe, purpose is not created in isolation.
It emerges through a relationship.

Birth as a Vibrational Timestamp

The moment of your birth is not simply a biological milestone—it is an energetic inscription, a precise moment in the unfolding of the universe when consciousness took form through you. Birth is the point at which spirit, matter, time, and space converge into a single, unrepeatable configuration.

At the instant you entered the world, the cosmos existed in perfect specificity. The planets occupied exact degrees within their orbits. The Moon exerted a particular gravitational influence over Earth's waters—within the oceans and within your own body. The Sun delivered a distinct spectrum of electromagnetic radiation. Day and night established circadian cues that would begin calibrating your biological rhythms. Surrounding it all was the constant hum of cosmic vibration—the background frequency of the universe itself.

Nothing about this moment was interchangeable.

Together, these conditions formed what can be understood as a **vibrational timestamp**—a unique energetic signature that marked your arrival into physical reality. Just as a digital timestamp records the exact coordinates of an event in time and space, your birth recorded the energetic conditions under which your nervous system, endocrine system, and cellular networks began their lifelong dialogue with the world.

This imprint occurs during a period of extreme biological openness. At birth, the human system is exquisitely plastic —highly sensitive to environmental cues, frequencies, and rhythms. The nervous system is organizing itself. Hormonal pathways are establishing baselines. Cellular communication is rapidly forming. Into this receptive field, the vibrational environment of the cosmos leaves its mark.

This is not symbolism—it is physiology.

Research in developmental biology and circadian science shows that timing at birth influences stress reactivity, sleep-wake cycles, emotional regulation, and sensory processing throughout life. Epigenetic mechanisms further demonstrate that environmental signals at early developmental stages influence how genes express themselves long-term. When viewed through this lens, the energetic conditions present at birth become not just contextual— but foundational.

Your birth moment functions like the **keynote frequency** of your life—setting the tone to which your system continually seeks coherence. Throughout your lifetime, you will encounter experiences that resonate with this original frequency: people who feel familiar, challenges that repeat in different forms, and environments that activate growth or discomfort. These are not arbitrary patterns; they are echoes of your initial imprint calling you toward alignment.

Just as a musical instrument is tuned to a specific pitch, your body-mind system carries an original tuning. When life events move you closer to that resonance, you experience flow, clarity, and purpose. When you move away from it, you may experience resistance, dissonance, or confusion—not as punishment, but as feedback.

From this perspective, destiny is not imposed from above by an external force. It is not a rigid script that removes choice or agency. Destiny is **imprinted**, not enforced—encoded as a vibrational orientation that interacts dynamically with free will, environment, and consciousness.

You are not here to fulfill a fate you cannot escape.
You are here to remember the frequency you were born carrying—and to learn how to live in harmony with it.

When you understand your birth as a vibrational timestamp, your life stops feeling random. It begins to feel intelligible. Your patterns gain meaning. Your timing makes sense. And purpose becomes less about searching outward, and more about tuning inward—back to the original resonance that marked your arrival into the world.

Frequencies at Birth and Energetic Imprinting

Everything in the universe is in motion. Nothing is static. At the most fundamental level of existence, reality expresses itself through vibration. Atoms oscillate. Cells pulse. Neural networks fire in rhythmic patterns. Thoughts generate measurable electromagnetic signals. Emotions alter heart rhythms, brainwaves, and hormonal cascades. Life itself is frequency in motion.

The human body is not a fixed structure—it is a dynamic orchestra of interacting frequencies, continuously tuning itself in response to both internal states and external environments. Health, emotion, perception, and consciousness emerge not from isolated parts, but from the *coherence* of these rhythms working together.

Birth marks one of the most critical moments in this tuning process.

At birth, the human system is exceptionally plastic and receptive. The brain is rapidly forming neural pathways. The nervous system is calibrating threat and safety responses. Hormonal systems are establishing baseline rhythms. Cellular communication networks are coming online. In this state of openness, the body is exquisitely sensitive to frequency—absorbing and encoding information from its environment.

This is when cosmic, environmental, and biological frequencies converge to establish what can be described as your **baseline energetic architecture**.

The timing of your birth—down to the hour and minute—shapes how your system organizes itself around key functions, including:

- **Nervous system sensitivity** – determining how quickly and intensely you respond to stimulation, stress, and novelty

- **Emotional processing** – influencing emotional depth, regulation capacity, and attachment patterns

- **Perceptual tendencies** – shaping how you interpret sensory information, meaning, and symbolism

- **Stress response patterns** – calibrating fight, flight,

freeze, or adaptive resilience mechanisms

- **Intuitive and cognitive wiring** – affecting creativity, pattern recognition, insight, and problem-solving styles

These tendencies are not personality labels—they are energetic predispositions that guide how consciousness interfaces with the world.

This understanding is strongly supported by modern science. **Circadian biology** shows that light exposure, seasonal timing, and daily rhythms at birth influence sleep cycles, mood regulation, and hormonal balance across the lifespan. **Neurodevelopmental research** demonstrates that early environmental signals shape neural connectivity and emotional regulation capacity. **Epigenetics** reveals that genes respond dynamically to timing, stress, rhythm, and environment—turning on or off based on informational input rather than genetic destiny alone.

In other words, biology listens.

Genes do not act independently; they respond to the vibrational context in which they operate. Frequency becomes the conductor, and genetic expression follows the lead. This reframes destiny not as something locked inside DNA, but as something that emerges through interaction between code and context.

Your destiny is not stored in a single gene.
It is stored in the **frequency that governs how your genes respond to life**.

This explains why individuals born into similar environments can experience vastly different life trajectories. It also explains why awareness, healing, and alignment practices can fundamentally change how destiny unfolds. When frequency shifts, expression changes.

From this perspective, challenges are not defects in design—they are signals pointing toward recalibration. Growth does not require rewriting who you are; it requires *retuning* your system back toward coherence.

Understanding frequencies at birth allows you to see yourself not as broken or deficient, but as exquisitely tuned for a specific journey of evolution. Your sensitivities, strengths, and struggles are not mistakes—they are information encoded in vibration, guiding you toward the experiences necessary for your becoming.

You were not simply born into the world.
You were *tuned* into it.

And learning to understand that tuning is the first step in consciously embodying your destiny.

The Body as a Microcosm of the Cosmos

Ancient wisdom traditions across cultures taught a simple yet profound truth: *"As above, so below; as within, so without."* What was once expressed through myth, philosophy, and sacred law is now being echoed—measured, observed, and validated—by modern science. The human body is not separate from the cosmos; it is a living reflection of it.

Your physiology is not arbitrary. It is rhythmic, cyclical, and synchronized with the larger movements of the universe.

The most immediate example of this relationship is the **circadian rhythm**—the internal biological clock that governs sleep, wakefulness, hormone secretion, digestion, immune function, and cognitive performance. This rhythm aligns directly with the Earth's 24-hour rotation, responding to cycles of light and darkness. Long before artificial lighting existed, human biology evolved in an intimate relationship with the Sun, calibrating bodily functions to planetary time.

Even today, disruption of circadian alignment—through shift work, chronic stress, or disconnection from natural light—has been linked to metabolic disorders, mood dysregulation, immune dysfunction, and cognitive decline. Alignment, therefore, is not philosophical; it is physiological.

Beyond the daily solar rhythm, the **Moon** exerts a powerful influence over human biology. The human body is composed of approximately 60–70% water, making it responsive to gravitational forces that govern tides and fluid movement on Earth. Research has associated lunar phases with fluctuations in sleep patterns, emotional states, fertility cycles, and hormonal regulation—particularly within the endocrine and reproductive systems.

Hormonal cycles, especially those related to reproduction, often mirror the approximately 28-day lunar cycle—a reminder that human life is governed by celestial timing as much as internal chemistry.

At the neurological level, the brain communicates through **neural oscillations**—electrical rhythms measured in hertz (Hz). These brainwave frequencies (delta, theta, alpha, beta, and gamma) resonate within ranges comparable to planetary electromagnetic frequencies. Certain states of consciousness —such as meditation, creativity, intuition, and deep emotional processing—occur when these rhythms fall into coherent patterns, suggesting a state of synchronization rather than separation.

Consciousness, then, is not generated in isolation. It emerges through resonance.

The heart plays a central role in this cosmic dialogue. Research conducted by the HeartMath Institute has shown that the heart generates the strongest electromagnetic field in the human body—significantly more powerful than that of the brain. This field extends several feet beyond the physical body and changes in response to emotional states, intention, and coherence.

When the heart is in a state of coherence—when emotional, cognitive, and physiological rhythms are aligned—it functions as a powerful integrative organ, influencing brain activity, hormonal balance, immune response, and perception. In coherent states, individuals demonstrate improved intuition, emotional regulation, and cognitive clarity.

The heart, in this sense, acts as both transmitter and receiver—a biological interface between the internal and external universe.

Taken together, these rhythms reveal a profound truth: the human body is not passively existing *on* Earth as a detached organism. It is actively living *with* Earth, continuously synchronizing with solar, lunar, and planetary cycles. Your biology is in constant conversation with the cosmos.

This understanding reframes how we view health, purpose, and destiny. When the body falls out of rhythm with natural cycles—through chronic stress, trauma, environmental disconnection, or emotional suppression—dissonance emerges. When alignment is restored, coherence follows.

You are not designed to dominate nature or transcend it.
You are designed to *resonate* with it.

To know your purpose, then, is not to escape the body or override its signals—but to listen more deeply to its rhythms. Your body is a living archive of cosmic intelligence, carrying within it the same order, timing, and wisdom that governs the stars.

You are not a small being in a vast universe.
You are the universe—expressing itself through form.

Schumann Resonance and Planetary Rhythm

The Earth is not a silent body drifting through space. It is a living, electrically active system, constantly emitting and responding to electromagnetic frequencies. One of the most significant of these is the **Schumann Resonance**—a naturally occurring electromagnetic standing wave that exists between the Earth's surface and the ionosphere.

Often referred to as the planet's "heartbeat," the fundamental Schumann Resonance frequency averages approximately **7.83 Hz**. This frequency is not arbitrary; it arises from the interaction between Earth's electromagnetic field, lightning activity, and atmospheric conditions. It is the baseline rhythm of the planet itself.

What makes this frequency extraordinary is its striking similarity to key human brainwave states. Human **alpha** and **theta** brainwaves—associated with intuition, creativity, emotional regulation, learning, deep meditation, and states of calm awareness—fall within the same range. These are the states in which insight emerges, nervous system regulation stabilizes, and the mind becomes receptive rather than reactive.

This overlap is not coincidental.

Human physiology does not merely tolerate the Earth's electromagnetic rhythm—it **synchronizes** with it. Research in chronobiology and neurophysiology suggests that the human nervous system is highly responsive to geomagnetic activity. Brainwave patterns, heart rate variability, sleep cycles, and emotional states have all been shown to fluctuate in response to changes in the Earth's electromagnetic environment.

In essence, the human body is tuned to the Earth's frequency in the same way a musical instrument is tuned to its reference pitch.

This synchronization implies something profound: humans

are biologically designed to resonate with planetary energy fields. Our nervous systems evolved in continuous interaction with Earth's electromagnetic environment, adapting over millennia to its rhythms and fluctuations. The Earth is not merely our habitat—it is an active regulator of human physiology and consciousness.

When this resonance is intact, the body tends toward coherence. Emotional regulation improves. Cognitive clarity sharpens. Intuition strengthens. The nervous system finds balance between arousal and rest. This state of alignment is not mystical—it is measurable through indicators such as heart rate variability, brainwave coherence, and hormonal regulation.

However, when these natural rhythms are disrupted, the consequences are felt deeply. Chronic stress, unresolved trauma, excessive artificial electromagnetic exposure, sleep deprivation, and disconnection from natural environments can interfere with the body's ability to synchronize with planetary frequencies. When coherence is lost, symptoms such as anxiety, emotional volatility, fatigue, cognitive fog, and somatic distress may emerge.

This disruption is often experienced as disconnection—from the body, from purpose, and from meaning.

From this perspective, healing is not about forcing the body into compliance, but about restoring **resonance**. Regulation occurs when the nervous system is allowed to return to its natural alignment with the rhythms it was designed to follow. Practices such as grounding, exposure to natural light, rhythmic breathing, meditation, and time spent in nature all support this recalibration because they reintroduce the body to the frequencies it recognizes as home.

Alignment, therefore, is not abstract.
It is not merely philosophical or spiritual.

It is **physiological**.

To live in alignment is to live in rhythm—with your body, with the Earth, and with the larger intelligence that governs both. When you understand this, destiny stops feeling like a distant concept and begins to feel embodied. Purpose becomes something you *feel* in your nervous system—not something you chase with your mind.

You are not meant to fight the rhythm of the planet.
You are meant to move with it.

And when you do, life begins to make sense—not because it becomes easier, but because it becomes coherent.

DNA as the Antenna of Consciousness

DNA has long been described as the blueprint of life—a static set of instructions dictating physical form and biological function. While this metaphor has been useful, it is also incomplete. A blueprint implies something fixed and unchanging, yet living systems are anything but static. DNA does not simply *store* information; it actively **receives, interprets, and transmits** it.

Emerging research in biophysics and molecular biology suggests that DNA functions less like an instruction manual and more like a **responsive communication system**. At a subcellular level, DNA emits and absorbs electromagnetic frequencies, responding to signals from within the body and from the environment. This behavior aligns with the understanding that biological systems are fundamentally energetic as well as chemical.

In this sense, DNA behaves like a **biological antenna**—capable of receiving vibrational information and translating it into biological expression.

This perspective radically expands how we understand consciousness. If DNA is responsive to electromagnetic and vibrational signals, then consciousness cannot be reduced solely to neural activity in the brain. Instead, awareness is mediated through the entire body—through cells, tissues, organs, and the biofield that surrounds them. The body becomes a distributed network of intelligence rather than a passive vessel controlled by the mind.

Your thoughts, emotions, beliefs, and perceptions are not abstract experiences floating above biology. They generate measurable signals—electrical, chemical, and electromagnetic—that interact directly with cellular function. These signals influence how DNA expresses itself, shaping physiology, behavior, and long-term adaptation.

This is where the science of **epigenetics** becomes especially relevant. Epigenetic research demonstrates that genes are not destiny in isolation; they are responsive to informational input. Stress, environment, emotional states, trauma, nourishment, and even meaning-making can influence which genetic pathways are activated or silenced. DNA listens to context.

Your DNA is not static.
It listens.
It responds.
It adapts.

This adaptability is what transforms destiny from a rigid script into a living process. Rather than being locked into predetermined outcomes, you are encoded with **potential ranges**—possibilities that unfold based on resonance, experience, and awareness. The original imprint at birth establishes a baseline frequency, but expression evolves continuously through interaction with life.

From this perspective, destiny is not something that happens *to* you. It is something that happens *through* you.

Every experience you encounter sends information into your

system. Every emotional response alters biochemical and energetic signaling. Every belief either constricts or expands the range of expression available to your biology. In this way, consciousness and DNA engage in an ongoing dialogue—one shaping the other in real time.

This understanding dissolves the false divide between fate and free will. You are not bound by your biology, nor are you separate from it. You are in a relationship with it. Your awareness influences your expression, and your expression influences your experience.

Destiny, then, is not deterministic—it is **dynamic**.

It is a conversation between your original encoding and your lived consciousness. When you become aware of this dialogue, you gain agency—not to erase your design, but to cooperate with it more skillfully. Healing becomes possible because adaptation is built into the system. Growth becomes inevitable because responsiveness is inherent to life.

You are not a prisoner of your genetic code.
You are a participant in its expression.

And when you understand DNA not as a fixed blueprint, but as an intelligent antenna of consciousness, you begin to see yourself not as a static being—but as a living signal in an ever-evolving universe.

Cellular Memory and Epigenetic Influence

For much of modern history, genetics was understood through a deterministic lens—the belief that DNA dictated destiny in a fixed and unchangeable way. However, the field of **epigenetics** has fundamentally altered this narrative. Epigenetics reveals that genes do not operate in isolation; they respond dynamically to information. It is not the gene itself that determines outcome, but how—and when—it is expressed.

In simple terms, **genes load the gun, but environment pulls**

the trigger.

Environmental signals, emotional states, beliefs, stress levels, nourishment, relationships, and even perception itself influence which genetic pathways are activated or silenced. These influences do not change the DNA sequence, but they modify how genes are read and expressed—shaping physiology, behavior, emotional resilience, and susceptibility or resistance to illness.

This means that destiny is not encoded as a fixed endpoint. It is encoded as a **range of potential**.

Your birth moment establishes your energetic baseline—the original frequency through which your system interfaces with the world. This baseline influences sensitivity, temperament, intuitive capacity, and predispositions. Yet from that moment forward, your lived experience continuously shapes how that blueprint unfolds. Biology listens to life.

Cells remember.

This concept of **cellular memory** suggests that experiences —particularly emotionally charged ones—leave imprints not only in the mind, but in the body itself. Trauma, love, fear, safety, and meaning are translated into biochemical and energetic signals that influence cellular behavior. Over time, repeated signals reinforce patterns of expression, embedding experience into physiology.

This understanding reframes how we view both healing and hardship.

You were encoded with **potential**, not limitation. Challenges do not appear as evidence of defect, but as **activators**—specific experiences that press certain energetic buttons designed to awaken growth, resilience, awareness, and transformation. Just as muscle fibers strengthen under resistance, the nervous system and psyche evolve through experience.

From this perspective, adversity is not punishment. It is information.

Certain life events activate latent capacities within you—strength you didn't know you possessed, wisdom forged through struggle, empathy born of pain, leadership shaped by survival. These qualities do not emerge despite hardship; they emerge *because* of it. The body-mind system adapts in response to what it encounters, sculpting identity through lived experience.

Epigenetic research supports this adaptive capacity. Studies have shown that trauma, stress, and emotional environments can alter gene expression across generations—yet healing, safety, and intentional intervention can also reverse or soften these imprints. This means that the same system that records pain is capable of recording restoration.

Your cells are not simply carrying your personal story—they are carrying ancestral stories as well. Patterns of resilience, creativity, survival, and wisdom are inherited alongside patterns of stress and fear. Awareness becomes the gateway to choice: when you recognize what has been carried forward, you gain the ability to transform it.

This is where destiny and responsibility meet.

Your life experiences are not random obstacles blocking your path. They are feedback mechanisms—signals inviting recalibration, expansion, and conscious participation in your own becoming. When you engage challenges with awareness rather than resistance, expression changes. When expression changes, destiny unfolds differently.

You are not here to suffer endlessly.
You are here to *activate* what was encoded within you.

Cellular memory reminds us that healing is not about becoming someone new—it is about allowing the fullest expression of who you were always designed to be. When you understand this, growth stops feeling like a battle and begins to feel like remembrance.

Your body knows how to evolve.
Your cells know how to adapt.
Your destiny responds to your awareness.

The Heart as a Gateway of Intelligence

For centuries, the heart has been symbolically regarded as the seat of wisdom, intuition, and truth. What was once dismissed as a poetic metaphor is now being substantiated by modern science. Research conducted by the **HeartMath Institute** has demonstrated that the heart is far more than a mechanical pump—it is a powerful center of intelligence, communication, and regulation within the human system.

The heart possesses its own intrinsic nervous system, often referred to as the **"heart brain."** This neural network contains tens of thousands of neurons capable of sensing, learning, and remembering independently of the brain. In fact, communication between the heart and the brain is bidirectional, with the heart sending more signals *to* the brain than the brain sends to the heart. These signals influence cognitive processing, emotional interpretation, and decision-making at a fundamental level.

Even more profound is the heart's electromagnetic influence. The heart generates the strongest electromagnetic field in the human body—measurably stronger and more far-reaching than that of the brain. This field extends several feet beyond the physical body and fluctuates dynamically based on emotional state, intention, and physiological regulation.

Emotion, then, is not just felt—it is broadcast.

This electromagnetic field plays a critical role in shaping perception and intuitive awareness. When the heart is in a state of stress, fear, or incoherence, the signals sent to the brain are erratic, disrupting cognitive clarity and narrowing perception. The world is experienced through a lens of threat or urgency. Decision-making becomes reactive rather than responsive.

However, when the heart enters a state of **coherence**—a harmonious alignment between emotional, mental, and physiological rhythms—the entire system reorganizes.

Heart coherence occurs when heart rhythms become smooth and ordered, often associated with emotions such as appreciation, compassion, gratitude, and calm presence. In this state, communication between the heart, brain, and nervous system becomes efficient and synchronized. Stress hormones decrease. Immune function improves. Cognitive flexibility increases. Intuition sharpens.

In coherence, the body becomes a **clear receiver of information**.

Purpose feels less like something to analyze and more like something to recognize. Decisions feel grounded rather than forced. Insight arises without strain. Life begins to flow with less resistance—not because challenges disappear, but because perception expands. You respond from alignment rather than survival.

This coherence is not mystical or subjective—it is **measurable**. Heart rate variability (HRV), brainwave synchronization, hormonal balance, and immune markers all reflect the physiological shift that occurs when the heart and nervous system move into coherence. These measurable changes demonstrate that alignment is a biological state, not merely a spiritual aspiration.

From this perspective, intuition is not a vague feeling—it is a coherent signal. The heart acts as a gateway through which deeper intelligence becomes accessible when the system is regulated and aligned. When coherence is lost, that signal becomes distorted. When coherence is restored, clarity returns.

This understanding reframes destiny and decision-making. You do not access purpose by overthinking or forcing direction. You access it by cultivating coherence—by bringing the heart, mind, and body into alignment. From this state, the next step becomes evident, not because it is predicted, but because it is *felt*.

The heart does not dictate destiny.
It **reveals** it—when you are aligned enough to listen.

In learning to regulate and attune the heart, you do not surrender logic; you integrate it. Intelligence becomes embodied. Wisdom becomes practical. Purpose becomes lived.

And in that state of coherence, you remember that alignment is not something you must chase.
It is a state you return to—again and again—through awareness, presence, and intention.

Reprogramming Destiny Through Frequency

If destiny is frequency, then transformation does not occur through struggle, control, or force—it occurs through **recalibration**. Just as a radio must be tuned to the correct station to receive a clear signal, the human system must be tuned to its natural resonance in order to express its highest potential. Change is not about becoming someone else; it is about restoring coherence to what already exists within you.

Modern neuroscience has demonstrated that the brain is not fixed, but **plastic**. Through the process of **neuroplasticity**, neural pathways reorganize themselves in response to experience, repetition, and intention. Thoughts you think consistently strengthen certain circuits. Emotional states you inhabit regularly reinforce particular physiological patterns.

Over time, these patterns become familiar, automatic, and self-perpetuating.

This is not destiny—it is conditioning.

The same research that reveals how patterns are formed also reveals how they can be changed. Intentional practices such as meditation, breathwork, visualization, and emotional regulation have been shown to alter brainwave activity, improve heart-brain coherence, reduce stress hormones, and enhance cognitive flexibility. These practices introduce new frequencies into the system—signals that invite the body and mind into alignment rather than survival.

At the cellular level, this recalibration influences **gene expression**. Epigenetic research shows that stress, safety, belief, and meaning alter which genetic pathways are activated. When the nervous system shifts from chronic threat to regulation, the body moves from defensive expression toward restorative and adaptive expression. Healing becomes possible not because the blueprint changes, but because its expression does.

This is the distinction between force and alignment.

Force attempts to override biology through willpower alone. Alignment works with the body's natural intelligence, inviting coherence through rhythm, awareness, and repetition. When frequency shifts, perception shifts. When perception shifts, choice expands. And when choice expands, destiny unfolds differently.

Importantly, recalibration does not erase your original design. It does not remove your sensitivities, challenges, or gifts. It allows them to be expressed in healthier, more integrated ways. What once manifested as anxiety may evolve into intuition. What once appeared as emotional intensity may become empathy and leadership. What once felt like disruption may reveal itself as innovation.

You are not here to escape your design.
You are here to **embody** it.

Embodiment means allowing your nervous system, emotional landscape, and belief structures to align with your true frequency rather than resist it. It means learning how to work with your biology instead of against it. It means recognizing that growth is not about transcending the body, but about inhabiting it more fully and consciously.

Destiny, in this context, is not a destination.
It is a state of resonance.

As you recalibrate your frequency—through awareness, practice, and intentional living—you do not create a new blueprint. You activate what was already encoded within you. Purpose stops feeling like something to chase and begins to feel like something to *live*.

This is the science of becoming.
This is the art of alignment.
And this is how destiny is reprogrammed—not by force, but by frequency.

The Inner Cosmos

When you begin to understand that your body is not merely *in* the universe, but **is a universe**, something profound shifts in the way you perceive your life. Chaos gives way to pattern. Confusion gives way to context. What once felt random starts to reveal an underlying order. Events no longer appear as isolated occurrences, but as interconnected movements within a larger design.

From this perspective, life stops feeling like a series of disconnected moments and starts feeling like a meaningful unfolding.

Patterns become visible—recurring themes in relationships,

familiar challenges that arise at different stages of life, talents that persist regardless of circumstance. These are not coincidences or failures to "get it right." They are expressions of an inner cosmos seeking alignment. Challenges cease to feel like obstacles and instead begin to reveal themselves as **initiatory gateways**—experiences designed to awaken specific qualities, wisdom, and awareness encoded within you.

Purpose, then, is no longer something to be hunted down externally. It is not hidden in achievements, titles, or destinations. Purpose becomes an act of **remembering**—a gradual recognition of what has always been present beneath conditioning, expectation, and fear. When you attune to your inner cosmos, clarity arises not because answers are imposed, but because resonance returns.

Science supports this shift in understanding. Every atom in your body was forged in the heart of a star. The same forces that govern planetary motion—gravity, electromagnetism, resonance—operate within your cells. The same intelligence that organizes galaxies into spirals organizes DNA into helixes. Structure, rhythm, and order are universal principles, expressed at every scale.

You are not separate from the stars.
You are made of the same intelligence that formed them.

This realization collapses the illusion of insignificance. You are not a small being navigating an indifferent universe; you are a conscious expression of the universe exploring itself through form. Your thoughts, emotions, and choices are not irrelevant —they are participatory forces within the greater field of existence.

From this vantage point, destiny ceases to feel imposed or external. It is not something waiting to happen to you in the future. It is something living within you—encoded in your frequency, activated through awareness, and expressed through alignment. The path forward becomes less about becoming someone else and more about **becoming congruent with who you already are.**

Your destiny lives not outside of you—in predictions, expectations, or external validation.
It lives within the frequency of your being—in your rhythms, responses, intuition, and inner knowing.

When you learn to listen to that frequency, life begins to move with coherence. Decisions feel aligned rather than forced. Timing feels intentional rather than delayed. Meaning emerges naturally—not because life becomes simpler, but because it becomes intelligible.

The inner cosmos is not something to be created.
It is something to be remembered.

And as you remember it, you step out of survival and into participation—no longer asking whether you belong in the universe, but recognizing that the universe has been expressing itself through you all along.

Reflection Prompt

Where in your life do you sense that you have been resisting your natural rhythm—rather than aligning with it?

CHAPTER 2

The Celestial Blueprint: Understanding Natal Charts

"Until you make the unconscious conscious, it will direct your life and you will call it fate."

— **Carl Jung**

The moment of your birth left more than an energetic imprint—it left a **map**.

A natal chart is not a prophecy. It is a blueprint of consciousness at the moment your soul entered form. It captures *how* you experience life, *where* growth is initiated, and *which archetypal forces* guide your evolution. Astrology, when understood correctly, does not tell you *what will happen*—it reveals **how you are wired to meet what happens**.

This is why astrology has endured across civilizations: it speaks the language of pattern, symbol, and psyche.

What a Natal Chart Really Is

A natal chart is not a belief system—it is a **mathematical and astronomical model**. It is a precise snapshot of the sky taken at the exact moment, date, and geographic location of your birth, calculated using verifiable celestial data. Long before psychology had language for temperament or neuroscience had tools to study cognition, humanity used the sky as its first mirror of consciousness.

At its core, a natal chart records four primary layers of information:

- **The position of the Sun, Moon, and planets** at the moment of birth

- **The zodiac signs** that those celestial bodies occupied

- **The twelve houses** of life, those energies were activating

- **The angular relationships (aspects)** formed between the planets

Each of these components adds depth and dimension. Separately, they describe tendencies; together, they create a **symbolic architecture of the inner world**—a multidimensional map of how consciousness organizes itself within form.

This architecture is not random. It is structured, patterned, and relational—much like the psyche itself.

A Map of Pattern, Not Prediction

One of the most misunderstood aspects of astrology is the assumption that a natal chart dictates fate. In truth, a natal chart does not override free will, nor does it predict specific events in a rigid or deterministic way. Instead, it reveals **patterns of perception, motivation, and response**—the lenses through which you experience life.

Your chart highlights:

- **Natural strengths and sensitivities** – areas of ease, talent, receptivity, and heightened awareness

- **Repeating life themes** – experiences that resurface in different forms, inviting deeper understanding rather than avoidance

- **Motivational drives and psychological needs** – what fuels you, what fulfills you, and what disrupts your sense of alignment

- **Life arenas of activation** – where growth, challenge, mastery, and fulfillment are most likely to unfold

These themes do not compel behavior; they *inform* it. They describe the energetic climate in which your choices are made.

In psychological terms, a natal chart functions much like a temperament profile or archetypal map—it does not tell you what to do, but it explains **why certain experiences feel more charged, meaningful, or transformative than others**.

Symbolic Architecture of the Psyche

The natal chart speaks in the language of symbols because the psyche itself operates symbolically. Long before rational thought engages, the unconscious responds to imagery, pattern, and meaning. Astrology encodes these patterns in a visual and mathematical form, allowing the psyche to be observed from the outside.

- **Planets** represent functions of consciousness

- **Signs** describe how those functions express themselves

- **Houses** reveal where in life those functions are emphasized

- **Aspects** show how different parts of the psyche interact—harmoniously or in tension

Seen this way, a natal chart is not mystical—it is **psychological cartography**.

It explains why two people can experience the same event and walk away transformed in completely different ways. It reveals why certain lessons repeat until they are integrated. It clarifies why fulfillment is found not by imitation, but by alignment.

How Destiny Speaks

Destiny does not shout. It communicates through patterns.

Your natal chart shows how destiny speaks to *you*—through emotion, thought, relationship, work, creativity, or transformation. It reveals the channels through which growth is initiated and the forms through which wisdom is earned.

Some individuals are designed to meet destiny through responsibility and mastery.
Others through emotional depth and relational healing.
Others through innovation, disruption, or spiritual surrender.

None are superior. All are necessary.

In this sense, a natal chart is not a sentence—it is an invitation.

It does not tell you *who you must become*.
It shows you **how you are designed to become**.

And when you understand that language—when you learn to read the architecture of your own consciousness—life stops feeling like a series of inexplicable detours and starts feeling like a coherent, intelligent unfolding.

That is the true purpose of a natal chart:
not to control your destiny, but to help you recognize the pattern it has always been speaking in.

The 12 Houses: Mirrors of Life's Arenas

The twelve houses of astrology represent the **primary domains of human experience**—the arenas in which life unfolds and consciousness evolves. If zodiac signs describe *how* energy behaves and planets describe *what* aspect of consciousness is active, the houses reveal **where that energy is lived, tested, and integrated**.

Think of the houses as rooms in the house of the psyche. Each room holds a different lesson, responsibility, and opportunity for mastery. You may move through all twelve over the course of a lifetime, but certain rooms are more frequently occupied —activated repeatedly until their lessons are understood and embodied.

Each house functions as a **psychological stage**, setting the scene for particular themes to arise. These themes are not arbitrary; they reflect universal developmental processes shared across humanity, expressed uniquely through each individual chart.

Overview of the Twelve Houses

First House — Identity, Self-Image, Embodiment

The First House represents the *experience of being*. It governs how you meet the world, how you see yourself, and how others perceive you. This is the house of embodiment—your physical presence, instinctual responses, and approach to life. Strong First House emphasis often brings themes of self-definition, leadership, or identity evolution.

Second House — Values, Security, Resources, Self-Worth

The Second House addresses what you value and how you create stability. It governs material resources, finances, and possessions—but also self-worth and internal security. Planets here often indicate lessons around abundance, scarcity, boundaries, and the relationship between value and survival.

Third House — Communication, Learning, Perception

This house governs the mind in motion—how you think, learn, communicate, and interpret reality. It includes language, siblings, early education, and mental patterns. A strong Third House highlights perception as a life theme: how meaning is constructed, exchanged, and revised.

Fourth House — Roots, Family, Emotional Foundation

The Fourth House is the inner sanctuary of the chart. It represents home, ancestry, emotional safety, and psychological grounding. This is where early conditioning leaves its imprint. Emphasis here often brings themes of healing lineage patterns, redefining home, or building emotional security from within.

Fifth House — Creativity, Pleasure, Self-Expression

The Fifth House governs joy, play, romance, and creative expression. It is the house of the inner child and authentic self-expression. Planets here seek to be *seen* and experienced fully. This house asks: *What brings you alive?*

Sixth House — Health, Service, Daily Rhythms

This house governs the rituals of daily life—work habits, health practices, service, and refinement. It reflects the relationship between mind, body, and routine. Strong Sixth House themes often indicate lessons around discipline, embodiment, and aligning daily actions with purpose

Seventh House — Relationships, Mirrors, Partnerships

The Seventh House is the realm of the *other*. It governs partnerships, intimate relationships, contracts, and projection. What is activated here often reflects qualities we are learning to integrate through relationship. This house teaches self-awareness through mirroring.

Eighth House — Transformation, Intimacy, Power

The Eighth House is the domain of deep psychological and energetic transformation. It governs intimacy, shared resources, power dynamics, death and rebirth processes, and shadow integration. Planets here often indicate initiatory experiences that catalyze profound personal evolution.

Ninth House — Meaning, Belief Systems, Higher Learning

This house governs the search for meaning. It includes philosophy, spirituality, higher education, travel, and worldview formation. Ninth House emphasis often brings a lifelong quest for truth, purpose, and expanded understanding beyond familiar horizons.

Tenth House — Purpose, Vocation, Public Contribution

The Tenth House represents how you are seen in the world and how you contribute to it. It governs career, legacy, authority, and responsibility. This house reflects the calling to *become* something meaningful in the public sphere—not for validation, but for service and impact.

Eleventh House — Community, Innovation, Collective Vision

The Eleventh House governs community, social movements, innovation, and future-oriented thinking. It represents the individual's role within the collective. Strong emphasis here often brings themes of activism, collaboration, and visionary leadership.

Twelfth House — The Unconscious, Spirituality, Surrender

The Twelfth House is the most subtle and often misunderstood domain. It governs the unconscious, dreams, spirituality, solitude, and transcendence. This house dissolves boundaries, inviting surrender and spiritual integration. Planets here often indicate deep intuition, compassion, and karmic resolution.

Activation Through Planetary Placement

When planets occupy these houses, they **activate those life arenas**, bringing repeated attention, experiences, and lessons to those domains. A planet does not force events—it *stimulates awareness*. Over time, recurring themes emerge, signaling where growth is asking to occur.

For example:

- Multiple planets in one house amplify its importance

- Empty houses are not inactive, but less emphasized

- Transits through houses temporarily activate those life arenas

Seen this way, the twelve houses are not compartments—they are **living classrooms**.

They show where consciousness is being educated through experience.

Understanding the houses allows you to stop resisting recurring lessons and begin working *with* them. Life becomes less about reacting to circumstances and more about recognizing **where you are being shaped**.

Because destiny does not arrive randomly—it unfolds through specific arenas of life, again and again, until awareness transforms experience into wisdom.

Zodiac Archetypes and Psychological Patterning

The zodiac is not a personality test, nor is it a system of labels meant to confine human behavior. At its core, the zodiac is a system of **archetypal psychology**—a symbolic language that describes universal patterns of consciousness and instinctive ways of engaging with life. These archetypes transcend culture, era, and belief system because they are rooted in fundamental modes of perception and response.

Each zodiac sign represents a **primary orientation of consciousness**—a patterned way energy initiates, stabilizes, interprets, or feels experience. These patterns are not learned; they are inherent. They reflect how awareness moves through the world before conditioning, expectation, or socialization intervenes.

Fire initiates.
Earth stabilizes.
Air conceptualizes.
Water feels.

These elemental principles form the foundation of psychological behavior. They describe how individuals respond to novelty, challenge, safety, meaning, and connection. Long before modern psychology developed terminology for temperament, these patterns were observed and encoded symbolically in the zodiac.

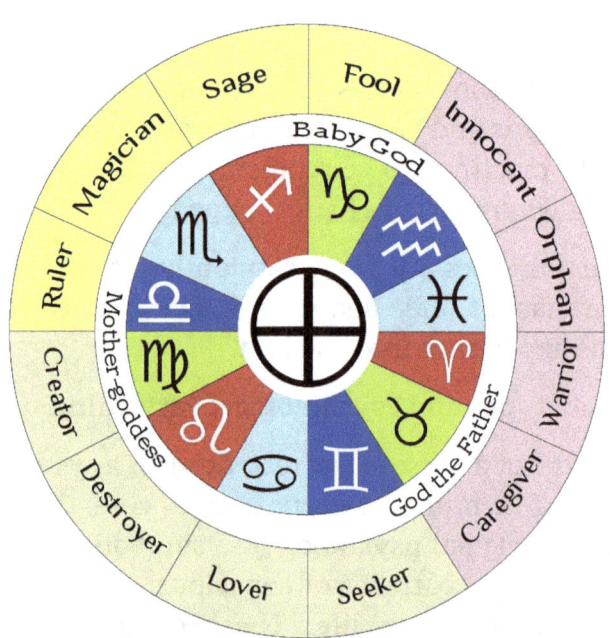

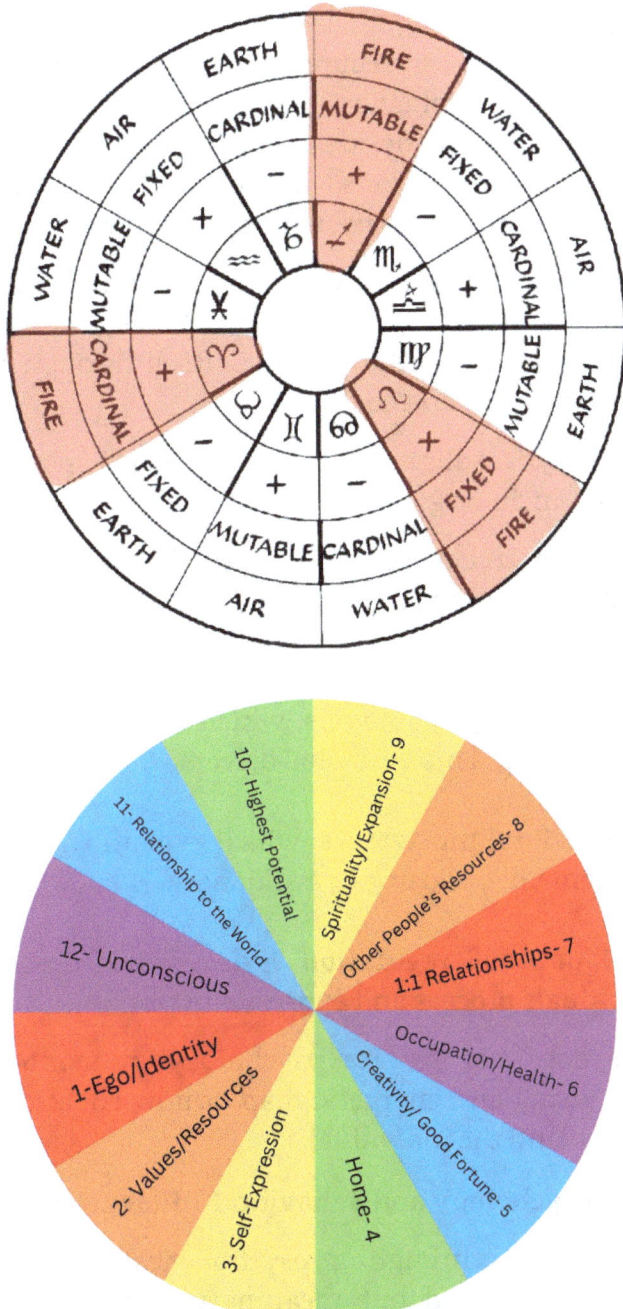

Archetypes as Psychological Language

Modern psychology acknowledges that the human psyche organizes itself through recurring patterns—archetypes that shape motivation, behavior, and perception. The work of **Carl Jung** introduced the idea that archetypes exist within the collective unconscious, influencing how individuals experience meaning, identity, and transformation.

Astrological archetypes parallel these insights. Each zodiac sign reflects a distinct psychological stance—an instinctual orientation toward life that expresses itself through behavior, emotional response, and cognitive style.

These archetypes align with contemporary psychological frameworks, including:

- **Jungian archetypes**, which describe universal psychic motifs such as the hero, the caregiver, the explorer, and the mystic

- **Personality typologies**, which categorize behavioral tendencies and motivational drivers

- **Behavioral motivators**, which explain what activates engagement, curiosity, or avoidance

- **Emotional regulation styles**, which describe how individuals process and express emotion

Astrology does not replace psychology—it **symbolizes it**, offering a visual and energetic map of how consciousness is organized within the individual.

Elemental Psychology and Behavioral Tendencies

When examined through a psychological lens, the four elements reveal broad but meaningful tendencies in how consciousness organizes itself:

- **Fire-dominant patterns** often correlate with high

novelty-seeking, motivation, enthusiasm, and initiative. Individuals with strong fire signatures tend to act first and refine later, driven by purpose, inspiration, and the desire to experience life fully.

- **Earth-dominant patterns** align with structure, responsibility, grounding, and practicality. These individuals often prioritize stability, reliability, and tangible results. Their psychological orientation values consistency and embodiment.

- **Air-dominant patterns** reflect cognitive flexibility, abstraction, communication, and conceptual thinking. Air-oriented individuals are motivated by ideas, connection through language, and understanding systems of meaning.

- **Water-dominant patterns** correlate with emotional depth, empathy, relational sensitivity, and intuitive awareness. These individuals process experience primarily through feeling and emotional resonance, often possessing heightened sensitivity to others and their environments.

These tendencies are not limitations. They are **energetic orientations**—starting points through which consciousness engages with experience.

Beyond Stereotype: Dynamic Expression

It is essential to understand that zodiac archetypes are not stereotypes. No individual embodies a single sign in isolation. A natal chart contains multiple archetypal influences interacting dynamically, creating nuance, complexity, and adaptability.

Archetypes do not dictate behavior; they **shape perception**. They influence how individuals interpret experience, what they notice first, and how they respond under stress or safety. Awareness of these patterns allows choice to emerge where unconscious reaction once dominated.

This is where astrology becomes a tool for growth rather than categorization.

When archetypal tendencies are unconscious, they can appear rigid or exaggerated. When brought into awareness, they become flexible strengths—resources that can be consciously integrated rather than unconsciously expressed.

Astrology as Symbolic Self-Knowledge

Understanding zodiac archetypes as psychological patterns allows astrology to be approached with maturity and depth. It shifts the conversation from *"This is who I am"* to *"This is how my consciousness organizes itself."*

That distinction is critical.

Astrology does not tell you what you are capable of—it reveals how you are inclined to approach life. When paired with awareness, intention, and lived experience, these archetypes become tools of empowerment rather than identity cages.

You are not your sign.
You are a **dynamic interplay of archetypal energies**, learning how to express them with wisdom and balance.

In this way, zodiac archetypes do not reduce human complexity—they honor it, offering a symbolic mirror through which the psyche can be seen, understood, and consciously evolved.

Planets as Energetic Teachers

In astrology, planets are not external forces acting *upon* you from the sky. They are symbolic representations of **functions of consciousness**—inner teachers that describe how different aspects of your psyche operate, mature, and seek expression over time. Planets do not cause events; they correspond to **processes of awareness** unfolding within you.

To understand planets as energetic teachers is to move beyond superstition and into psychological and spiritual literacy.

Each planet symbolizes *what part of you is being activated*, refined, or challenged through lived experience. Together, they describe the curriculum of your life—not as punishment or reward, but as growth through engagement.

The Personal Planets: Core Identity and Daily Functioning

These planets shape personality, emotional life, and everyday experience.

Sun — Identity, Vitality, Purpose

The Sun represents the core self—the organizing principle of identity and conscious purpose. It reflects how you experience aliveness, confidence, and direction. The Sun's placement reveals *where* you are meant to shine and *how* you express your authentic self. Growth here involves self-actualization and purposeful embodiment.

Moon — Emotional Processing, Attachment, Instinct

The Moon governs the emotional body and unconscious responses. It reflects how you seek safety, process feelings, and form attachment. Lunar themes often operate beneath conscious awareness, shaping habits, moods, and reactions. The Moon teaches emotional literacy, self-soothing, and intuitive trust.

Mercury — Thought, Communication, Perception

Mercury represents the mind in motion—how you think, learn, interpret, and communicate. It governs language, cognition, and pattern recognition. Mercury teaches discernment, adaptability, and meaning-making. Challenges here often involve miscommunication or cognitive rigidity, while mastery brings clarity and connection.

Venus — Values, Love, Pleasure, Relating

Venus reflects what you value and how you experience connection, pleasure, and harmony. It governs attraction, aesthetics, intimacy, and self-worth. Venus teaches receptivity, balance, and relational awareness. Lessons here often revolve around boundaries, attachment, and the ability to receive.

Mars — Drive, Boundaries, Assertion

Mars symbolizes action, motivation, and survival energy. It governs how you assert yourself, pursue goals, and protect boundaries. Mars teaches healthy aggression, courage, and self-direction. When misaligned, Mars energy may manifest as reactivity or suppression; when integrated, it becomes purposeful momentum.

The Social Planets: Growth and Structure

These planets shape belief systems, responsibility, and integration within society.

Jupiter — Growth, Meaning, Expansion

Jupiter represents expansion through experience. It governs belief systems, optimism, wisdom, and the search for meaning. Jupiter teaches trust, perspective, and growth beyond limitation. Its lessons often involve discernment—knowing when expansion is nourishing and when it becomes excess.

Saturn — Structure, Discipline, Mastery

Saturn is often misunderstood as restrictive, yet it is one of the greatest teachers of mastery. Saturn governs responsibility, boundaries, time, and commitment. It teaches patience, resilience, and earned wisdom. Saturn's lessons mature consciousness through effort and accountability, transforming fear into authority.

The Transpersonal Planets: Collective

and Transformational Forces

These planets operate at a generational and evolutionary level, shaping deep transformation and collective consciousness.

Uranus — Innovation, Liberation, Disruption

Uranus represents awakening and change. It governs innovation, rebellion, and the breaking of outdated structures. Uranus teaches freedom through authenticity, often arriving through sudden shifts or disruptions that realign you with your truth.

Neptune — Imagination, Spirituality, Dissolution

Neptune dissolves boundaries between the seen and unseen. It governs imagination, spirituality, compassion, and transcendence. Neptune teaches surrender, faith, and unity—but also challenges discernment. Its lessons involve distinguishing intuition from illusion.

Pluto — Transformation, Power, Rebirth

Pluto governs deep psychological transformation. It represents death and rebirth processes, power dynamics, shadow integration, and regeneration. Pluto's lessons are rarely gentle, but they are profoundly liberating. Through Pluto, consciousness sheds what is no longer authentic and reclaims inner power.

Learning Through Relationship and Interaction

The planets do not operate independently. Their **interactions—called aspects—describe how different parts of the psyche communicate**. Harmony suggests ease and flow; tension signals growth through challenge. Neither is superior. Both are teachers.

Equally important is **placement**. Where a planet falls in the chart reveals *where* its lessons are lived—through relationships, career, health, creativity, or inner life. Two people with the same planet may experience it entirely differently depending on house placement and interaction.

This is why astrology does not dictate experience—it contextualizes it.

Wisdom, Not Determinism

Planets do not determine whether lessons exist; they reveal **how lessons are encountered**. Every human experiences love, challenge, growth, and transformation. Astrology simply describes the *path of engagement*—the style through which consciousness evolves.

Seen this way, planets are not rulers of fate. They are **teachers of awareness**.

When their lessons are unconscious, life feels repetitive and frustrating. When they are understood and integrated, experience becomes purposeful. The same energies that once felt disruptive become sources of strength and wisdom.

You are not controlled by the planets.
You are **learning through them**.

And as you mature in awareness, those teachers shift—from demanding instruction through experience, to offering guidance through insight.

Natal Charts and Personality Correlation

As psychology and neuroscience have evolved, researchers have increasingly turned their attention to **patterns**—recurring constellations of traits, behaviors, and perceptual styles that shape human experience. Interestingly, many of these modern frameworks echo distinctions that astrology has symbolically mapped for thousands of years. While astrology does not claim to *cause* personality traits, meaningful **correlations** between astrological archetypes and psychological typologies continue to be observed.

This distinction is essential: astrology is not a deterministic science—it is **symbolic cartography**. Its value lies not in prediction, but in pattern recognition.

Convergence with Modern Psychological Frameworks

Across disciplines, psychology and astrology are asking the same foundational question from different vantage points: **How does consciousness organize itself within the human experience?** The language differs, the methods diverge, yet the patterns they describe often converge with striking consistency.

Several well-established psychological models align conceptually with astrological archetypes—not as causal equivalents, but as **parallel maps of human orientation**.

The Big Five Personality Traits and Elemental Orientation

The Big Five model—**Openness, Conscientiousness, Extraversion, Agreeableness, and Neuroticism**—is one of the most widely accepted trait-based frameworks in modern psychology. It describes broad, stable tendencies in behavior and emotional regulation across populations.

Astrological archetypes approach these same domains symbolically:

- **Openness** parallels archetypes associated with curiosity, exploration, imagination, and meaning-making

- **Conscientiousness** aligns with archetypes emphasizing structure, responsibility, discipline, and mastery

- **Extraversion** resonates with outwardly expressive, initiating, or relational archetypes

- **Agreeableness** reflects relational sensitivity, harmony-seeking, and cooperative orientations

- **Neuroticism** overlaps with sensitivity to stress, emotional reactivity, and internal processing intensity

Rather than scoring these traits on a linear scale, astrology contextualizes them—showing *where* and *how* they are likely to emerge in lived experience. The emphasis is not on ranking traits, but on understanding **their role in the psyche's overall ecology.**

MBTI Cognitive Functions and Perceptual Orientation

The MBTI framework focuses on **how individuals perceive information and make decisions**, distinguishing between sensing and intuition, thinking and feeling, introversion and extraversion. These distinctions mirror astrological insights into cognitive and perceptual style.

Astrology expresses these differences through:

- Elemental emphasis (sensory vs. conceptual vs. emotional processing)

- Planetary symbolism (thinking, feeling, intuition, and action functions)

- House placement (internal vs. external orientation of awareness)

Where MBTI describes *how* information is processed, astrology illustrates **the energetic pathway through which perception flows**—whether inwardly reflective, outwardly expressive, emotionally intuitive, or analytically conceptual.

Both systems acknowledge that no single mode is superior; effectiveness depends on alignment between perception, environment, and purpose.

Temperament Theory and Innate Responsiveness

Temperament theory identifies biologically rooted tendencies in emotional intensity, adaptability, and self-regulation. These traits appear early in life and influence how individuals respond to novelty, stress, and social interaction.

Astrological archetypes similarly describe **baseline responsiveness**:

- How quickly one reacts to change

- How deeply one feels the experience

- How much stimulation one seeks or avoids

- How one regulates emotion under pressure

The key overlap lies in the recognition that **not all nervous systems are wired the same way**. Astrology honors this diversity symbolically, emphasizing that temperament is not something to overcome, but something to understand and work with consciously.

Different Languages, Shared Insight

These frameworks differ in methodology—psychology relies on observation, measurement, and statistical modeling; astrology relies on symbolic interpretation and pattern recognition. Yet both aim to describe **how individuals process stimuli, relate to others, and navigate the world.**

Psychology tends to define traits as relatively stable characteristics. Astrology frames these same tendencies as **dynamic, energetic orientations**—patterns that evolve through awareness, experience, and integration.

This distinction matters.

Astrology does not assign fixed traits; it describes **potentials and proclivities**. It shows how certain energies are more readily accessible, where growth is catalyzed, and how challenges function as teachers rather than flaws. In doing so, it complements psychological models by adding depth, context, and meaning to observed behaviors.

Symbolic Orientation Rather Than Fixed Identity

Where psychology often asks, *"What traits does this person have?"*
Astrology asks, *"How does consciousness move through this person?"*

Planets, signs, and houses do not label identity—they describe **orientation**. They illustrate how attention flows, how energy responds to experience, and how the psyche seeks equilibrium. This symbolic approach allows for nuance, contradiction, and evolution—acknowledging that humans are not static profiles, but living systems.

Seen together, modern psychology and astrology do not compete. They **converge**—each illuminating the same human complexity from different angles.

Astrology becomes most powerful not when it replaces psychological insight, but when it **adds a symbolic dimension** to it—helping individuals understand not only *what* they do, but *why certain paths feel more natural, charged, or meaningful than others.*

In this convergence, astrology stands not as an alternative to science, but as a **complementary language of self-awareness**—one that translates inner experience into pattern, meaning, and possibility.

Observed Areas of Pattern Alignment

When astrology is examined alongside contemporary psychological research—not as a predictive tool, but as a system of symbolic pattern recognition—clear areas of alignment emerge. Across observational studies, comparative analyses, and clinical reflection, astrology consistently mirrors the same **orientations of consciousness** identified by empirical psychology. The value lies not in causation, but in correspondence.

Astrology does not *produce* these traits. It **describes the same underlying tendencies** through a different language.

Introversion vs. Extroversion: Direction of Energy Flow

One of the most consistent areas of alignment appears in how individuals orient energy—**inward or outward**.

Charts that emphasize inward, reflective archetypes—often associated with introspective, receptive, or internally focused symbolism—frequently correlate with **introverted processing styles**. These individuals tend to recharge through solitude, reflection, and internal meaning-making. Their engagement with the world is thoughtful, selective, and depth-oriented.

Conversely, charts emphasizing outward, expressive archetypes often align with **extroverted engagement**. These individuals process experience through interaction, action, and external stimulation. They gain energy from exchange, expression, and movement within their environment.

This distinction mirrors core constructs found in both the **Big Five** (Extraversion) and **MBTI** (Introversion–Extraversion), reinforcing the idea that astrology symbolically maps **directional attention**, not behavior itself. It reveals *where energy naturally flows*, not how it must be used.

**Emotional Reactivity and Regulation:
Sensitivity of the Nervous System**

Another area of strong alignment involves **emotional processing and regulation**.

Certain archetypal configurations correlate with heightened emotional sensitivity—greater depth of feeling, stronger affective response, and increased attunement to emotional nuance. Individuals with these configurations often experience emotions as immersive and embodied, requiring intentional regulation strategies to maintain balance.

Other configurations align with more contained emotional expression—where feelings are processed cognitively, behaviorally, or through action rather than internal sensation. These individuals may appear emotionally steady or reserved, though their emotional life is no less meaningful—simply regulated differently.

These distinctions parallel findings in affective neuroscience and emotional regulation research, which demonstrate that nervous systems vary widely in **emotional intensity, recovery time, and processing style**. Astrology symbolically encodes this variation, offering insight into emotional needs without pathologizing sensitivity or restraint.

Risk Tolerance and Novelty-Seeking: Orientation Toward Change

Patterns also emerge around **risk tolerance and novelty-seeking behavior**.

Archetypes associated with initiation, exploration, and movement often correlate with higher tolerance for uncertainty and a stronger drive toward new experiences. These individuals may thrive in environments that reward experimentation, adaptability, and growth through challenge.

In contrast, stabilizing archetypes tend to align with cautious decision-making, strategic planning, and a preference for consistency. These individuals often excel in roles requiring reliability, foresight, and sustained effort over time.

This mirrors research in behavioral psychology and temperament theory, which identifies biologically rooted differences in **novelty-seeking, impulse regulation, and risk assessment**. Astrology does not label these tendencies as strengths or weaknesses—it contextualizes them as

functional orientations, each essential in different life arenas.

Cognitive Processing Styles: How Meaning Is Made

Cognitive psychology recognizes that individuals differ in how they process information—whether through abstraction, sensory detail, relational awareness, or intuitive patterning. Astrology symbolically reflects these differences as well.

Some configurations emphasize **conceptual thinking**, pattern recognition, and abstraction. These individuals often excel at systems thinking, theoretical analysis, and future-oriented visioning.

Others favor **sensory processing and pragmatism**, focusing on tangible experience, practical outcomes, and real-world application.

Still others demonstrate strong **emotional or intuitive cognition**, processing information through feeling states, relational context, and subtle cues rather than linear logic.

These distinctions align closely with learning style research and cognitive typologies, reinforcing astrology's role as a symbolic mirror of **how consciousness organizes meaning**, rather than a predictor of intelligence or ability.

Symbolic Description, Not Determination

What is most notable across these observed alignments is not that astrology predicts personality traits—but that it **describes the same orientations** consistently identified through empirical psychological observation.

Psychology measures tendencies through data and testing. Astrology reflects those tendencies through symbol and pattern.

Both arrive at similar conclusions: humans differ not because some are better or worse, but because **consciousness expresses itself through diverse configurations**. Astrology's contribution lies in its capacity to contextualize these differences within a broader narrative of purpose, growth, and meaning.

In this way, astrology functions not as a system of prediction, but as a **language of correspondence**—one that translates psychological diversity into symbolic insight.

It does not tell you who you must be.
It helps you understand **how you are inclined to experience, interpret, and evolve through life**.

And when those inclinations are recognized consciously, choice expands, agency strengthens, and destiny becomes something you participate in—rather than something you feel subjected to.

Symbol, Not Sentence

Astrology's enduring power lies not in prediction, but in **description**. Its strength is its ability to capture *qualitative experience*—the felt sense of how a person moves through life, encounters challenge, seeks meaning, and responds to the world. Where many psychological models rely on measurement and categorization, astrology works through **symbol and narrative**, offering a mirror rather than a verdict.

Where psychology measures, astrology mirrors.
Where psychology classifies, astrology contextualizes.

This distinction is critical. Numbers and categories are invaluable for research and diagnosis, but they often strip experience of nuance. Astrology restores that nuance by placing traits, tendencies, and behaviors within a **living framework of meaning**. It does not isolate characteristics; it shows how they interact, evolve, and express themselves over time.

For this reason, astrology is best understood as a **language of pattern**, not a system of fate.

Pattern as Information, Not Imprisonment

Patterns do not dictate outcomes. They describe **tendencies**—probable orientations of perception, emotion, and behavior. A tendency is not a command; it is a starting point. It indicates where energy flows most naturally, not where it must remain.

When tendencies operate unconsciously, they can feel deterministic. Reactions repeat. Circumstances echo. Life seems to happen *to* us rather than *with* us. This is when astrology is often misunderstood as fate—because unconscious patterns can create the illusion of inevitability.

Awareness changes this.

When individuals recognize their inclinations—how they tend to respond under stress, where they seek comfort, what triggers defensiveness or inspiration—they gain access to **choice**. The same pattern that once governed behavior becomes a signal that invites conscious response.

Astrology, at its best, does not lock identity in place.
It **illuminates the terrain** so navigation becomes possible.

From Reaction to Response

The shift from unconscious reaction to conscious response is where astrology reveals its greatest value. Symbolic insight allows individuals to see themselves with compassion and clarity rather than judgment. Instead of asking, *"What's wrong with me?"*, the question becomes, *"How is my energy oriented—and how can I work with it wisely?"*

This reframing is profound.

A pattern of emotional intensity becomes a capacity for empathy and depth when regulated.
A tendency toward caution becomes discernment rather than fear.
A drive toward independence becomes leadership rather than

isolation.

Astrology provides the **context** in which these tendencies make sense, transforming self-criticism into self-understanding.

Astrology as Conscious Language

Symbols are not rigid definitions—they are **living references**. They allow the psyche to recognize itself without being confined by labels. Astrology uses these symbols to reflect inner experience in a way that honors complexity, contradiction, and growth.

Rather than saying, *"This is who you are,"* astrology asks, *"This is how your consciousness tends to organize itself—what will you do with that awareness?"*

In this way, astrology becomes a language of empowerment. It does not predict destiny; it **reveals the pathways through which destiny is negotiated**. It does not remove responsibility; it deepens it—by making unconscious patterns visible and therefore workable.

Freedom Through Understanding

Freedom is not the absence of pattern—it is the ability to move within pattern consciously.

When astrology is approached as a symbol rather than a sentence, it becomes a tool for liberation rather than limitation. It invites curiosity instead of fear, responsibility instead of resignation. It reminds us that we are not prisoners of our tendencies, but participants in their expression.

Astrology does not tell you what will happen.
It helps you understand **how you are likely to meet what happens**.

And in that understanding, choice emerges—quietly, steadily, and powerfully.

Because destiny is not written in stone.
It is written in **pattern**—and patterns are meant to be understood, not obeyed.

Astrology as Integrative Insight

When approached with discernment and responsibility, astrology does not compete with psychology—it **complements it**. Where psychology often examines specific components of the human experience in isolation, astrology offers a **holistic lens**, integrating emotion, cognition, instinct, motivation, and meaning into a single, coherent symbolic framework.

This integrative quality is astrology's greatest contribution.

Rather than fragmenting the self into symptoms, traits, or diagnoses, astrology views the individual as a **dynamic system**—one in which inner processes interact continuously with external experience. Thoughts influence emotions. Emotions shape behavior. Instinct informs perception. Meaning guides motivation. Astrology reflects these interactions symbolically, allowing patterns to be seen in context rather than in pieces.

A Tool for Reflection, Not Replacement

Astrology is not a substitute for psychological assessment, therapy, or scientific inquiry. Instead, it functions as an **interpretive framework**—a way of making sense of experience through pattern recognition and symbolic meaning. Used in this way, astrology becomes especially valuable for:

- **Self-reflection**, by helping individuals recognize recurring themes and internal dynamics

- **Therapeutic insight**, by offering language for emotional processes that may be difficult to articulate directly

- **Personal development**, by clarifying motivations,

sensitivities, and growth edges

For practitioners, astrology can provide a supplementary map—one that enriches understanding of the client's inner world without replacing evidence-based approaches. For individuals, it offers a narrative lens through which life experiences can be integrated rather than compartmentalized.

Shifting the Question

Perhaps the most profound contribution astrology offers is a shift in inquiry.

Rather than asking,
"What will happen to me?"—a question rooted in fear, control, or avoidance—
astrology invites a more empowering question:

"How am I designed to experience, interpret, and grow through what happens?"

This reframing moves the individual from passive recipient to active participant. Life is no longer something that *happens to* the person; it becomes something that unfolds *with* them. Challenges are no longer signs of failure, but **invitations to develop specific capacities** encoded within the psyche.

Illuminating Pathways, Not Predicting Outcomes

Seen through this lens, natal charts do not predict destiny. They **illuminate pathways**—routes through which personality, purpose, and potential are most likely to unfold. They reveal the terrain, not the destination. They show where growth is catalyzed, where resistance may arise, and where fulfillment can be cultivated.

This understanding restores nuance to the concept of destiny. Rather than a fixed outcome, destiny becomes a **process of engagement**—a conversation between predisposition and choice, pattern and awareness.

Astrology, then, is not a tool of limitation.
It is a **language of self-awareness**.

Agency Through Understanding

Crucially, astrology does not ask individuals to surrender agency. On the contrary, it **returns agency** by making unconscious patterns visible. When tendencies are understood, they can be navigated consciously. When motivations are clarified, decisions become intentional. When challenges are contextualized, resilience deepens.

Understanding does not remove responsibility—it refines it.

In recognizing their patterns, individuals are not confined by them. They gain the freedom to respond with wisdom rather than reflex. Growth becomes purposeful rather than reactive. Identity becomes flexible rather than fixed.

Astrology, used wisely, does not tell you who to be.
It helps you understand **how you are becoming**.

And in that understanding, individuals do not lose control of their lives.
They reclaim it—grounded in awareness, aligned with purpose, and empowered by choice.

Case Pattern Illustrations (Conceptual)

When natal charts are examined across populations—not to predict outcomes, but to observe **recurring symbolic themes** —distinct patterns consistently emerge. These patterns do not function as destiny scripts. They operate as **developmental invitations**, highlighting where consciousness is most likely to be shaped through experience.

What follows are conceptual illustrations—not rigid rules— meant to demonstrate how archetypal emphasis tends to correlate with lived themes over time.

Emphasis on the Tenth House: Vocation, Responsibility, and Public Contribution

Charts with strong emphasis on the **Tenth House** —through planetary placements, angular emphasis, or repeated activation—often correlate with early awareness of responsibility, visibility, or vocation. Individuals with this pattern frequently feel a pull toward purpose-driven work, leadership roles, or public contribution earlier in life than their peers.

This does not necessarily mean conventional career success or public fame. Rather, it reflects a psychological orientation toward **impact, accountability, and contribution**. These individuals may feel internally compelled to "become something" or to represent integrity, authority, or mastery within their chosen field.

Challenges often arise around pressure, self-expectation, or identity being overly tied to achievement. Growth occurs when purpose is defined internally rather than externally— when contribution becomes aligned with authenticity rather than obligation.

Heavy Eighth or Twelfth House Placements: Transformation and Initiation

Charts with significant emphasis in the **Eighth** or **Twelfth Houses** often align with profound inner transformation. These individuals may encounter early life experiences that expose them to intensity—psychological depth, loss, power dynamics, trauma, or spiritual inquiry.

The Eighth House frequently correlates with experiences that require **psychological rebirth**—situations that strip away superficial identity and demand emotional truth, boundary renegotiation, or empowerment through vulnerability. Themes of intimacy, trust, and shared resources often act as catalysts for growth.

The Twelfth House, by contrast, often aligns with **spiritual initiation**, unconscious processing, and deep empathy. Individuals with strong Twelfth House patterns may feel different, unseen, or deeply sensitive from a young age. They are often attuned to collective emotion, suffering, or unseen dimensions of experience.

In both cases, these placements do not indicate suffering as fate. They indicate **depth as a curriculum**. Healing, insight, and compassion often emerge as strengths precisely because of what has been navigated.

Strong Mercury or Air Placements: Thought, Communication, and Meaning-Making

Charts with strong emphasis on **Mercury** or the **Air element** frequently appear in individuals drawn to teaching, writing, speaking, research, counseling, or systems-based thinking. These individuals tend to process life cognitively—seeking understanding, language, and connection through ideas.

Such placements often correlate with early curiosity, verbal agility, and pattern recognition. The mind becomes the primary interface with the world, and meaning is constructed through dialogue, analysis, or conceptual frameworks.

Challenges may include overthinking, disconnection from the body, or emotional detachment. Growth occurs when intellect is integrated with embodiment and emotional awareness—allowing insight to become wisdom rather than abstraction.

Patterns as Invitations, Not Conclusions

What is essential to understand is that these patterns do not represent fate. They are **recurring invitations**—themes that life revisits until they are consciously engaged.

Two individuals with similar chart emphasis may live vastly

different lives depending on awareness, environment, support, and choice. One may feel burdened by responsibility; another may feel empowered by purpose.

One may feel overwhelmed by emotional depth; another may become a healer, guide, or advocate.

The chart does not decide the outcome.
It reveals **where growth is asking to happen**.

Patterns repeat not to punish, but to educate. They surface again and again, not because one has failed, but because consciousness evolves through repetition until insight transforms experience.

Astrology, in this context, does not lock life into inevitability.
It highlights **the curriculum of becoming**.

When patterns are recognized consciously, they stop feeling like cycles to escape and begin to feel like **paths to walk with intention**. And in that recognition, destiny shifts—from something that happens unconsciously, to something that is actively participated in, shaped by awareness and choice.

PRACTICAL TOOL: BIRTH CHART BREAKDOWN WORKSHEET

Mapping Your Celestial Blueprint

This guided exercise is designed to help you begin translating your natal chart into lived understanding. You do not need to "master astrology" to benefit from this process. The goal is **recognition, not perfection**.

Have your natal chart available (from a reputable chart calculator) as you work through the steps.

Step 1: Identify Your Core Triad

Sun, Moon, and Rising (Ascendant)

These three placements form the foundation of your chart and describe the core architecture of your experience.

- **Sun Sign (Identity & Purpose):**
  What sign is your Sun in?
  What qualities do you recognize in how you express yourself, seek fulfillment, or define purpose?

- **Moon Sign (Emotional Processing & Safety):**
  What sign is your Moon in?
  How do you tend to process emotion, seek comfort, or respond under stress?

- **Rising Sign (Interface with the World):**
  What sign is rising on the eastern horizon at your birth?
  How do you tend to approach life, new situations, and first impressions?

Notes / Observations:

Step 2: Identify Your Most Activated Life Arenas

House Emphasis

Look at which houses contain the most planets or significant points.

- Which **houses** appear most populated?
- Are there life areas that seem to demand repeated attention, growth, or resolution?

Consider how these themes show up in your lived experience:

- Relationships
- Career or public contribution
- Emotional foundations
- Health and daily rhythms
- Creativity or spirituality

Key Houses Activated:

Life Themes You Recognize:

Step 3: Observe Elemental Patterns

Fire · Earth · Air · Water

Notice which elements appear most frequently in your chart.

- **Fire (Action, Motivation, Inspiration):**
  Do you act quickly? Seek meaning through experience?

- **Earth (Stability, Structure, Practicality):**
  Do you prioritize security, responsibility, or tangible results?

- **Air (Thought, Communication, Conceptualization):**
  Do you process life through ideas, dialogue, or analysis?

- **Water (Emotion, Intuition, Relational Depth):**
  Do you experience life primarily through feeling and emotional resonance?

Dominant Element(s):

How This Shows Up in Your Life:

Step 4: Identify Dominant Planetary Themes

Which planets appear repeatedly, are closely clustered, or occupy significant positions (such as the 1st, 7th, or 10th houses)?

- Are themes of communication, responsibility, transformation, creativity, or healing especially strong?

- Do certain lessons seem to recur around boundaries, authority, intimacy, or purpose?

Dominant Planet(s):

Recurring Life Lessons or Strengths:

Reflection Prompt

Which life areas feel most activated in your experience so far?

Where do you notice repetition—not as failure, but as invitation?
What themes seem to return, asking for deeper understanding, integration, or expression?

Reflection Space:

Closing Note to the Reader

Your natal chart is not a verdict.
It is a **map of awareness**.

This worksheet is not about defining who you are—it is about recognizing how your consciousness has been organized to learn, grow, and evolve through experience. As you continue through this book, return to this worksheet often. Each chapter will illuminate new layers of what you have already begun to see.

Key Takeaway

Your natal chart does not dictate identity. It does not assign a role you must play or a path you are obligated to follow. It does not define your worth, your limitations, or your future. Instead, it offers something far more valuable: **orientation**.

Your natal chart reveals **how you are designed to grow**.

It illuminates the mechanisms through which your consciousness learns—how challenge refines you, how fulfillment is accessed, and how meaning is constructed through experience. The chart shows *where* energy naturally concentrates, *how* it tends to respond, and *which arenas of life* act as catalysts for development.

In this way, astrology does not describe destiny as an endpoint. It describes destiny as a **process of becoming**.

Where Life Asks Its Questions

Life does not test everyone in the same way. Some are shaped through responsibility and leadership. Others through emotional depth and relational healing. Some through innovation and disruption, others through surrender and spiritual integration.

Your natal chart highlights **where life is most likely to ask its questions**.

These questions may appear as recurring themes:

- Repeated relationship dynamics

- Vocational crossroads

- Cycles of transformation or reinvention

- Persistent calls toward creativity, service, or truth

These patterns are not signs of failure. They are signals of curriculum—areas where growth is intentional, and wisdom is meant to be earned through engagement rather than avoidance.

Where You Hold the Capacity to Respond

Just as importantly, your chart reveals **where you are most capable of answering those questions with wisdom**.

Your strengths are not random gifts; they are compensatory intelligences—capacities designed to meet the very challenges you encounter. The same placements that highlight struggle also highlight resources. Sensitivity carries empathy. Responsibility cultivates mastery. Curiosity generates insight. Depth births transformation.

Astrology, when approached consciously, shows not only where difficulty arises—but **how you are equipped to meet it**.

From Limitation to Liberation

When astrology is read unconsciously, it can feel limiting—like a set of labels or constraints. But when read with awareness, it becomes a mirror of liberation.

It frees you from self-judgment by contextualizing your tendencies.
It dissolves comparison by honoring unique design.
It replaces confusion with coherence.

Instead of asking, *"What's wrong with me?"*
You begin asking, *"What is this experience teaching me?"*

This shift changes everything.

Astrology as Conscious Reflection

Astrology does not remove uncertainty. It deepens understanding. It does not replace responsibility. It clarifies it. It does not confine growth. It **directs it**.

When read with consciousness, astrology becomes less about

identity and more about **integration**—bringing together instinct and intention, challenge and capacity, destiny and choice.

Your natal chart is not a map of who you must be.
It is a mirror reflecting how you are invited to evolve.

And in seeing that reflection clearly, you do not lose freedom.
You reclaim it—aligned, informed, and awake.

CHAPTER 3
Time, Place, and Purpose: Astrocartography and Energy Portals

You are not meant to experience every version of yourself in the same place.

Just as your birth encoded a vibrational signature into your body, **geography activates that code** in different ways. Where you live, travel, work, and heal matters—not only socially or economically, but energetically. Certain places draw out aspects of your soul. Others challenge you, refine you, or initiate profound transformation.

Astrocartography reveals *why*.

The Energetic Relationship Between Geography and the Soul

Astrocartography is the study of how the energetic blueprint encoded at your birth interacts with the physical geography of the Earth. It examines how planetary energies from your natal chart are projected onto the globe, revealing **where specific archetypal forces are amplified, tested, or awakened based on location**. In this way, astrocartography answers a question that many people intuitively feel but rarely articulate: *Why does life feel so different in different places?*

At its foundation, astrocartography is not mystical speculation —it is **mathematics applied to consciousness**. Using precise astronomical calculations, your natal planetary positions are translated into longitudinal lines that wrap around the Earth. These lines mark locations where each planet was rising, setting, culminating, or at its lowest point at the moment of your birth. Each position corresponds to a specific mode of expression—how that planetary energy manifests through experience.

What this creates is a **geographic extension of your natal chart**.

Rather than existing solely within the psyche, your blueprint becomes spatial. It stretches across continents and oceans, embedding your destiny into the physical world itself. Place, therefore, is not neutral. It is an active participant in your evolution.

Each planetary line represents an **archetypal current**:

- Identity and visibility

- Love and attraction

- Power and transformation

- Growth and opportunity

- Healing and spiritual initiation

When you live, work, or travel near one of these lines, the corresponding themes become louder. Experiences accelerate. Lessons intensify. Awareness sharpens. What might have remained dormant elsewhere rises to the surface—not because the planet causes events, but because the **environment resonates with a particular frequency within you**.

This is why the same person can feel confident and expansive in one city, emotionally raw in another, and spiritually awakened in a third. The soul is not inconsistent—the environment is activating different dimensions of the same design.

In simple terms:

Your soul responds differently depending on where you are standing on Earth.

This response is both psychological and physiological. Changes in geomagnetic fields, light exposure, environmental rhythm, and cultural energy all interact with the nervous system. When these external frequencies align with specific aspects of your natal imprint, inner shifts occur naturally. Motivation changes. Emotional patterns reorganize. Life direction recalibrates.

Astrocartography provides a language for understanding these shifts—not as coincidence, but as **resonance**.

From this perspective, destiny is not confined to time alone. It is **spatially distributed**. Certain places call forth leadership. Others invite healing. Some demand transformation, while others offer rest, love, or creative expression. None are accidental.

Understanding the energetic relationship between geography and the soul empowers conscious movement. It allows you to choose locations not only for survival or success, but for **alignment**. It reframes relocation as a form of initiation, travel as activation, and place as a teacher.

You are not meant to become everything everywhere.
You are meant to become specific aspects of yourself in specific places.

Astrocartography reveals that the Earth itself is part of your blueprint—a living map of where your soul remembers, awakens, and evolves.

Why Place Matters More Than We've Been Taught

Modern culture has largely reduced geography to a matter of logistics. We are taught to choose where we live based on affordability, opportunity, proximity, or convenience—treating land as a neutral backdrop upon which life simply unfolds. Yet this perspective is historically and energetically incomplete. For most of human civilization, **place was**

never incidental. It was understood as alive, intelligent, and directive.

Ancient cultures across the world—Kemetic, Indigenous, Mayan, Vedic, Celtic, Andean, and many others—recognized land as a living participant in human evolution. Sacred sites were not chosen arbitrarily. Temples, initiation grounds, healing centers, and seats of governance were established in locations where energy was known to concentrate, flow, or amplify intention. These societies understood that **where you stand shapes who you become**.

Science is now beginning to echo what ancestral wisdom preserved.

The Earth as an Energetic System

The Earth is enveloped in a dynamic electromagnetic field generated by its molten core, rotation, and interaction with solar radiation. This field is not static—it fluctuates in response to solar activity, geomagnetic storms, and planetary rhythms. Human nervous systems, hearts, and brains are biologically sensitive to these fluctuations.

Research in neurocardiology and chronobiology demonstrates that:

- Heart rate variability responds to geomagnetic activity
- Sleep cycles and mood shift with changes in light exposure and magnetic conditions
- Emotional regulation and cognitive clarity are influenced by environmental rhythm

When you change location, you do not simply change scenery —you change **frequency**.

These shifts are often subtle, but their effects accumulate over time. A place may calm the nervous system or activate it. It may ground awareness or heighten emotional sensitivity. It may stimulate creativity or initiate introspection. None of this is random.

Why Certain Places Feel Charged

This energetic sensitivity explains experiences that many people report but struggle to articulate:

- **Some places feel like home immediately**, even without a logical explanation. The body relaxes. Breath deepens. Orientation feels natural.

- **Some locations trigger deep healing or discomfort**, bringing unresolved emotion, memory, or identity to the surface.

- **Some environments expand creativity, confidence, or visibility**, making expression feel effortless and aligned.

- **Others initiate karmic lessons**, catalyzing endings, confrontations, or periods of shadow work that reshape identity.

These responses occur not because a place is "good" or "bad," but because it **activates specific frequencies within the individual**.

What feels supportive for one person may feel destabilizing for another—because each nervous system carries a unique energetic imprint. Place interacts with that imprint in highly personal ways.

Astrocartography as Interpretive Language

Astrocartography provides a framework for understanding these experiences with clarity and intention. It translates the intuitive knowing that *place matters* into a symbolic and mathematical map that explains **why certain locations affect**

you the way they do.

Rather than dismissing strong reactions to place as coincidence or mood, astrocartography reframes them as **feedback**—signals that an environment is interacting with your blueprint in meaningful ways.

This understanding restores agency. You no longer need to wonder why a place felt inexplicably heavy, expansive, draining, or inspiring. You can recognize those sensations as part of an energetic dialogue between your soul and the land beneath your feet.

From Convenience to Conscious Choice

When a place is understood as energetic rather than incidental, relocation becomes more than a practical decision—it becomes an act of alignment. Travel becomes initiation. Movement becomes intentional.

You stop asking, *"Where should I go to succeed?"*
And begin asking, *"Where does my soul come alive, heal, or evolve?"*

Astrocartography does not dictate where you must live. It illuminates how **place collaborates with destiny**. It invites conscious choice in a world that often treats movement as mechanical.

Because the land you stand on is not passive.
It is communicating with you—constantly.

And when you learn to listen, place transforms from background into guide, from setting into teacher, from location into **activation**.

Lines of Destiny: Power, Love, Growth, and Karma

In astrocartography, each planetary line represents an **activation pathway**—a geographic corridor where a specific archetypal force is amplified. These lines do not *cause* events;

they **activate themes** already encoded within your natal blueprint. When you live, work, or spend meaningful time near a line, the corresponding lessons grow louder, clearer, and often faster.

Think of planetary lines as **currents** in a living ocean. You can swim anywhere—but when you enter a current, your movement changes. You are carried in a particular direction, asked to engage a specific aspect of yourself, and invited to grow through that engagement.

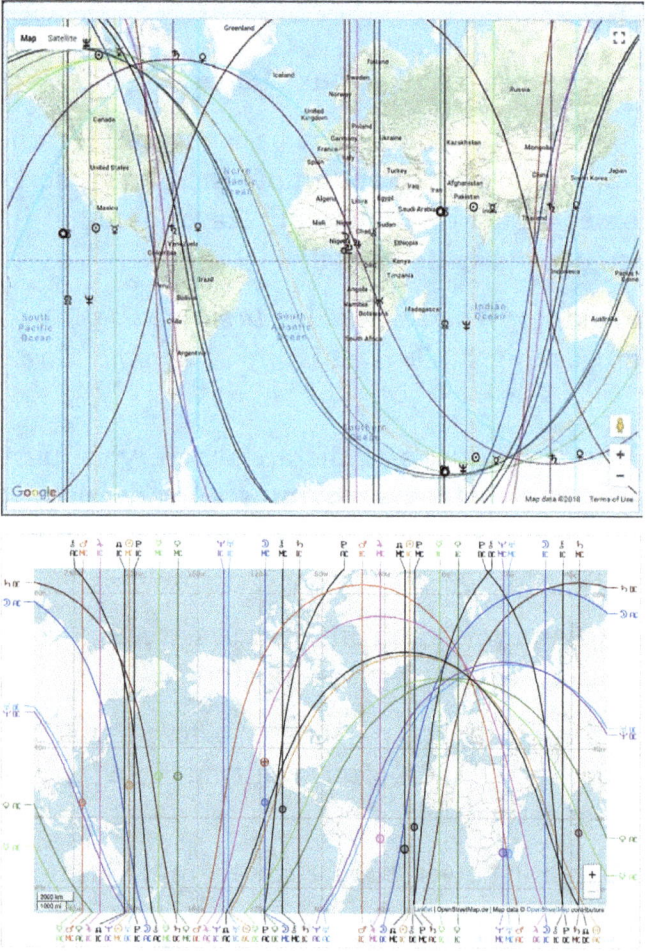

ENCODED IN THE STARS | 87

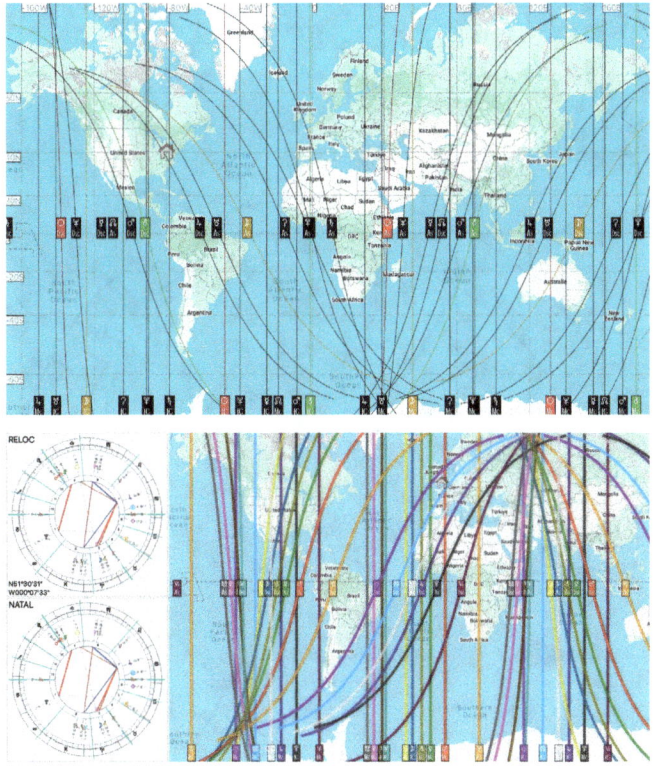

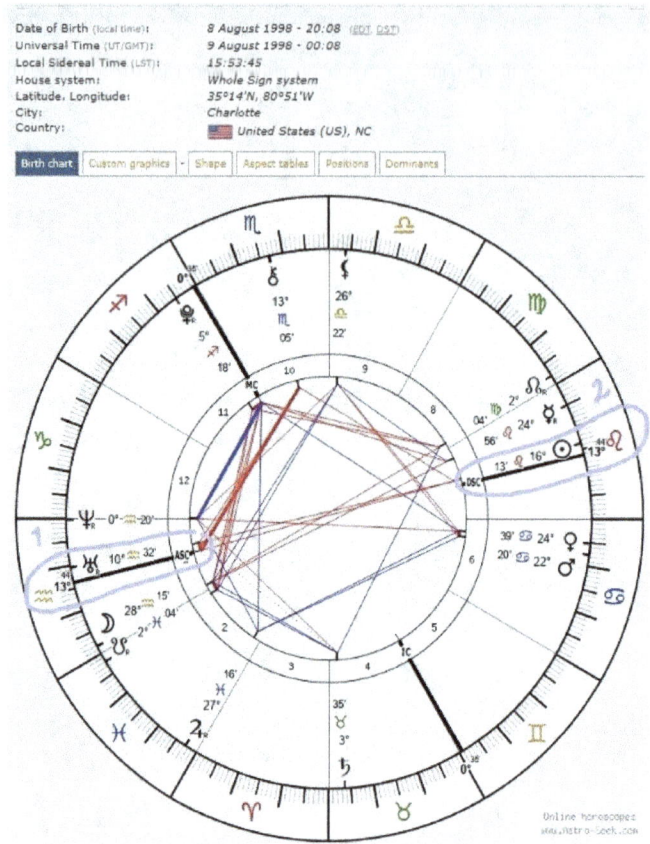

Planetary Lines and Their Core Teachings

Sun Lines — Visibility, Identity, Leadership, Purpose

Sun lines illuminate identity. Near these locations, people often feel *seen*, energized, and called to step into leadership or self-expression. Confidence and recognition tend to increase —not always comfortably, but purposefully. These places ask: *Who are you when you are fully visible?*

Common experiences: career momentum, leadership roles, renewed vitality, public recognition.

Moon Lines — Emotional Life, Family, Intuition, Inner Healing

Moon lines amplify feeling. They often evoke deep emotional memory, attachment themes, and intuitive awareness. These locations can feel like home—or expose unresolved emotional patterns that seek healing. They teach emotional literacy and self-nurturing.

Common experiences: family focus, mood sensitivity, caregiving roles, and ancestral healing.

Venus Lines — Love, Beauty, Pleasure, Harmony, Attraction

Venus lines soften experience. They enhance connection, aesthetics, romance, and the ability to receive. These places often support relationships, creativity, and enjoyment—but can also reveal where balance, boundaries, or self-worth need attention.

Common experiences: romantic partnerships, artistic inspiration, social ease, pleasure, and comfort.

Mars Lines — Action, Conflict, Drive, Boundaries, Courage

Mars lines activate momentum. They bring drive, assertion, and courage—but can also intensify conflict if boundaries are unclear. These locations are powerful for initiating projects, reclaiming agency, and learning healthy self-assertion.

Common experiences: rapid movement, competition, leadership through action, boundary testing.

Jupiter Lines — Growth, Abundance, Education, Expansion

Jupiter lines expand horizons. They often bring opportunity, learning, travel, and optimism. Growth here can feel effortless, but discernment is key—expansion without integration can become excess.

Common experiences: career growth, higher education, mentorship, spiritual or philosophical expansion.

Saturn Lines — Discipline, Responsibility, Tests, Mastery

Saturn lines refine through challenge. They demand patience, accountability, and sustained effort. While not always easy, these locations build resilience and long-term mastery. What is earned here tends to endure.

Common experiences: increased responsibility, delayed gratification, authority testing, and personal maturation.

Uranus Lines — Awakening, Disruption, Liberation, Change

Uranus lines awaken the unexpected. They disrupt routine, catalyze liberation, and invite authenticity—often suddenly. These places are excellent for innovation and reinvention, but rarely predictable.

Common experiences: sudden life changes, breakthroughs, unconventional paths, freedom from old constraints.

Neptune Lines — Spirituality, Imagination, Illusion, Surrender

Neptune lines dissolve boundaries. They heighten spirituality, creativity, and compassion—but can blur clarity if grounding is absent. These places teach surrender, faith, and discernment between intuition and illusion.

Common experiences: spiritual exploration, artistic inspiration, heightened sensitivity, and idealization.

Pluto Lines — Power, Transformation, Death/Rebirth Cycles

Pluto lines transform at the root. They bring intensity, shadow work, and profound rebirth. These locations often coincide with endings that make space for empowerment and renewal.

Common experiences: deep psychological change, power dynamics, loss and regeneration, reclamation of inner authority.

Teachers, Not Judgments

No planetary line is inherently "good" or "bad." Each line **teaches**.

- Some locations **support**—offering ease, growth, or harmony.

- Others **initiate**—awakening dormant gifts or awareness.

- Some **demand transformation**—requiring release, courage, or deep integration.

What feels supportive at one stage of life may feel constraining at another. A place meant for healing may not be meant for permanence. Astrocartography invites discernment: *Is this location for building, becoming, or letting go?*

Choosing with Consciousness

Understanding your planetary lines empowers conscious choice. You can select environments that align with your current intention—whether that is love, mastery, creativity, healing, or reinvention—while respecting that each choice carries a curriculum.

You are not meant to bloom the same way everywhere.
Some places are classrooms.
Some are sanctuaries.
Some are initiations.

Astrocartography doesn't promise ease—it promises **meaningful alignment**. And when you engage a place with awareness, geography becomes a collaborator in destiny rather than a backdrop to it.

Energy Portals and Karmic Activation Zones

Certain places on Earth function as **energy portals**—geographic zones where the interaction between your natal blueprint and the planet's energetic grid becomes intensified. In these locations, dormant aspects of the psyche rise to the surface. Memory activates. Gifts awaken. Unfinished lessons demand attention. Life accelerates—not because fate intervenes, but because **frequency meets readiness**.

People often describe these places as feeling *charged*, *fated*, or *inevitable*. The pace of life shifts. Events cluster. Decisions carry weight. Inner changes happen quickly, sometimes uncomfortably, often irrevocably.

Common experiences reported in these zones include:

- **Sudden life changes**, where familiar structures dissolve rapidly

- **Accelerated growth**, compressing years of development into months

- **Spiritual awakenings**, marked by expanded awareness or existential reorientation

- **Intense relationships**, catalytic connections that mirror deep truths

- **Career breakthroughs—or collapses**, forcing realignment with purpose

These experiences are not random. They arise because **location activates latent codes** already present in the natal chart. What was subtle elsewhere becomes unmistakable here. The environment amplifies specific archetypal themes—bringing clarity, confrontation, or completion.

Activation Does Not Mean Permanence

A crucial truth about energy portals is that **they are not always meant to be permanent homes**.

Some places are designed as **thresholds**, not destinations. They serve a specific function in the arc of becoming, then release you onward. When their work is complete, the same location that once felt alive may begin to feel heavy, stagnant, or restrictive.

This is not failure—it is completion.

Certain locations are designed for:

- **Learning** — acquiring insight, skill, or perspective

- **Healing** — processing grief, trauma, or emotional fragmentation

- **Awakening** — remembering truth, purpose, or spiritual identity

- **Releasing** — ending cycles, relationships, or outdated identities

When a place has fulfilled its role, staying beyond that point can **stall growth**. The nervous system adapts to frequency; when stimulation no longer invites evolution, inertia replaces expansion.

This is why people often *outgrow* cities, homes, or regions that once felt aligned. The soul has moved forward—even if the geography has not.

Karmic Lessons and Energetic Boundaries

Karmic activation zones often carry a double edge. They may bring profound insight and equally profound discomfort. These places can surface unresolved patterns—power dynamics, abandonment wounds, self-betrayal, or fear—so they can be seen clearly and integrated consciously.

Importantly, **learning the lesson does not require lifelong**

residence.

This is why the truth rings so deeply when people say:
"You cannot grow in the same space where you were hurt."

This is not only psychological wisdom—it is **energetic law**.

The body remembers environments. Nervous systems encode context. When a place becomes associated with chronic threat, grief, or depletion, remaining there can continually reactivate survival patterns, even after insight has been gained. Growth requires **a new frequency** to stabilize the new self.

Leaving, then, is not avoidance.
It is **integration**.

Movement as Evolution

Astrocartography reframes movement not as instability, but as **evolutionary intelligence**. The soul moves when it is ready to embody a new frequency. Geography becomes a collaborator —guiding transitions through resonance rather than force.

Some places break you open.
Some places hold you while you heal.
Some places remind you who you are becoming.

And some places must be left—not because they were wrong, but because their work is done.

Understanding energy portals and karmic activation zones allows you to release guilt around change. It replaces confusion with clarity. It honors the truth that **growth is dynamic**, and that alignment sometimes requires movement.

You are not meant to stay where you were initiated forever.
You are meant to **carry the wisdom forward**—into the places where your next becoming can breathe.

Relocation Charts: How the Self Reorganizes by Place

When you move, your natal chart does not disappear. It

reorganizes.

Astrology recognizes that while your birth moment anchors your core identity, **place determines how that identity is expressed**. A relocation chart recalculates your natal chart as if you were born in the new location—using the same date and time, but a different latitude and longitude. The planets remain in the same zodiac signs, yet the **house structure shifts**, reassigning where life emphasis unfolds.

In practical terms, your *essence* stays the same, but the **stage changes**.

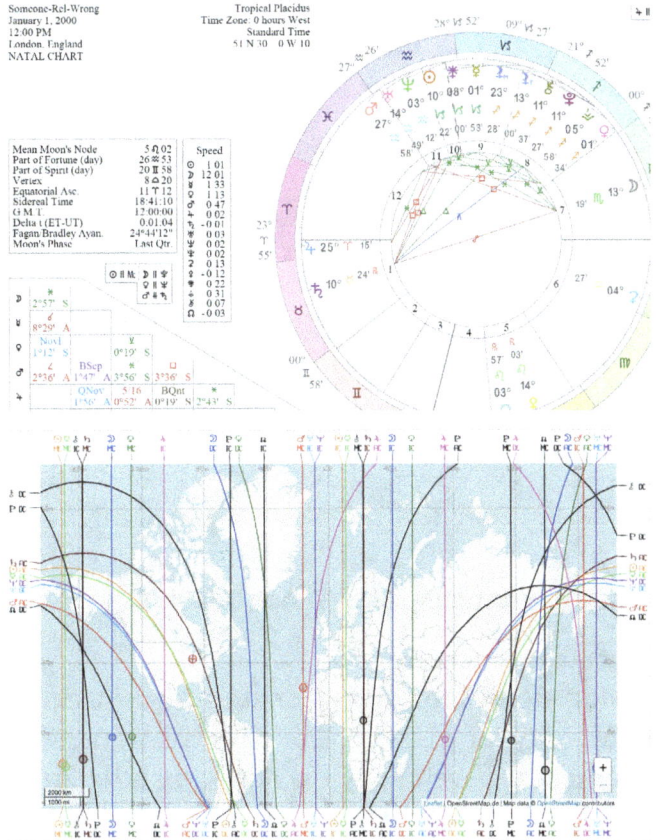

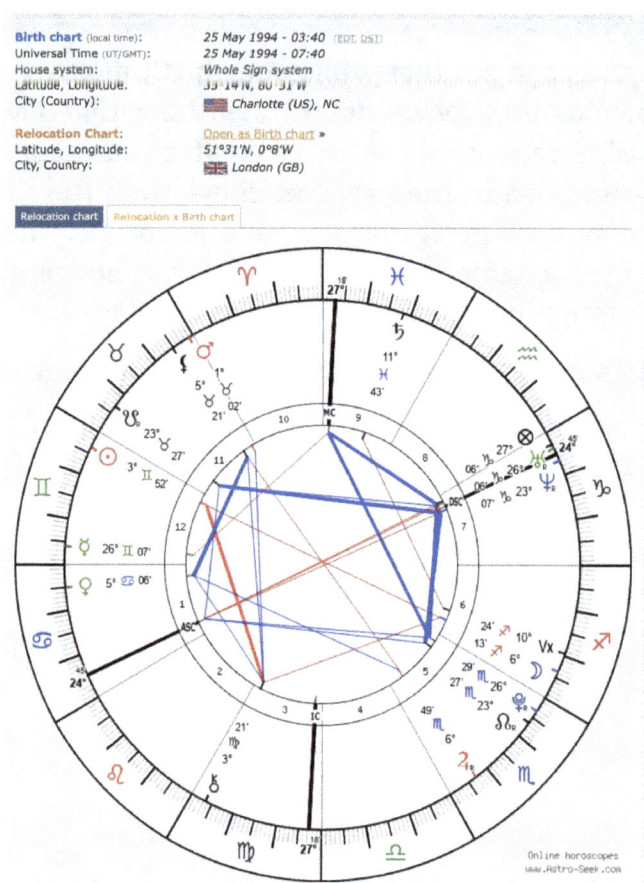

What Actually Changes—and What Doesn't

- **What stays constant:**
  Your Sun sign, Moon sign, planetary sign placements, and core archetypal makeup. Your motivations, values, and fundamental psychology do not vanish when you cross borders.

- **What changes:**
  The **houses**—the arenas of life where those planetary

energies express themselves. A planet that once emphasized home and inner life may now emphasize career and visibility; another that once centered relationships may shift toward creativity or service.

This is why relocation can feel like a personality change—without actually being one.

Why Experience Shifts So Dramatically

Relocation charts explain common, lived experiences that otherwise feel mysterious:

- **Feeling more confident and visible in one city**
  When identity- or vitality-related energies move into angular or public houses, self-expression feels easier. Leadership opportunities arise naturally. You feel *seen* without forcing it.

- **Experiencing emotional intensity in another location**
  When emotional or memory-oriented energies become emphasized, inner life deepens. Family themes, intuition, and sensitivity increase—sometimes bringing healing, sometimes demanding it.

- **Finding love or connection where life once felt neutral**
  When relational or attraction-oriented energies shift into interpersonal houses, partnership becomes a focal point. Encounters feel meaningful rather than coincidental.

- **Encountering career tests after relocating**
  When responsibility- or mastery-oriented energies move into vocational houses, life may demand discipline, structure, or patience before reward. Growth becomes earned rather than effortless.

These experiences are not coincidences. They are **contextual activations**.

Activation, Not Replacement

Relocation does not make you someone else.
It **activates a different layer of who you already are**.

Every individual carries multiple potentials within their natal design. Place determines which potentials are foregrounded. One environment may amplify confidence and creativity; another may deepen emotional intelligence; another may refine discipline and mastery.

This is why timing and intention matter. A place that feels restrictive at one stage of life may feel stabilizing at another. A location meant for initiation may not be where you settle long-term.

Relocation charts offer discernment: *Is this place asking me to build, to heal, to lead, or to release?*

Choosing a Place with Awareness

Understanding relocation charts empowers conscious movement. Rather than asking whether a place will make you "happy," you can ask a more precise question:

What part of myself will this place invite me to embody right now?

With this awareness, relocation becomes an act of collaboration with destiny rather than a gamble. You are no longer chasing change—you are **aligning expression**.

You are not losing yourself when you move.
You are reorganizing how your self meets the world.

And when a place is chosen with intention, relocation stops feeling destabilizing and starts feeling **purposeful**—a strategic activation of the next chapter in your becoming.

Scientific Support: Earth Resonance and Bioenergetics

The idea that place shapes human experience is no longer

confined to ancient wisdom or intuitive knowing. Modern science increasingly supports the conclusion that **location influences physiology, nervous system regulation, and states of consciousness**. The Earth is not an inert platform beneath our feet—it is an active, dynamic system in constant communication with the human body.

We are bioelectrical beings living within a planetary electrical field.

The Earth's Electromagnetic Environment

The Earth generates a vast and fluctuating electromagnetic field created by its molten core, rotation, solar interaction, and atmospheric dynamics. Human biology—particularly the heart, brain, and nervous system—is exquisitely sensitive to this field.

Research across biophysics, neurocardiology, and chronobiology demonstrates that **external electromagnetic conditions directly influence internal biological rhythms**. When you change location, you change your relationship to these fields—often in subtle ways that accumulate into significant physiological and psychological effects over time.

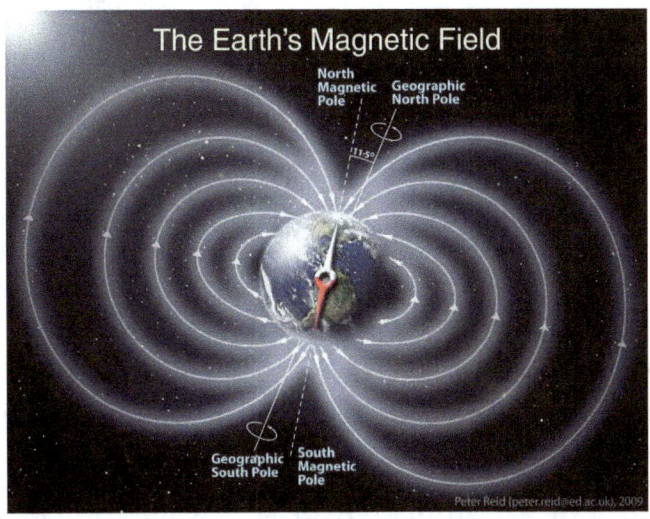

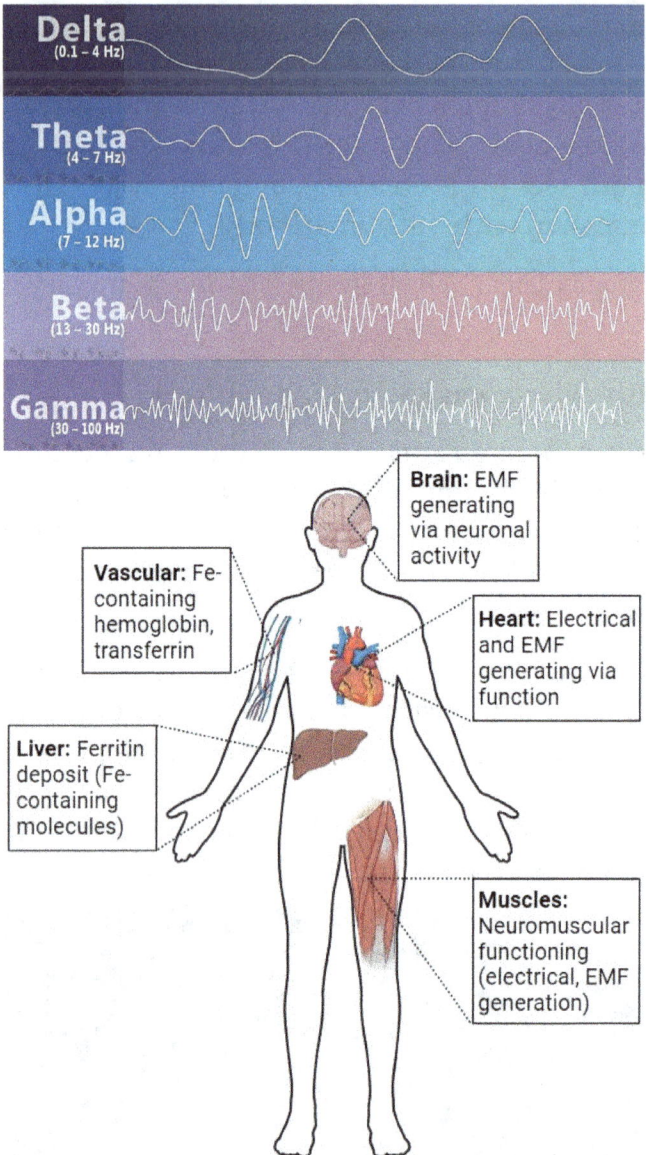

Geomagnetic Fields and Human Regulation

One of the most studied areas of environmental influence involves **geomagnetic fields**. Variations in geomagnetic activity have been correlated with measurable changes in:

- **Heart rate variability (HRV)** — a key indicator of nervous system resilience and emotional regulation

- **Sleep cycles and circadian rhythms**, affecting mood, cognition, and immune function

- **Stress hormone regulation**, influencing anxiety, irritability, and emotional reactivity

When geomagnetic conditions are stable and supportive, the nervous system tends to regulate more easily. When they are erratic or misaligned with an individual's sensitivity, stress responses can increase—even in the absence of psychological triggers.

This helps explain why some locations feel calming and restorative, while others feel overstimulating or draining without any obvious external cause.

Ley Lines and Sacred Geography

For thousands of years, ancient civilizations identified and mapped what are often referred to as **ley lines**—energetic pathways believed to run through the Earth's surface. These lines were not abstract concepts; they were identified through repeated observation of places where energy felt intensified, perception shifted, or healing and ritual were most effective.

Remarkably, many of these mapped pathways coincide with:

- Ancient temples and pyramids

- Sacred mountains and burial sites

- Historic cities and ceremonial grounds

While modern science does not universally adopt the term "ley lines," emerging research into **geophysical anomalies, telluric currents, and subtle electromagnetic concentrations** suggests that certain locations do, in fact, exhibit unique energetic properties.

Ancient cultures did not choose these sites by chance. They listened to the land.

Earth Resonance and Nervous System Coherence

The Earth produces natural resonance frequencies—most notably those occurring between the surface of the planet and the ionosphere. These frequencies overlap with ranges known to support **calm focus, creativity, intuition, and emotional regulation** in the human nervous system.

When the body synchronizes with these environmental rhythms, **coherence emerges**. Heart rhythms stabilize. Brainwave patterns harmonize. Emotional processing becomes more fluid. This is not mystical—it is measurable.

Disruption occurs when:

- Environmental frequencies clash with individual sensitivity

- Chronic stress overrides biological rhythm

- The nervous system remains in a prolonged fight-or-flight

In such cases, dysregulation increases—manifesting as anxiety, fatigue, emotional volatility, or cognitive fog.

Human Biofields and Planetary Interaction

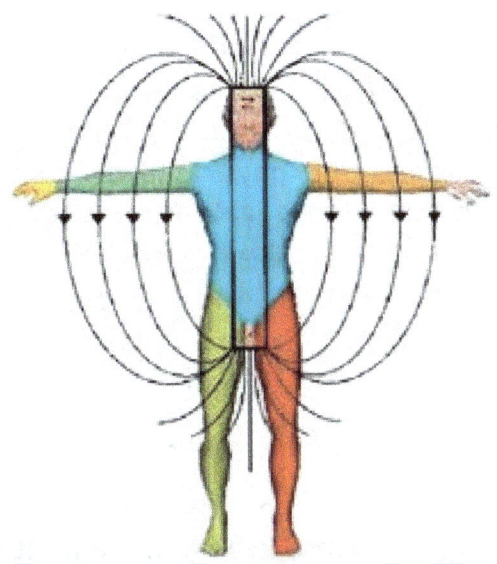
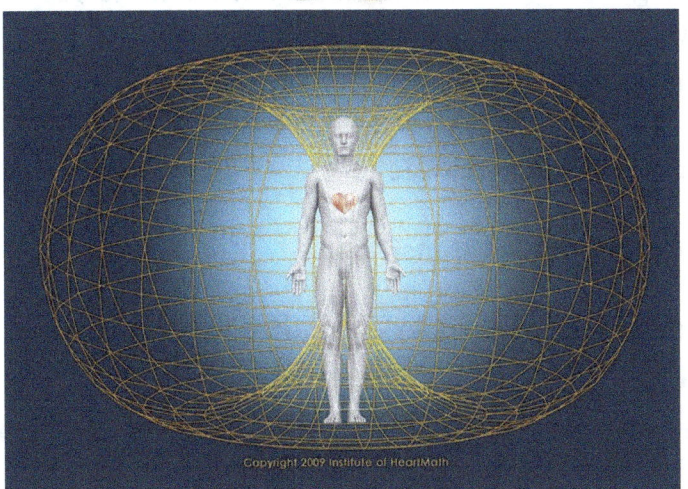

Electromagnetic Field of the Heart

Our thoughts and emotions affect the heart's magnetic field, which energetically affects those in our environment whether or not we are conscious of it.

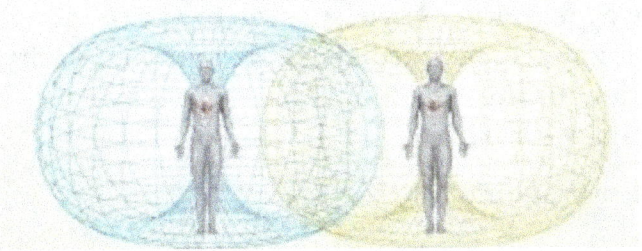

The human body is not only biochemical—it is **bioelectrical**. Every heartbeat, neural impulse, and cellular exchange generates electromagnetic activity, creating a dynamic field that extends beyond the physical body. This field—often referred to as the **human biofield**—is measurable, responsive, and deeply relational. It does not exist in isolation. It is in constant dialogue with the larger electromagnetic environment of the Earth.

Your body is continuously *listening* to the planet.

The Biofield as an Interface, Not a Barrier

The biofield functions as an interface between internal physiology and the external environment. It responds to changes in:

- **Geographic location**
- **Altitude and latitude**
- **Geomagnetic intensity**
- **Solar and atmospheric conditions**

These variables subtly influence nervous system tone, heart rhythm coherence, hormonal balance, and emotional regulation. The body adapts moment by moment—often without conscious awareness—to the energetic conditions of the environment.

This is why relocation, travel, or even brief exposure to certain places can produce immediate shifts in mood, clarity, energy, or emotional state. The biofield is not passive; it is **adaptive and communicative**.

Coherence vs. Conflict

When the frequency of the human biofield aligns harmoniously with planetary fields, the body enters a state of **coherence**. In this state:

- Heart rate variability stabilizes
- Nervous system regulation improves
- Emotional processing becomes fluid
- Cognitive clarity increases
- Intuition sharpens

Coherence feels like ease, groundedness, and alignment. It often manifests as a sense of *belonging*—that ineffable feeling of being in the right place at the right time.

When there is misalignment—when planetary conditions clash with individual sensitivity or biological rhythm—the body compensates. This can activate stress responses without a clear psychological cause. Symptoms may include:

- Restlessness or anxiety
- Fatigue or mental fog
- Emotional irritability or heaviness
- Sleep disruption

Importantly, this does not mean the place is "wrong." It means the environment is **activating something specific**—perhaps a growth edge, a karmic lesson, or a phase of recalibration.

Why Place Feels Personal

This interaction helps explain a phenomenon many people intuitively recognize: **the same environment can feel** radically different to different individuals.

One person may thrive in a high-energy urban center, while another becomes dysregulated. One may feel spiritually awakened near the ocean, while another feels emotionally overwhelmed. These differences are not a matter of preference alone—they reflect **unique biofield sensitivities and natal energetic imprints**.

Your biofield carries your blueprint. The Earth provides the amplifier.

Astrocartography bridges this interaction by identifying where planetary frequencies intersect most strongly with your natal design—offering insight into why certain places feel supportive, catalytic, or destabilizing.

Place as Feedback, Not Judgment

When a location feels profoundly supportive, it is often because your biofield is resonating with the planetary environment in a way that promotes coherence. When a place feels unsettling, it may be activating unfinished integration or demanding adaptation.

Neither experience is inherently positive or negative. Both are **informational**.

The body responds honestly to place. It does not filter through logic or expectation. It communicates through sensation, emotion, and intuition—signaling whether an environment is stabilizing, stimulating, or challenging your current state of becoming.

Listening to the Field

Understanding human biofields and planetary interaction reframes intuition as biological intelligence. The question shifts from *"Why do I feel this way here?"* to *"What is this place activating within me?"*

When you listen to that feedback, place becomes a guide rather than a mystery.

Alignment does not always feel comfortable—but it is always clarifying.

And when coherence is present, the body knows before the mind does.

Because you are not merely living *on* the Earth.
You are living **in a relationship with it**—field to field, frequency to frequency, becoming shaped not only by time, but by place.

Place as a Shaping Force

When viewed through the combined lenses of science, bioenergetics, and symbolic systems, geography is no longer a passive setting. It emerges as a **shaping force**—a biological, neurological, and energetic variable that actively participates in human development.

Place influences **rhythm**.
Rhythm influences **regulation**.
Regulation shapes **perception, behavior, and meaning-making**.

This chain is foundational. It explains why identical life circumstances can be experienced radically differently depending on location, and why internal shifts often follow external movement. Geography does not simply host experience—it **conditions how experience is processed**.

From Environment to Experience

Environmental rhythm—light cycles, electromagnetic patterns, altitude, climate, and cultural tempo—interacts continuously with the nervous system. When rhythm supports biological regulation, the body settles. When rhythm disrupts regulation, the nervous system compensates, often through heightened vigilance, emotional reactivity, or fatigue.

Over time, these physiological states shape:

- How safe the world feels

- How easily connection is formed

- How clearly purpose is sensed

- How meaning is constructed from experience

In this way, place quietly sculpts identity—not by force, but by **repetition**.

Place, therefore, is not just where life happens.
It is **how life is shaped**.

Astrocartography as Integrative Bridge

Astrocartography bridges scientific insight with symbolic intelligence. It offers a framework for understanding why certain environments promote **coherence, embodiment, and expansion**, while others demand **adaptation, transformation, or release**.

Rather than labeling places as good or bad, astrocartography reveals *function*:

- Some environments stabilize and nourish

- Others initiate growth through challenge

- Some awaken dormant gifts

- Others expose what must be healed or released

This perspective removes moral judgment from experience. A difficult place is not a failure—it is often a **training ground**. A supportive place is not a reward—it is a **resonant match** for the current phase of becoming.

The Body as the First Responder

The body responds to place before the mind understands why. Subtle shifts in breath, sleep, mood, and energy offer real-time feedback about environmental alignment. When a place is chosen consciously, the body often relaxes into coherence —heart rhythms stabilize, nervous system tone improves, and clarity increases.

When a place is ignored, the nervous system compensates.

This compensation may appear as:

- Chronic stress without clear cause

- Emotional exhaustion or irritability

- Difficulty settling or committing

- Persistent feeling of misalignment

These are not personal failures. They are **signals**—indicating that the environment is asking more of the system than it can sustainably offer at that time.

Restoring an Ancient Knowing

Ancient cultures understood that land was not inert. Mountains were teachers. Rivers were conduits. Cities were chosen, not placed. What science now confirms is what ancestral wisdom never forgot:

The land you stand on participates in who you become.

Astrocartography restores this knowing in a modern language —one that honors both empirical insight and lived experience. It allows individuals to move through the world with intention, recognizing that alignment is not only internal, but spatial.

When a place is honored as a collaborator rather than a backdrop, movement becomes meaningful. Relocation becomes initiation. Staying becomes intentional rather than habitual.

You do not simply inhabit geography.
You **co-evolve** with it.

And when you learn to listen—to your body, your biofield, and the land beneath you—place transforms from circumstance into guidance, shaping not just where you live, but how fully you become who you are meant to be.

Case Pattern Illustrations

When astrocartography maps are examined alongside lived experience, clear **patterned responses** to place consistently emerge. These patterns are not deterministic outcomes, nor are they universal guarantees. They are **activation tendencies**—ways the psyche and nervous system often respond when particular planetary frequencies are emphasized by location.

What follows are conceptual illustrations meant to deepen understanding, not prescribe expectation.

**Sun and Jupiter Lines: Expansion,
Visibility, and Opportunity**

Individuals who relocate to or spend extended time near **Sun or Jupiter lines** frequently report a noticeable expansion in confidence, opportunity, and visibility. Life may feel more buoyant. Doors open more easily. There is often a renewed sense of purpose or optimism that encourages forward movement.

On Sun lines, people often feel *recognized*—as though their presence matters more, or their identity is more clearly reflected back by the world. Leadership roles, creative expression, or public-facing opportunities may arise naturally, not through force, but through a sense of resonance.

Jupiter lines, similarly, tend to amplify growth. These locations often correspond with educational advancement, mentorship, travel, philosophical expansion, or professional opportunity. Yet even here, discernment matters. Expansion without grounding can lead to excess, overextension, or inflated expectations.

In both cases, the growth experienced is not created by the place—it is **drawn out** by it.

Pluto and Saturn Lines: Restructuring and Deep Transformation

Time spent on **Pluto or Saturn lines** often coincides with periods of intense personal restructuring. These are not typically light or casual experiences. Instead, they mark phases where identity, responsibility, or power dynamics are confronted directly.

Saturn lines tend to slow life down. Progress may feel delayed or effortful. External pressures increase. Responsibility becomes unavoidable. Yet what is built here often lasts. Saturn teaches mastery through patience, accountability, and endurance. Individuals may emerge from these locations with greater self-respect, clarity, and inner authority—earned rather than bestowed.

Pluto lines, by contrast, tend to catalyze deep psychological transformation. Endings, power struggles, or profound emotional reckonings may surface. What is no longer authentic is stripped away. These experiences can feel destabilizing in the moment, but they often result in empowerment, clarity, and rebirth.

These locations are not punitive. They are **initiatory**.

Neptune Lines: Spiritual Opening and the Need for Grounding

Neptune lines frequently activate spiritual sensitivity, imagination, compassion, and mystical awareness. Many individuals report heightened intuition, creativity, or a sense of connection to something larger than themselves when in these locations.

However, Neptune dissolves boundaries. Without grounding, clarity can blur. Idealization, confusion, escapism, or disillusionment may arise if discernment is not practiced. What feels transcendent can become disorienting if the nervous system lacks anchors in routine, structure, or embodied presence.

These locations often teach surrender—but they also demand **integration**.

Activation, Not Causation

What is critical to understand is that these shifts do not occur because a place *causes* change. The land is not imposing experience upon you. Rather, location acts as an **amplifier**, activating latent aspects of the psyche, nervous system, and energetic blueprint.

The same Sun line that empowers one individual may overwhelm another, depending on readiness and awareness. The same Pluto line that catalyzes rebirth for one person may feel destabilizing for someone resisting change. Place does not override agency—it **reveals what is already present**.

Place as a Catalyst, Not a Verdict

Astrocartography reframes experience from randomness to resonance. It explains why certain chapters of life unfold where they do—and why leaving a place after its lesson is complete often feels not only right, but necessary.

Patterns emerge not to dictate destiny, but to **invite participation**.

When understood consciously, these locations stop feeling like forces acting upon you and begin to feel like **classrooms, initiations, or sanctuaries**—each with a role in your becoming.

The place did not change you.
It called forth something within you that was ready to be known.

INTERACTIVE TOOL: MAPPING YOUR SOUL'S ACTIVATION ZONES

Reader Exercise: Astrocartography Mapping

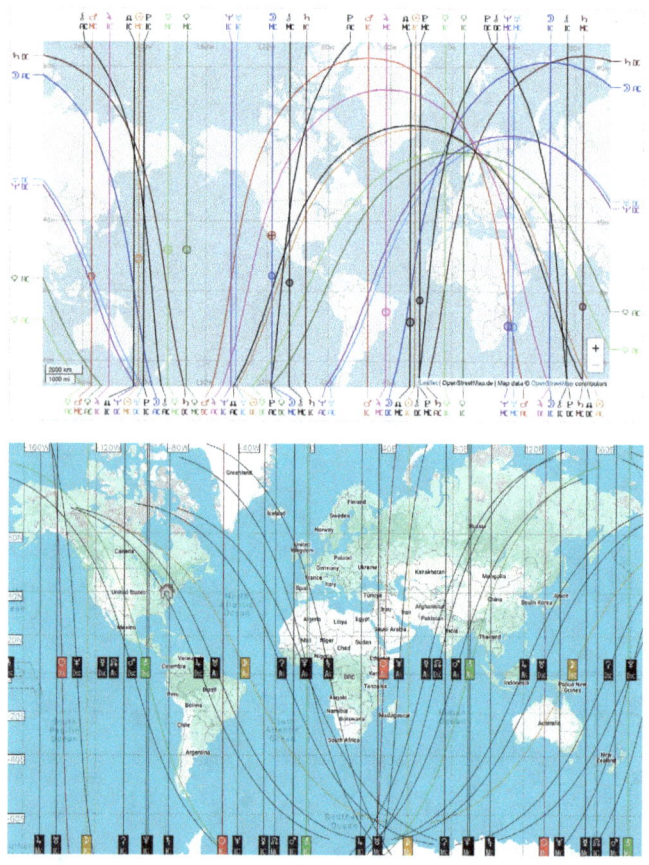

This guided exercise helps you translate astrocartography from theory into lived awareness. You are not searching for a "perfect place." You are learning how **place collaborates with your becoming**.

Have your birth data ready (date, exact time, and location).

Step 1: Generate Your Astrocartography Map

Use a reputable astrocartography calculator to create your personal map. Ensure your birth time is accurate, as even small variations can shift line placement.

Record your key planetary lines (Sun, Moon, Venus, Mars, Jupiter, Saturn, Uranus, Neptune, Pluto):

_____
_____

Step 2: Identify Activated Locations

Look for planetary lines that pass *through* or *near* locations where you have:

- Lived

- Traveled

- Felt a strong pull toward

Proximity matters—lines within a few hundred miles can still be active.

List the locations and nearby planetary lines:

_____
_____

Step 3: Reflect On Lived Experience

For each location, reflect honestly on what unfolded there. Focus on *patterns*, not isolated events.

Consider:

- Did life accelerate or slow down?

- Were relationships intensified or clarified?

- Did your confidence, creativity, or purpose expand?

- Did challenges demand growth, release, or restructuring?

Notes on experiences (growth, challenge, or change):
_____
_____

Step 4: Identify Conscious Activation Zones

Now look forward. Based on your current intentions—healing, expansion, love, mastery, creativity—which planetary energies would you like to **work with consciously**?

This is not about escape. It is about **alignment**.

Planetary lines you feel called to engage next:
_____

Why these energies feel relevant now:
_____
_____

Reflection Prompt

> **Which places in your life felt activating—and what part of you came alive there?**

Where did you feel more *yourself*?
Where were you challenged into growth?
Where did something end so something truer could begin?

Reflection Space:
_____
_____
_____

Closing Insight

This exercise is not about predicting outcomes. It is about **listening to the conversation between your soul and the Earth**. Patterns you recognize here will deepen as you continue through this book—revealing that movement, when chosen consciously, is not instability.

It is intelligence in motion.

Your soul does not wander randomly.
It activates—place by place—until purpose becomes embodied.

Key Insight of This Chapter

You are not meant to bloom everywhere in the same way.

Just as a single seed expresses itself differently depending on soil, climate, and light, **your soul expresses different facets of itself in different places**. Geography is not a backdrop to destiny—it is one of its instruments. Place shapes timing, rhythm, challenge, and emergence.

Some places are for **becoming**.
They stretch you forward. They call you into visibility, leadership, courage, or expansion. Growth feels active, sometimes uncomfortable, often exhilarating. These are places where identity evolves, and new versions of self are forged.

Some places are for **remembering**.
They soften you. They reconnect you to ancestry, intuition, creativity, or inner truth. These environments feel familiar in ways you cannot logically explain. They restore what was fragmented and remind you of who you were before the world asked you to harden.

Some places are for **releasing**.
They initiate endings—of roles, relationships, beliefs, or identities that can no longer travel with you. These locations may feel heavy or intense, yet profoundly necessary. What you leave behind there makes space for what comes next.

None of these places are mistakes.
Each serves a phase of becoming.

Astrocartography teaches that destiny is not only written in the stars—it is **mapped across the Earth**. Your blueprint does not live solely in time; it lives in space. When you understand this, movement gains meaning. Relocation becomes intentional. Staying becomes a choice rather than a habit.

When you choose a location consciously, you stop wandering and start **aligning**.

Alignment does not always feel comfortable. In fact, comfort often signals familiarity, not growth. Purpose rarely emerges from stagnation. It emerges where awareness is sharpened, where old patterns are disrupted, and where dormant capacities are called into action.

You do not find purpose by staying where you are most at ease. You discover it by standing where your soul is **called to awaken**.

And when you answer that call—whether through travel, relocation, or intentional engagement with place—you begin to experience life as participatory rather than accidental. Destiny stops feeling like something that happens to you and starts feeling like something you *move with*.

This chapter invites you to see geography not as coincidence, but as **collaboration.**
The Earth is not merely beneath you—it is working with you.

Where you stand matters.
Not because it decides your fate,
but because it reveals **which part of you is ready to rise next.**

CHAPTER 4
The Mathematics of the Soul: Numerology and Life Path Numbers

The universe does not speak only in words or symbols.
It speaks in **numbers**.

Before language, before myth, before philosophy, there was **pattern**. From the spiral arms of galaxies to the double helix of DNA, from the rhythmic cadence of heartbeats to the precise orbits of planets, reality reveals itself through proportion, sequence, and mathematical order. Mathematics is not merely a human invention used to describe the universe—it is the **structural intelligence through which the universe organizes itself**.

Nature does not improvise randomly.
It follows rhythm.

This is why the same ratios appear repeatedly across existence: in flowers and shells, in sound waves and light frequencies, in biological cycles and celestial motion. These patterns are not coincidental; they are **expressions of coherence**—the way energy stabilizes into form.

Numerology arises directly from this truth.

ENCODED IN THE STARS | 121

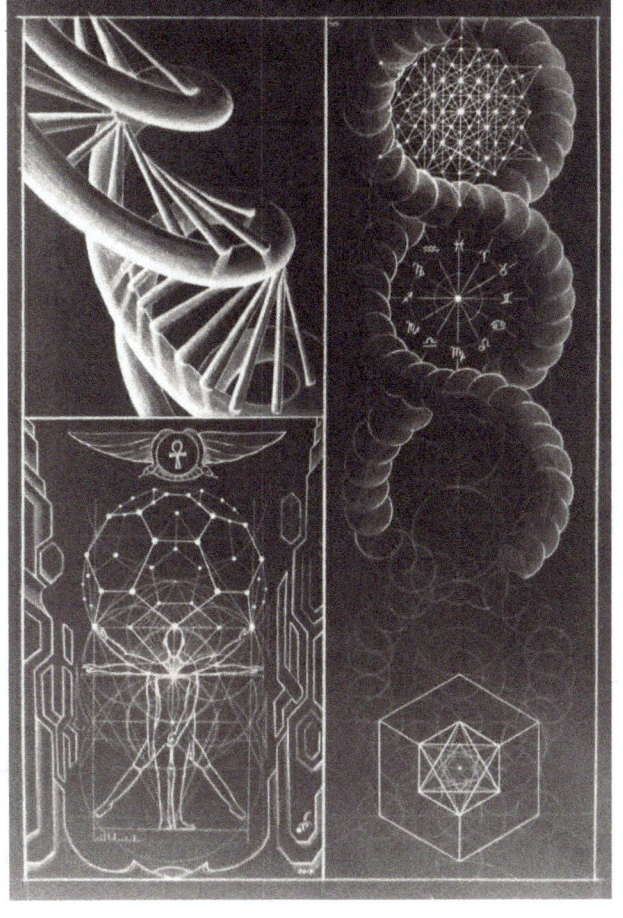

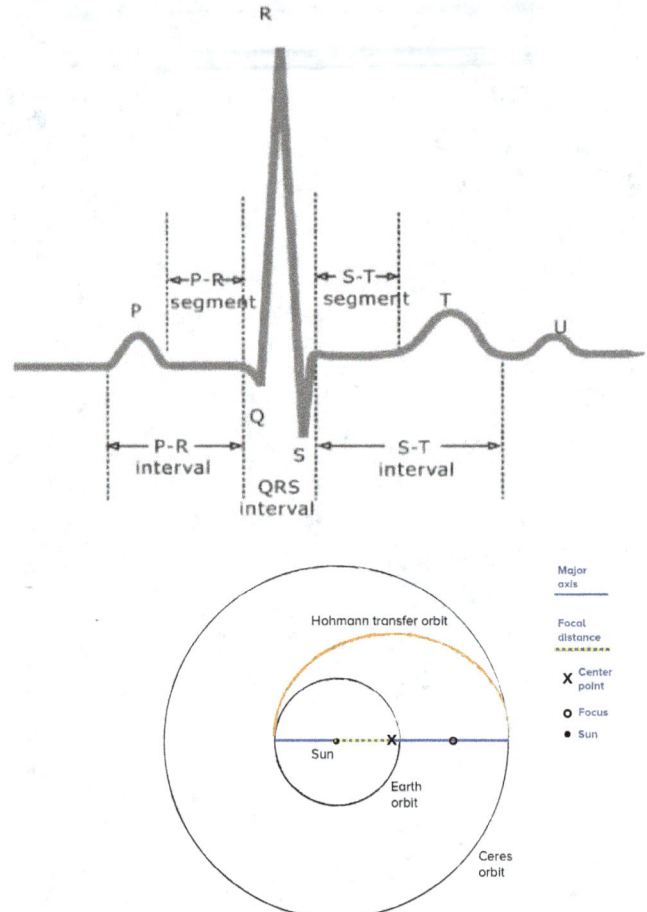

Numbers as Living Frequencies

Numerology is the study of numbers not as quantities, but as **vibrational intelligences**. Each number carries a distinct frequency—a specific way energy moves, organizes, and expresses itself. These frequencies influence personality tendencies, developmental themes, relational dynamics, and the timing of life experiences.

In this sense, numbers function much like musical notes. A single note carries a tone; a sequence creates a melody; harmony emerges through relationship. Change the frequency, and the entire composition shifts.

Your life follows a similar principle.

Numerology suggests that the numbers encoded in your birth date form a **vibrational signature**—a rhythmic pattern that shapes how your consciousness engages with experience. This does not dictate events, but it influences *how experience is metabolized*: how challenges are approached, how meaning is extracted, and how growth unfolds over time.

From Prediction to Recognition

When misunderstood, numerology is treated as a predictive tool—something that tells you what will happen. But this approach misses its deeper power. Numerology is not about forecasting outcomes; it is about **recognizing pattern**.

Recognition brings agency.

When you understand your numerical frequencies, you begin to see why certain themes repeat, why specific lessons recur, and why particular paths feel more aligned than others. What once appeared random starts to reveal structure. What once felt like resistance becomes intelligible as curriculum.

Numerology, when approached consciously, shifts the question from:
"What is going to happen to me?"
to:
"What frequency am I here to learn through?"

The Soul as Equation

Your soul is not chaotic.
It is **encoded**.

Life Path Numbers, in particular, function as **vibrational algorithms**—mathematical expressions of how your soul evolves through time. They describe the rhythm of your becoming, the style of your learning, and the terrain through which wisdom is earned.

This is why numerology resonates across cultures and eras. It does not depend on belief; it depends on **pattern recognition**. It reveals that destiny is not imposed from outside—it emerges from within, through the consistent repetition of frequency seeking expression.

Mathematics as Sacred Language

Ancient philosophers understood this deeply. Figures like **Pythagoras** taught that number was the essence of all things—that reality itself was structured through harmonic resonance. To study number was to study the soul of the universe.

Modern science now echoes this insight. From chaos theory to systems biology, from quantum mechanics to neuroscience, research continues to reveal that order emerges through **mathematical relationship**, not randomness.

Numerology stands at this intersection—where ancient wisdom meets modern understanding.

A New Way of Seeing Your Life

When you begin to view your life through the lens of number, experience gains coherence. You stop fighting your rhythm and start moving with it. You recognize that growth does not come from forcing change, but from **aligning with frequency**.

Numerology does not tell you who to be.
It reveals **how your soul learns best**.

And in that recognition, destiny shifts—from something you fear or chase, to something you consciously participate in.

Because you are not an accident in the universe.
You are a **mathematical expression of meaning**, moving through time, learning through rhythm, and evolving through number.

Ancient Roots, Modern Understanding

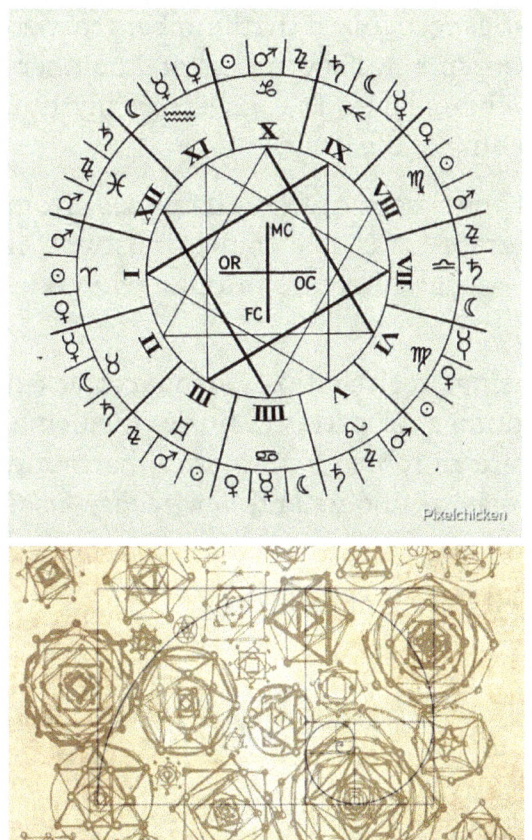

Numerology is one of humanity's oldest metaphysical sciences

—born not from superstition, but from **observation of pattern**. Across ancient Egypt, Babylon, China, India, and Greece, scholars and mystics recognized that numbers carried meaning far beyond measurement. They understood numbers as **energetic principles**—living codes that governed rhythm, proportion, and the unfolding of life itself.

These civilizations did not separate mathematics from spirituality. To them, number was not cold or abstract; it was **sacred intelligence**—the architecture through which the cosmos expressed order.

Temples were designed using precise ratios. Calendars tracked cosmic cycles through numerical pattern. Music, medicine, astronomy, and ethics were all rooted in numerical harmony. To understand number was to understand *how reality holds itself together*.

Pythagoras and the Sacred Nature of Number

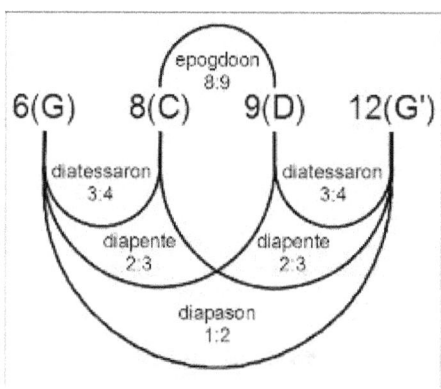

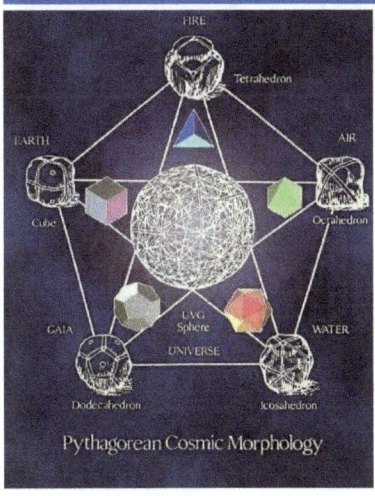

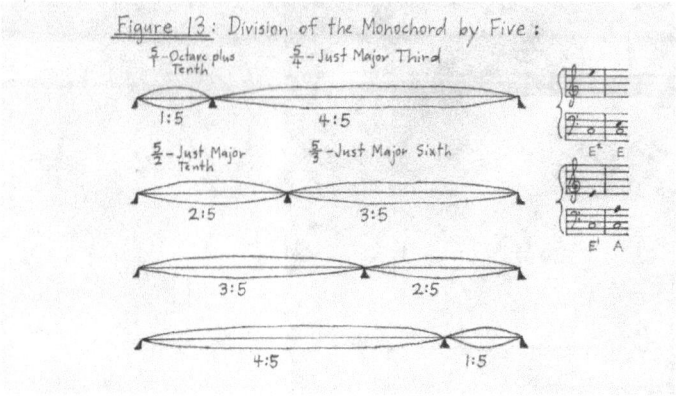

Figure 13: Division of the Monochord by Five.

The Greek philosopher **Pythagoras** articulated one of the most profound insights in human intellectual history with remarkable clarity: **number is the essence of all things**. To Pythagoras, reality was not constructed randomly nor governed by chaos—it was structured through **harmonic ratio and vibration**. Existence itself, he taught, was a living symphony.

In Pythagorean thought, the universe was not silent. It *sounded*.

This did not mean sound as the ear hears it, but vibration as the body and soul experience it. Every object, movement, and process carried a frequency. These frequencies interacted, overlapped, and resolved into harmony or dissonance according to precise mathematical relationships. Life, therefore, was not merely lived—it was **tuned**.

Mathematics as a Spiritual Practice

To Pythagoras, mathematics was not a tool for abstraction; it was a **path to truth**. Numbers were sacred because they revealed the hidden order beneath appearances. To study number was to study the architecture of reality—and by extension, the architecture of the soul.

In this worldview, spirituality was not separate from reason. It was embedded within it.

The Pythagorean school treated mathematics as a form of initiation. Students did not merely learn equations; they learned **attunement**—how to perceive harmony in sound, form, motion, and human conduct. Ethics, music, astronomy, and geometry were all expressions of the same underlying numerical order.

To live well was to live *in harmony* with that order.

Musical Harmony and Universal Law

One of Pythagoras' most influential observations came through music. Using the monochord—a single-stringed instrument—he demonstrated that harmonious musical intervals emerged from **simple numerical ratios**. A string divided in half produced an octave. Ratios of 2:3 or 3:4 produced consonant tones. Dissonance arose when ratios were complex or irregular.

This revelation changed everything.

Pythagoras recognized that harmony was not subjective preference—it was **mathematical law**. Beauty, resonance, and coherence emerged from proportion. From this insight, he extended the principle outward—from sound to geometry, from geometry to astronomy, and from astronomy to life itself.

If music obeyed number, so must the cosmos.

The Music of the Spheres

From this realization emerged the concept later known as the **"music of the spheres."** Pythagoras proposed that the movements of celestial bodies followed harmonic ratios, producing a form of cosmic music inaudible to the human ear but perceptible to the soul. Planetary motion, he believed, was not random—it was choreographed through number.

The universe, then, was not a machine.

It was an **orchestra**.

Each planet contributed its tone. Each orbit followed its rhythm. Together, they formed a coherent whole—an ordered cosmos governed by vibrational mathematics.

Number as Discovered Truth, Not Human Invention

Crucially, Pythagoras did not view numbers as symbols invented by human minds. He viewed them as **principles discovered through observation**—universal truths that existed independently of language, culture, or belief.

Humans did not create harmony.
They recognized it.

In this worldview, numbers were not abstractions layered onto reality. They were the **bones of reality itself**. Geometry revealed the structure of space. Ratio revealed the nature of movement. Sequence revealed the unfolding of time.

Implications for the Soul

When applied to human life, this philosophy reframes destiny entirely. If reality is governed by harmonic order, then the soul is not chaotic or accidental. It, too, is structured through number—through rhythm, repetition, and resonance.

Numerology draws directly from this lineage. It carries forward the Pythagorean understanding that **numbers describe how energy moves**, how consciousness learns, and how meaning unfolds across time.

Your life is not random noise in the universe.
It is a **distinct frequency within a greater symphony**.

To know your numbers is not to limit yourself.
It is to recognize the key you are written in.

And when you live in harmony with that key, life stops feeling like resistance and begins to feel like **resonance**—not because challenges disappear, but because you understand the rhythm through which your soul was always meant to learn and evolve.

From Sacred Ratio to Scientific Resonance

Modern science is now circling back to insights that ancient wisdom held intuitively—armed with advanced instruments, mathematical models, and empirical rigor, yet asking the **same foundational questions** humanity has always asked:

How does order arise?
Why does reality organize itself the way it does?
What governs the movement from chaos into coherence?

Across disciplines, the answer continues to converge: **resonance**.

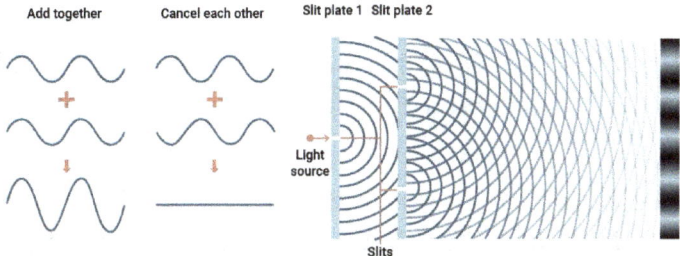

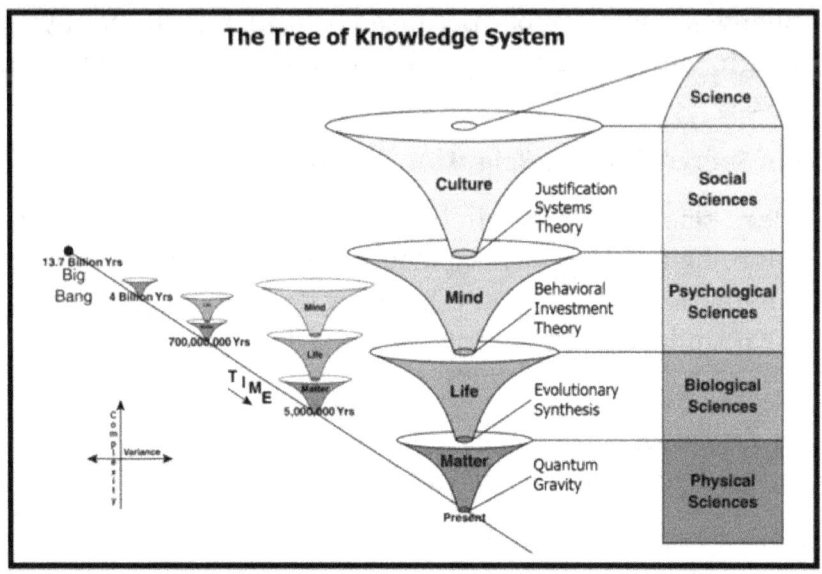

Physics: Reality as Wave and Probability

At the most fundamental level, physics has revealed that matter is not solid in the way it appears. Subatomic particles behave not as fixed objects, but as **waves of probability**—existing in multiple potential states until interaction collapses them into form.

These behaviors are not random. They follow **precise mathematical laws**. Wave functions, frequencies, amplitudes, and harmonic relationships govern how particles interact, bond, and stabilize. Reality, at its smallest scale, is rhythmic.

This discovery fundamentally altered our understanding of the universe. Matter is not static—it is **vibrational**. Existence is not built from things, but from **patterns of movement**.

Systems Theory: Order from Simple Rules

Systems theory further reinforces this truth. It demonstrates that complex, intelligent order can emerge from the repetition of **simple numerical rules**. From ant colonies to weather systems, from neural networks to ecosystems, complexity does not require external control—it arises naturally through iteration and feedback.

A few governing principles, applied repeatedly, generate intricate and adaptive structures.

This mirrors numerological insight precisely: life unfolds not through randomness, but through **algorithmic rhythm**. Repetition creates pattern. Pattern creates meaning. Meaning creates form.

Neuroscience: The Brain as a Rhythmic Organ

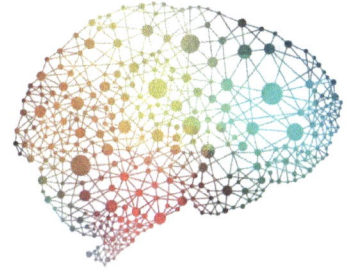

Neuroscience adds yet another layer of confirmation to an ancient truth: **the brain is rhythmic**. It does not operate as a linear processor moving step-by-step through information. Instead, it functions as a dynamic orchestra of **oscillatory rhythms**—electrical patterns that rise, fall, synchronize, and desynchronize across neural networks in real time.

These rhythms, commonly referred to as **brainwaves**, coordinate communication between brain regions. They determine *how* information is integrated, *which* networks are prioritized, and *what* state of consciousness is dominant at any given moment. Perception, emotion, memory, attention, and decision-making all depend on the timing and alignment of these oscillations.

In other words, the brain thinks in **frequency**.

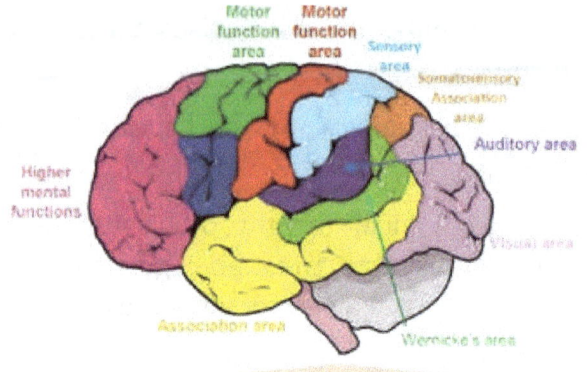

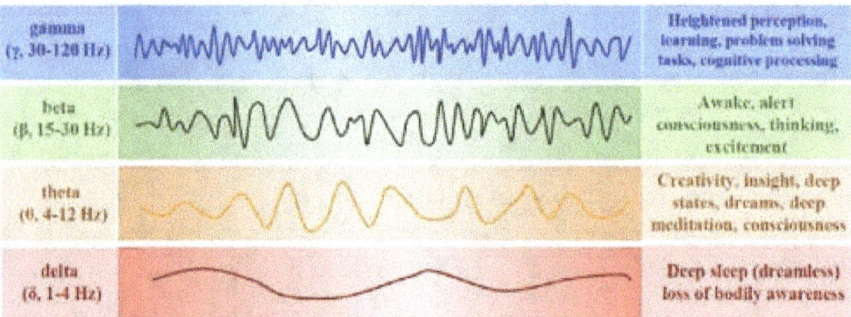

Frequency as the Organizer of Conscious Experience

Different brainwave frequencies are associated with distinct functional states:

- **Focused attention and alertness** emerge when faster rhythms coordinate task-relevant networks, enabling concentration, learning, and goal-directed action.

- **Creativity and insight** arise when mid-range rhythms allow cross-network communication, supporting pattern recognition, imagination, and flexible thinking.

- **Emotional regulation** depends on synchronized rhythms between cortical and limbic regions, enabling the mind to interpret feeling without being overwhelmed by it.

- **Rest and restoration** occur when slower rhythms

dominate, supporting memory consolidation, cellular repair, and nervous system recovery.

These states are not isolated; they blend and transition continuously. What matters is **coherence**—the degree to which oscillations are appropriately synchronized across regions.

Coherence vs. Dysregulation

When brain rhythms are coherent, cognition flows. Attention stabilizes. Emotional responses are proportionate. Memory integrates smoothly. The individual experiences clarity, presence, and adaptability.

When rhythms are disrupted—by chronic stress, trauma, sleep deprivation, or environmental mismatch—communication between neural networks becomes inefficient. This can manifest as:

- Mental fog or racing thoughts
- Emotional volatility or numbness
- Difficulty concentrating or remembering
- Heightened anxiety or shutdown

Importantly, these states are not moral failures or character flaws. They are **rhythmic mismatches**—signals that the system is struggling to maintain alignment.

The Brain Within a Larger Field

Crucially, brain rhythms do not exist in isolation from the body or environment. They interact with heart rhythms, breath cycles, hormonal pulses, and external electromagnetic conditions. The nervous system is constantly calibrating—responding to internal state and external field simultaneously.

This is why practices that restore rhythm—such as breathwork, meditation, movement, music, and sleep—are so effective. They do not "fix" the mind; they **retune** it.

And this is where neuroscience converges with numerology and cosmology.

Frequency Alignment as Universal Principle

The brain's reliance on oscillatory alignment mirrors the universe's reliance on resonance. Just as particles stabilize through harmonic interaction, neural networks stabilize through rhythmic synchronization. The same principle governs both scales.

The mind, like the universe, organizes itself through frequency alignment.

This insight reframes mental health, cognition, and consciousness not as static traits, but as **dynamic states of resonance**. Clarity is not forced—it is tuned. Insight is not hunted—it emerges when rhythms align.

Understanding the brain as a rhythmic organ restores agency. You are not broken when clarity fades; you are **out of sync**. And synchronization—through awareness, environment, and practice—is always possible.

This rhythmic intelligence is the bridge between mathematics and meaning, between number and mind. It reminds us that consciousness is not a thing we possess—it is a **pattern we participate in**, moment by moment, frequency by frequency.

And when alignment is restored, both the brain and the soul remember how to move in harmony with the greater symphony of existence.

The Universe as a Mathematical Symphony

Everything vibrates.

Everything oscillates.
Everything follows rhythm.

This is not poetic metaphor—it is physical law.

At every scale of existence, from subatomic particles to galaxies, reality expresses itself through **movement and repetition**. Sound travels in waves. Light propagates as oscillation. The heart beats in rhythm. Neurons fire in pulses. Even matter, once thought to be solid and still, is now understood as energy in constant motion.

The universe is not static.
It is **musical**.

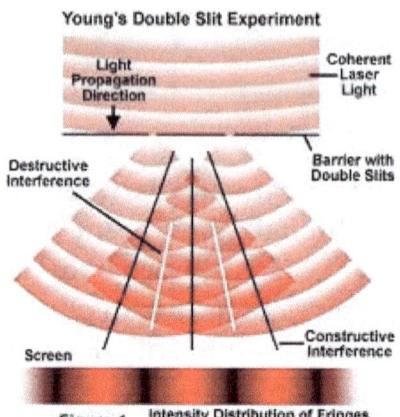

Figure 4 Intensity Distribution of Fringes

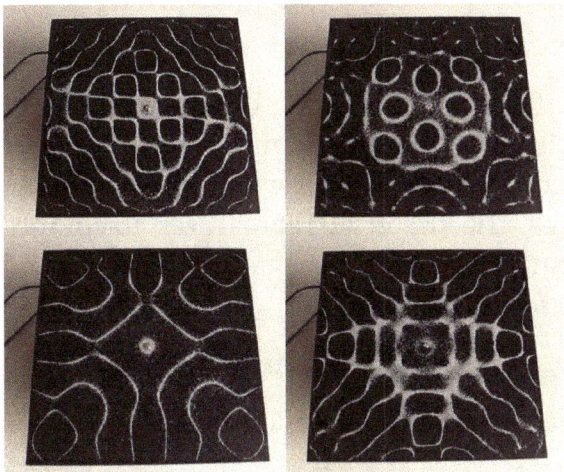

Mathematics as the Language of Motion

Mathematics provides the framework for understanding this motion. It allows us to describe how waves interact, how frequencies interfere, and how harmony or dissonance emerges. Just as music follows scales, intervals, and ratios, the universe follows **numerical harmonics**.

When ratios are simple and aligned, coherence emerges.
When ratios are complex or unstable, turbulence arises.

This is true in sound, in physics, and in life.

The same mathematical principles that govern musical harmony also appear in:

- Orbital mechanics

- Light spectra

- Biological rhythms

- Neural oscillations

Reality does not express itself randomly. It follows **structured vibration**.

Cymatics: Making Vibration Visible

Cymatics offers one of the most striking demonstrations of this truth. In cymatic experiments, sound frequencies are applied to substances such as sand, water, or liquid. As the frequency changes, the material reorganizes itself into **distinct geometric patterns**—circles, hexagons, spirals, and complex symmetrical forms.

Change the frequency, and the pattern changes.

Nothing else is altered. No force is added. No structure is imposed.
Only frequency shifts—and form responds.

This reveals a profound principle: **vibration precedes structure**.

Form is not imposed on matter.
It *emerges* from frequency.

From Matter to Meaning

This principle extends beyond physical matter into lived experience. Emotional states, thought patterns, and behavioral tendencies also operate through frequency. Stress carries one rhythm. Calm carries another. Creativity, fear, clarity, and confusion each have distinct energetic signatures.

When internal frequencies are coherent, experience feels aligned.
When they are fragmented, life feels chaotic or resistant.

Numerology applies this same understanding to consciousness over time.

Numbers as Vibrational Algorithms

Numerology proposes that numbers function as **vibrational algorithms**—structured frequencies that shape how consciousness organizes experience across a lifetime. Just as a musical composition follows a key signature, human development follows energetic sequences.

Your Life Path Number does not dictate events.
It sets the **rhythm through which learning occurs**.

Certain frequencies emphasize initiation. Others emphasize refinement, integration, or release. These patterns repeat not to punish, but to teach—because repetition is how rhythm stabilizes into mastery.

Consciousness as a Participatory Instrument

When viewed through this lens, consciousness is not separate from the universe's music. It is an **instrument within it**—responding, adapting, learning through resonance.

You do not move through life randomly.
You move through it **rhythmically**.

Numerology does not assign meaning arbitrarily. It listens for pattern. It translates vibration into language. It reveals how the soul learns through repetition, harmony, tension, and resolution.

Just as music is not noise but organized sound, your life is not chaos but **organized frequency**.

And when you recognize the rhythm you are moving to, you stop resisting the tempo and begin to participate consciously in the symphony.

Because the universe is not silent.
It is singing—
and you are one of its recurring themes.

Life Path Numbers: Your Core Algorithm

Your **Life Path Number** is the most influential number in numerology because it represents the **primary frequency through which your soul learns, evolves, and expresses**

purpose across this lifetime. It is derived from your full birth date—the moment your consciousness entered form and synchronized with time itself.

This number does not describe who you *appear* to be.
It describes **how you are designed to grow**.

Think of your Life Path Number as your **operating system**. Just as different operating systems run different programs more efficiently, your Life Path determines the energetic pathway through which lessons are integrated, challenges are metabolized, and wisdom is earned.

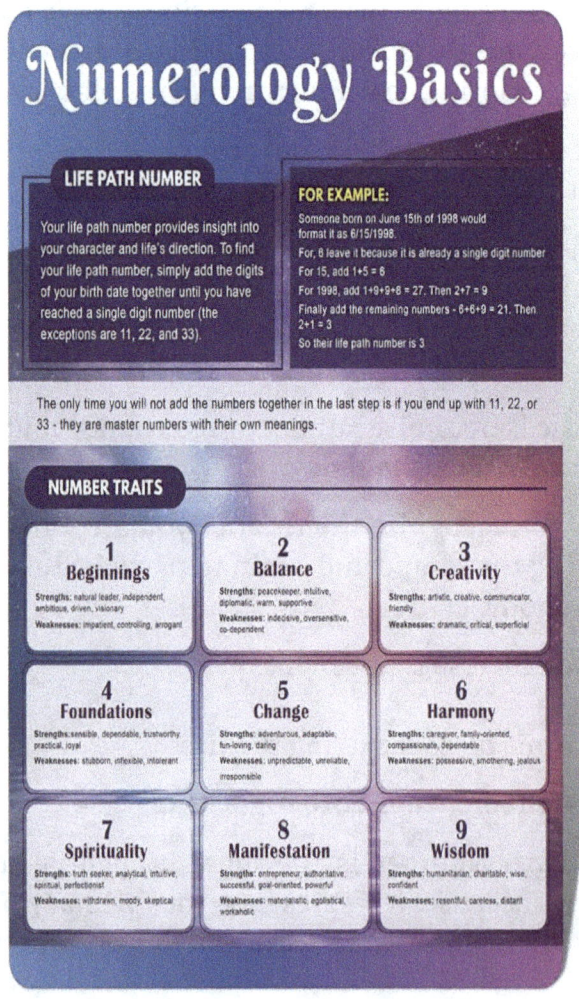

An Algorithm, Not a Label

An algorithm is not a destiny—it is a **process**.

In mathematics and systems theory, an algorithm describes a sequence of operations that determine *how* something unfolds, not *what* the final outcome must be. The same algorithm can produce countless expressions depending on input, context, and choice. Numerology applies this same principle to human development.

Your **Life Path Number** functions as an **energetic algorithm**—a patterned sequence through which your soul learns, adapts, and evolves across time.

It does not dictate events.
It governs **process**.

What Your Life Path Algorithm Influences

Your Life Path Number shapes:

- **The kinds of experiences that repeat until mastered**
  Certain lessons will resurface in different forms—relationships, careers, challenges, or internal conflicts—not because you are failing, but because repetition is how systems learn. The lesson changes shape, but the core frequency remains until integration occurs.

- **The themes through which meaning is extracted**
  Every Life Path pulls insight from different arenas. Some extract meaning through leadership and initiation, others through relationship, service, inquiry, or transformation. Meaning is not universal; it is frequency-specific.

- **The style in which growth unfolds**
  Some people grow through action and experimentation. Others grow through reflection and synthesis. Some

through structure and responsibility. Others through disruption and release. The algorithm determines *how learning feels*, not whether it happens.

- **The rhythm by which purpose is revealed**
  Purpose does not arrive all at once. It unfolds rhythmically—through cycles of expansion, contraction, testing, and integration. Your Life Path defines that rhythm. When you resist it, growth feels delayed. When you honor it, clarity accelerates.

Same Algorithm, Infinite Expressions

This is why individuals with the same Life Path Number can live vastly different lives while encountering **similar core lessons**. The algorithm is the same; the variables are not.

Culture, family, trauma, opportunity, belief systems, and personal choice all influence expression. One person may embody the algorithm consciously and evolve with relative ease. Another may resist it and experience the same lessons as struggle.

The difference is not fate.
It is **relationship to process**.

Numerology does not flatten individuality. It explains why individuality unfolds along certain energetic contours.

Liberation From Labels

When misunderstood, numerology is used as a label: *"I am a 7."*
But this reduces a dynamic system into a static identity.

You are not your number.
You are **moving through it**.

Your Life Path Number does not define your personality. It defines the **pathway through which wisdom is earned**. It reveals the terrain—not the destination.

How Becoming Actually Happens

Numerology does not say *what* you must become.
It reveals **how becoming happens for you**.

Some souls evolve by initiating.
Some by stabilizing.
Some by questioning.
Some by healing.
Some by transforming.

None of these are better or worse. Each is necessary for the whole.

When you understand your Life Path as an algorithm rather than a label, shame dissolves. Comparison loses its power. You stop forcing growth through methods that are not aligned with your frequency.

You stop asking, *"Why am I not like them?"*
And begin asking, *"How does my soul learn best?"*

That shift is not limiting—it is **liberating**.

Because when you stop trying to become someone else's expression of purpose and start honoring your own algorithm, growth stops feeling like resistance and starts feeling like

flow—not because life gets easier, but because you are finally moving in rhythm with the way your soul was always designed to evolve.

Learning Through Frequency

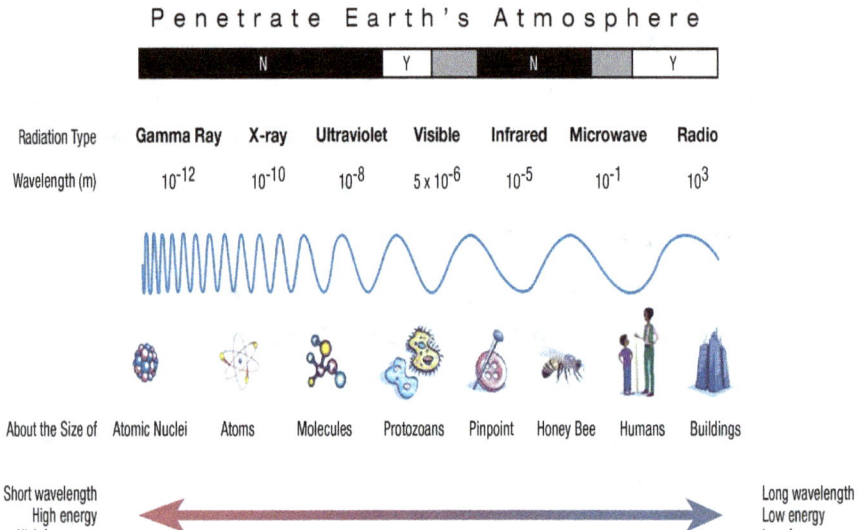

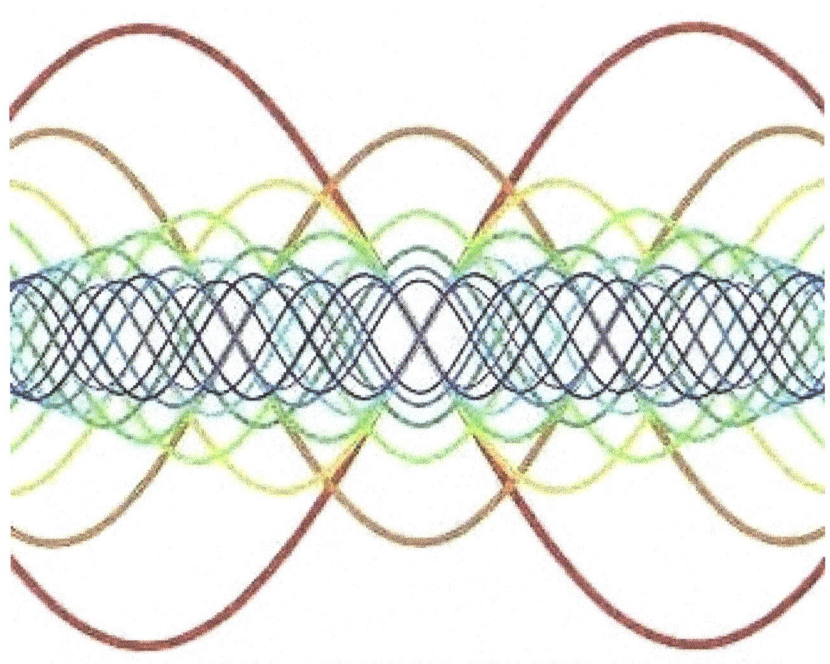

MBTI INTP Learning Styles

Each Life Path carries a **distinct frequency**—a characteristic rhythm that shapes how consciousness organizes experience, extracts meaning, and integrates wisdom over time. This frequency influences *how* lessons arrive, *where* growth concentrates, and *which* forms of intelligence are most naturally cultivated.

Some paths learn through **initiation and leadership**. Growth arrives through action—decisions, risk, responsibility, and the courage to begin. Insight emerges when momentum is claimed and direction is chosen.

Others learn through **relationship and emotional intelligence**. Meaning is refined through connection, attunement, and reciprocity. Lessons arrive via partnership, collaboration, and the nuanced work of empathy and balance.

Some evolve through **structure and discipline**. Mastery is earned by building foundations, honoring process, and committing to steady refinement. Growth is cumulative, forged through patience and integrity.

Others learn through **freedom, exploration, or transformation**. Expansion comes from movement, experimentation, and the willingness to release what no longer fits. Insight emerges through change itself—sometimes sudden, sometimes profound.

Different Frequencies, Different Intelligences

None of these pathways are superior. Each represents a **different mode of intelligence**—a distinct way consciousness learns how to become whole. What feels like struggle on one path may feel like ease on another, not because one is "better," but because each system is **optimized for different lessons**.

A highly structured environment may stabilize one Life Path while constricting another. Constant novelty may energize one frequency while dysregulating a different one. Ease and difficulty are not moral judgments; they are **signals of resonance or mismatch**.

This understanding dissolves comparison. It explains why advice that works brilliantly for one person can feel ineffective—or even harmful—for another.

Resistance vs. Resonance

When individuals resist their Life Path frequency—attempting to grow through methods that are not aligned—life often feels unnecessarily difficult. Effort increases, clarity decreases, and progress stalls. This resistance is not a lack of discipline or willpower; it is a **misalignment of rhythm**.

By contrast, when individuals work *with* their Life Path frequency, effort becomes more efficient. Insight arrives faster. Patterns resolve with less friction. Growth feels demanding yet meaningful, challenging yet coherent.

Alignment does not eliminate difficulty.
It **reduces waste**.

You stop expending energy fighting your natural learning style and start investing it where it compounds.

Practical Recognition

Learning through frequency means asking better questions:

- *Am I trying to grow in a way that contradicts my rhythm?*

- *Where does effort feel productive versus draining?*

- *Which environments amplify my clarity rather than fragment it?*

These questions shift development from force to **attunement**.

When you honor your Life Path frequency, you are not choosing comfort—you are choosing **efficiency of evolution**. You learn faster not because lessons disappear, but because you meet them in the language your soul understands best.

Growth, then, becomes less about pushing harder and more about **listening more accurately**—to rhythm, to pattern, to the frequency through which your life is asking to be lived.

Purpose as Process, Not Destination

Importantly, your **Life Path Number** does not point to a single job title, role, or external achievement. Purpose is not a fixed destination waiting to be reached. It is a **process of becoming**—one that unfolds through repeated engagement with your core frequency over time.

Purpose is not something you arrive at.
It is something you **practice**.

Each time life presents a familiar theme—leadership, intimacy, discipline, freedom, service, inquiry—it is inviting you to embody that frequency with greater maturity, nuance, and self-awareness. What changes is not the lesson itself, but **the level at which you meet it**.

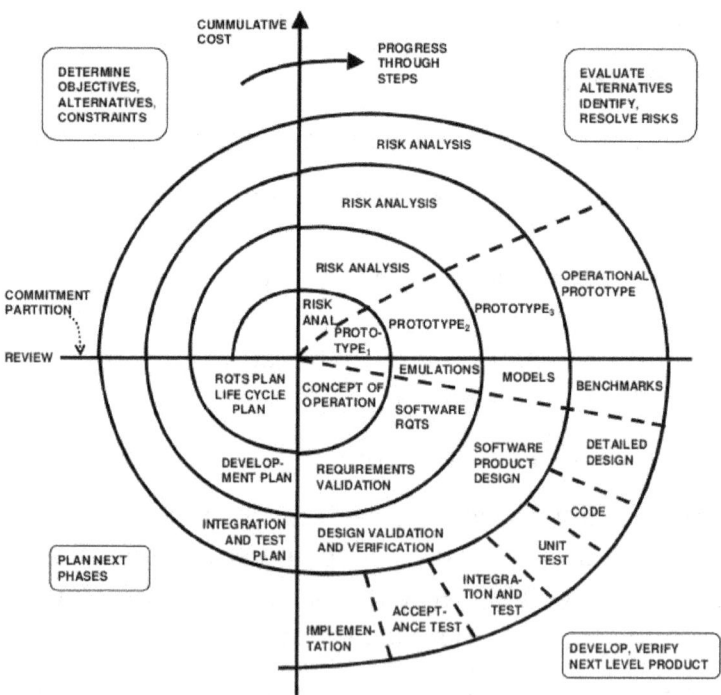

ENCODED IN THE STARS | 151

24 Ancient Spiral Symbols

Hopi Hand

Trefoil

Spiral Goddess

Kundalini Spiral

Double Spiral

3rd Eye Chakra Spiral
(Clockwise + AntiClockwise Spirals)

Golden Spiral

Unalome

Cretan Labyrinth

Koru Spiral

Triskelion

Spiral Sun

Cosmic Egg

Spiral Galaxy

Torus

Hunab Ku

Shiva's eye shell

Sankofa

Theodorus Spiral
(made of right-angled triangles)

Dwennimmen

Logarithmic Spiral

Om Spiral

Quadruple Spiral

Hopi Maze

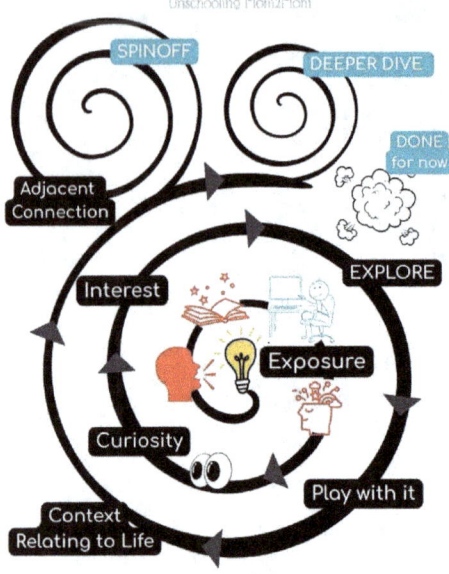

Reframing Frustration And Delay

Seen through this lens, frustration takes on a different meaning. Delay is no longer evidence of failure; it is information about **where integration is still underway**.

- If a lesson repeats, it is not punishment—it is **reinforcement**.

- If growth feels cyclical, it is not stagnation—it is **rhythmic learning**.

- If you revisit similar dynamics in different forms, it is not regression—it is **spiral evolution**.

Just as mastery in music requires repetition of scales, mastery in life requires revisiting core themes until embodiment replaces effort.

Why Patterns Recur

Your Life Path Number explains why certain experiences keep resurfacing—not to trap you, but to **train you**. Each recurrence asks a deeper question:

- Can you respond with more clarity than last time?

- Can you choose with greater integrity?

- Can you embody the lesson rather than intellectualize it?

The curriculum remains consistent because the **frequency is consistent**. What evolves is your relationship to it.

This is why two people with the same Life Path can be at entirely different stages of fulfillment. One may still be learning the lesson through resistance. Another may be expressing it through wisdom. The difference is not the number—it is **integration**.

Purpose Reveals Itself Through Embodiment

Purpose is not revealed all at once. It clarifies as you embody your frequency more fully—through choices, boundaries, relationships, and commitments that align with how your soul learns best.

When you stop asking, *"What am I supposed to do?"*
and start asking, *"What am I being asked to embody?"*
purpose becomes less elusive and more lived.

Your Life Path Number does not demand that you become something specific.
It invites you to **become more fully yourself**, again and again, at deeper levels of expression.

Purpose, then, is not a finish line.
It is the **ongoing refinement of resonance**—a process through which meaning is earned, not assigned.

And when you understand this, impatience softens. Comparison dissolves. Trust deepens.

Because you realize that you are not behind.
You are **in rhythm**.

And every return to a familiar lesson is not a setback—it is an opportunity to embody your purpose with greater presence, precision, and power than ever before.

Agency Through Awareness

Understanding your **Life Path Number** does not limit choice—it **expands it**.

Awareness is not a cage; it is a **map**. When you recognize your operating system—the frequency through which your soul learns—you stop measuring yourself against standards that were never meant to define you. You release the quiet self-blame that comes from trying to thrive in environments, roles, or relationships that are fundamentally misaligned with your rhythm.

Clarity replaces criticism.

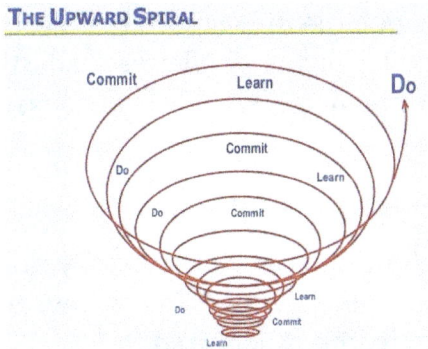

From Self-Judgment to Strategic Choice

Without awareness, effort is often misdirected. You may work harder, push longer, or stay committed to paths that drain rather than develop you—mistaking resistance for discipline. Awareness changes this. It allows you to distinguish between **growth-edge discomfort** and **energetic mismatch**.

When you understand your Life Path frequency, you begin choosing:

- **Strategies** that match how you learn best

- **Relationships** that support your mode of integration

- **Directions** that amplify rather than fragment your energy

This is not avoidance of challenge. It is **intelligent engagement** with it.

Alignment Replaces Force

When awareness deepens, something subtle but powerful shifts. You stop forcing evolution. You stop trying to become through pressure what can only be embodied through resonance.

You are no longer pushing against yourself.
You are moving **with** yourself.

Alignment does not mean ease at all times. It means effort produces return. It means challenge leads to clarity rather than burnout. It means growth feels purposeful even when it is demanding.

Rhythm as Wisdom Training

Your Life Path Number does not control your life. It does not dictate decisions or outcomes. What it reveals is the **rhythm through which wisdom is acquired**.

Just as fluency in language comes through immersion and repetition, fluency in wisdom comes through honoring your learning rhythm. Over time, the same frequency that once felt confusing becomes familiar. What once felt like struggle becomes skill. What once felt like searching becomes knowing.

This is how agency matures—not through rebellion against design, but through **relationship with it**.

Purpose Becomes Inevitable Through Alignment

When you honor your rhythm, purpose stops feeling elusive. Not because it is fixed, promised, or guaranteed—but because you are no longer **out of sync** with the way your soul was designed to grow.

Most people struggle not because they lack purpose, but because they are moving against their own frequency. They chase meaning through comparison, urgency, or borrowed definitions of success. Alignment changes that dynamic entirely.

You stop chasing meaning
and start **generating it**.

Meaning emerges naturally when your actions, choices, and environments reinforce your internal rhythm rather than contradict it. Life begins to feel responsive instead of resistant —not because challenges disappear, but because your system knows how to meet them.

UNALOME
THE SACRED YANTRA

Alignment
Clarity
Connection with the divine
Path to enlightenment

↑

Loops
Ups and downs
Twists and turns in life

↑

Spiral
Awakening
Beginning of the spiritual path

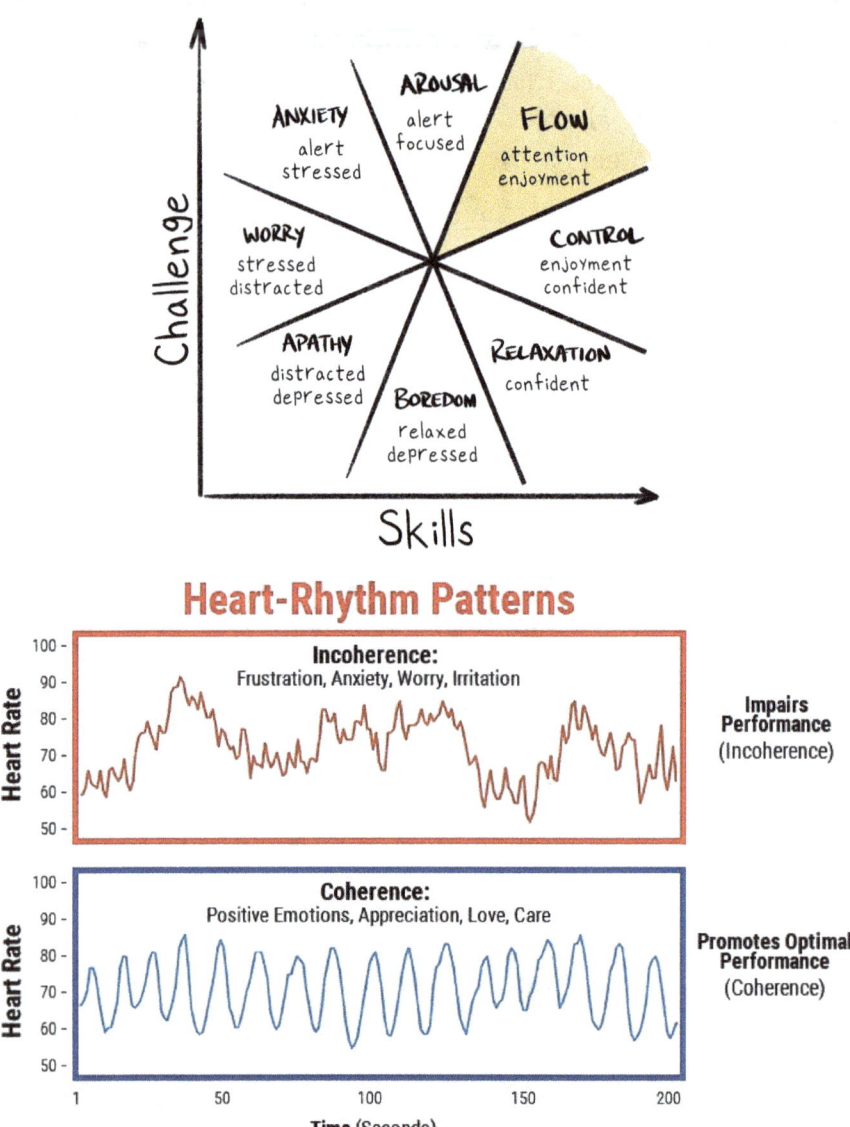

Inevitability as Coherence, Not Fate

Inevitability here does not mean predestination. It does not imply that your future is scripted or that choice is an illusion. Inevitability means **coherence**.

When your internal signal is clear, the feedback loop between you and life tightens.

Your choices begin to:

- Reinforce your learning rather than delay it
- Deepen embodiment rather than fragment attention
- Build momentum rather than scatter effort

You are no longer undoing yourself with each step forward.

Life responds with clarity because **your signal is clear**.

Opportunities align more easily. Patterns resolve faster. Decisions feel grounded rather than forced. This is not luck—it is resonance.

Accuracy Creates Momentum

Awareness gives you agency because it gives you **accuracy**.

Accuracy means you know where effort belongs and where it is wasted. You recognize which challenges are initiatory and which are misaligned. You discern when to persist and when to pivot—not from fear, but from intelligence.

Over time, accuracy creates momentum.

Momentum builds confidence.
Confidence builds trust.
Trust allows surrender to rhythm rather than control of outcome.

This is how purpose stabilizes—not as a single calling, but as a **way of moving through life** that continuously generates meaning.

Fluency Over Force

You are not here to override your design.
You are here to become **fluent** in it.

Fluency comes from repetition, engagement, and lived experience. Just as language becomes effortless through use, wisdom becomes embodied through rhythm honored over time.

When you become fluent in your frequency:

- You stop translating yourself for the world
- You stop forcing yourself into roles that cost too much
- You stop waiting for permission to be aligned

Purpose no longer arrives as a dramatic revelation from outside. It does not descend as a lightning strike or a final answer.

It **emerges naturally**—from alignment, from repetition, from lived wisdom accumulated through experience.

The Soul as Author

Your path was not written *for* you.
There is no fixed script imposed upon your life, no rigid storyline you are required to follow.

But there is a deeper truth—one far more empowering:

Your soul is writing through you, moment by moment.

Every choice, response, pause, and pivot becomes a sentence in that living manuscript. Time is the page. Experience is the ink. Consciousness is the hand moving across it.

How the Soul Writes

The soul does not write in words.
It writes in **rhythm, frequency, and pattern**.

It writes through repetition—lessons returning until they are embodied.

It writes through resonance—what expands when aligned and constricts when misaligned.

It writes through timing—knowing when something ripens and when it must be released.

When you learn how your soul writes, something profound happens:

you stop trying to **edit the story into something it was never meant to be**.

You stop forcing plot twists driven by fear.
You stop rewriting chapters to meet external expectations.
You stop comparing your narrative to someone else's pacing.

Instead, you allow **coherence** to guide the narrative.

Agency Refined, Not Removed

Purpose becomes inevitable not because you surrender agency, but because you finally **use it accurately**.

Accuracy is knowing which choices deepen alignment and which fracture it.

Accuracy is discerning when resistance is growth and when it is self-betrayal.

Accuracy is recognizing the difference between discomfort that refines and discomfort that depletes.

This is mature agency—not control, but attunement.

When agency is used accurately, life stops pushing back. Not because it becomes easy, but because it becomes **responsive**. The feedback loop tightens. The signal clarifies. Movement becomes meaningful.

From Searching to Expressing

In this state, life no longer feels like a search.

You are no longer asking, *"What am I supposed to be?"*

You are living the answer through expression.

Expression is purpose in motion.

It is purpose lived through how you speak, choose, build, love, lead, create, and respond. It is purpose embodied—not as an idea to be found, but as a frequency to be lived.

The Living Manuscript

Your soul does not rush.
It does not waste chapters.
It does not repeat lessons out of cruelty, but out of commitment to coherence.

And when you stop fighting the rhythm of its writing, the story does not shrink—it **clarifies**.

You realize you were never lost.
You were mid-sentence.

And now, fluent in your frequency, aligned with your rhythm, you write with intention—not because the ending is known, but because the expression is true.

That is the moment purpose stops being a destination.
And becomes **authorship**.

Calculating Your Life Path Number

Your **Life Path Number** is calculated from your full birth date. This process translates your entry point into time into a single, coherent frequency—your core learning rhythm for this lifetime.

Follow the steps below carefully.

NUMEROLOGY WORKSHEET (Use actual birth name not married or adopted names)

I. Life Path
- Month of Birth reduced to single digit _____
- Day of Birth reduced to single digit _____
- Year of Birth reduced to single digit _____
- _____ + _____ + _____ = _____

II. Destiny
(Add together) — First Name / No. Value _____ = _____ = _____
(Add together) — Middle Name / No. Value _____ = _____ = _____
(Add together) — Second Middle Name / No. Value _____ = _____ = _____
(Add together) — Last Name / No. Value _____ = _____ = _____

Add and reduce down final number to single digit unless final total is 11 or 22   _____ + _____ + _____ = _____

Reference key:
- AJS = 1   IR = 9
- BKT = 2
- CLU = 3
- DMV = 4
- ENW = 5
- FOX = 6
- GPY = 7
- HQZ = 8

III. Soul/Heart
(Vowels Only) — First Name / No. Value _____ = _____ = _____
(Vowels Only) — Middle Name / No. Value _____ = _____ = _____
(Vowels Only) — Second Middle Name / No. Value _____ = _____ = _____
(Vowels Only) — Last Name / No. Value _____ = _____ = _____

Add and reduce down final number to single digit unless final total is 11 or 22   _____ + _____ + _____ = _____

IV. Life Stages
- Month reduced to single digit _____
- Personal Year @ 28 years old _____
- Personal Year @ 56 years old _____

V. Life Challenge
- Difference between Day of Birth _____ and month of birth _____ (_____ − _____ = _____) Largest # / Smallest #
- Difference between Day of Birth _____ and year of birth _____ (_____ − _____ = _____) Largest # / Smallest #
- Difference between Day of 1st number _____ and 2nd number _____ (_____ − _____ = _____) Largest # / Smallest #

VI. Special Traits
- How many #1s _____   How many #6s _____   Avg. # of 1s = 3   Avg. # of 6s = 2
- How many #2s _____   How many #7s _____   Avg. # of 2s = 1   Avg. # of 7s = 1
- How many #3s _____   How many #8s _____   Avg. # of 3s = 2   Avg. # of 8s = 1
- How many #4s _____   How many #9s _____   Avg. # of 4s = 1   Avg. # of 9s = 3
- How many #5s _____   Avg. # of 5s = 4

VII. Personal Year
Day of Birth _____ + Month of Birth _____ + Current Year _____ = _____

VIII. Inner Dreams
(Consonants Only) — First Name / No. Value _____ = _____ = _____
(Consonants Only) — Middle Name / No. Value _____ = _____ = _____
(Consonants Only) — Second Middle Name / No. Value _____ = _____ = _____
(Consonants Only) — Last Name / No. Value _____ = _____ = _____

Add and reduce down final number to single digit unless final total is 11 or 22   _____ + _____ + _____ = _____

Step-by-Step Calculation

Step 1: Write your full birth date
Use the format **MM/DD/YYYY**.

Step 2: Reduce each component to a single digit

Add the digits of the month, day, and year separately.

Step 3: Add the reduced numbers together
Combine the three results.

Step 4: Reduce the final sum to a single digit
Continue reducing until you reach one digit.
Exception: *Master Numbers 11, 22, and 33 are not reduced.*

Worked Example

Birthdate: 07/14/1986

- Month: 0 + 7 = **7**

- Day: 1 + 4 = **5**

- Year: 1 + 9 + 8 + 6 = 24 → 2 + 4 = **6**

Final Sum:
7 + 5 + 6 = 18 → 1 + 8 = **9**

Life Path Number: 9

Why This Matters

This number is not a label—it is a **frequency**. It reveals:

- How lessons repeat until embodied

- Where meaning is extracted most naturally

- The rhythm through which purpose unfolds

As you continue through this chapter, you will learn how to interpret your Life Path Number—not as fate, but as **a map for conscious alignment**.

Take your time with this calculation. Accuracy matters—not for prediction, but for resonance.

Life Path Numbers as Vibrational Archetypes

Each **Life Path Number** represents a **vibrational archetype**—a core lesson and evolutionary direction through which the soul gains fluency in wisdom. These numbers are not labels for identity or personality traits. They are **curricula**: structured learning pathways that shape how growth is encountered, integrated, and expressed.

You are not your number.
You are **learning through it**.

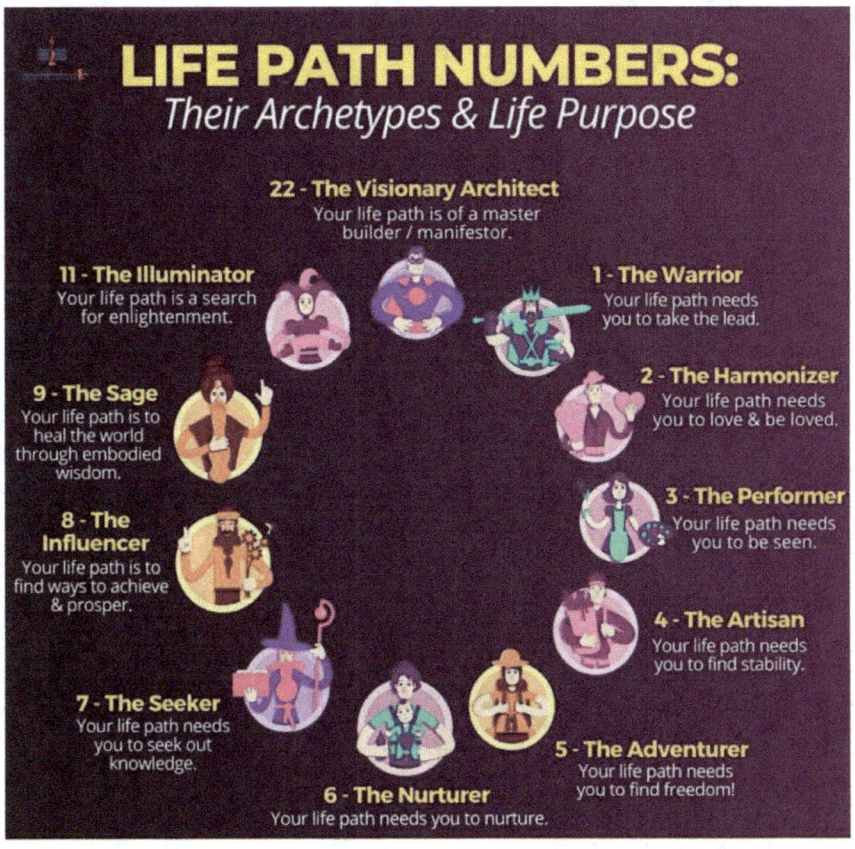

Life Path Archetypes

1 – Initiation, Leadership, Individuality
The curriculum of beginnings. Life asks you to claim direction, cultivate courage, and trust your capacity to lead. Mastery comes through self-definition rather than approval-seeking.

2 – Harmony, Partnership, Emotional Intelligence

The curriculum of attunement. Growth unfolds through relationship, diplomacy, and emotional literacy. Wisdom is earned by balancing self with other without self-erasure.

3 – Expression, Creativity, Communication
The curriculum of voice. Life invites playful creation, storytelling, and emotional expression. Mastery comes when expression is authentic rather than performative.

4 – Structure, Discipline, Foundation
The curriculum of building. Growth arrives through commitment, consistency, and integrity. Wisdom is forged by transforming effort into stability and vision into form.

5 – Freedom, Change, Exploration
The curriculum of movement. Life teaches adaptablity, curiosity, and liberation from stagnation. Mastery emerges when freedom is balanced with responsibility.

6 – Responsibility, Care, Community
The curriculum of stewardship. Growth unfolds through service, nurturing, and ethical leadership. Wisdom comes from caring without controlling and giving without depletion.

7 – Insight, Analysis, Spiritual Inquiry
The curriculum of truth-seeking. Life asks for reflection, discernment, and inner authority. Mastery is achieved by integrating intellect with intuition.

8 – Power, Material Mastery, Authority
The curriculum of influence. Growth comes through ethical leadership, resource stewardship, and embodiment of power without domination. Wisdom is earned through accountability.

9 – Compassion, Completion, Service
The curriculum of integration. Life invites forgiveness, humanitarian vision, and release. Mastery emerges when endings are honored as gateways to renewal.

Master Numbers: Advanced Curricula

11 – Intuition, Illumination, Spiritual Messenger

A heightened curriculum of sensitivity and insight. Life demands nervous-system regulation and grounded intuition so inspiration can be transmitted clearly.

22 – Architect of Reality, Legacy Builder

A curriculum of large-scale manifestation. Growth requires translating vision into enduring structures that serve the collective over time.

33 – Compassionate Teacher, Healer of the Collective

A curriculum of embodied love. Life asks for self-mastery so compassion can be offered without martyrdom, burnout, or self-neglect.

Master Numbers intensify learning. They are not "better"—they are **broader**.

Curriculum, Not Character

These numbers do not describe who you *are*. They describe **how you learn**.

Two people with the same Life Path may live entirely different lives, yet encounter similar lessons—because the **curriculum is the same, while the expression is unique**. When lessons feel repetitive, it is not failure; it is the curriculum returning at a deeper level of integration.

When you approach your Life Path as a vibrational archetype rather than a personality label, comparison dissolves and agency sharpens. You stop asking, *"What's wrong with me?"* and begin asking, *"What is this teaching me to embody more fully?"*

That shift transforms numerology from description into **direction**—not a sentence, but a syllabus for becoming.

Numbers as Frequency, Not Fate

Numerology does not dictate what will happen.
It describes **how experience is metabolized**.

This distinction is essential. Numbers do not predict events or impose outcomes. They illuminate the **processing style of consciousness**—the way lessons are received, interpreted, and integrated over time. In this way, numerology functions much like a metabolic map of meaning.

Life happens to everyone.
Numerology reveals **how life moves through you**.

Reframing Common Misinterpretations

When misunderstood, Life Path Numbers are often mistaken for personality flaws, obstacles, or limitations—labels that quietly teach people to resist themselves. This misunderstanding does real harm, because it frames **frequency as deficiency**.

In truth, each Life Path Number represents a **necessary frequency** in the ecosystem of human intelligence. None are mistakes. None are inferior. None are problems to be fixed.

Difficulty does not arise from the number itself.
It arises from **misalignment with its needs**.

Life Path 5: Freedom Misread as Chaos

A **Life Path 5** does not "cause" chaos. It is calibrated for **movement, change, exploration, and adaptability**. When this frequency is confined—by rigid routines, restrictive environments, or chronic obligation—the nervous system becomes restless. Stagnation breeds impulsivity, dissatisfaction, and reactivity.

This is not dysfunction. It is **signal**.

When given space to move, explore, and experiment, the 5 becomes an innovator, catalyst, and bridge between worlds.

What looks like instability from the outside is often an advanced capacity for **rapid adaptation** when aligned.

Life Path 4: Structure Misread as Limitation

A **Life Path 4** is often mislabeled as rigid, slow, or restrictive. In reality, this frequency is designed for **foundation-building, mastery, and integrity**. The 4 understands that lasting creation requires patience, process, and commitment.

When pressured to rush, improvise constantly, or bypass steps, the 4 can feel trapped or inadequate—not because it lacks creativity, but because its intelligence is **architectural**.

What others may experience as limitation, the 4 experiences as **stability, trustworthiness, and long-term success**. Its power lies not in speed, but in sustainability.

Life Path 7: Solitude Misread as Isolation

A **Life Path 7** is frequently misunderstood as withdrawn, aloof, or emotionally distant. In truth, this frequency is oriented toward **depth, inquiry, and inner authority**. The 7 must periodically withdraw from noise in order to integrate meaning.

Solitude for the 7 is not avoidance—it is **incubation**.

Without time for reflection, study, or spiritual inquiry, the 7 becomes mentally overwhelmed or existentially disconnected. When honored, this rhythm produces wisdom, discernment, and profound insight that benefits others as much as the self.

The Real Source of Struggle

In each of these examples, challenge does not arise from the Life Path Number. It arises from **living out of rhythm** with it—often due to external expectations, cultural norms, or internalized comparison.

A 5 forced into rigidity

A 4 pressured into constant flux
A 7 denied depth and quiet

Each scenario produces friction not because the individual is flawed, but because the **frequency is being misused**.

From Self-Correction to Self-Alignment

Reframing these misinterpretations is liberating. It shifts the internal question from:

"What's wrong with me?"
to
"What does my frequency need in order to function well?"

This shift dissolves shame and restores agency.

Life Path Numbers are not diagnoses.
They are **design specifications**.

When those specifications are honored, what once looked like a weakness reveals itself as a strength. What once felt like a struggle becomes a skill. What once felt like resistance becomes resonance.

The work, then, is not self-correction.
It is **self-alignment**.

And when alignment replaces misunderstanding, the Life Path stops feeling like a burden and starts functioning as what it always was:
a **precise, intelligent pathway for growth**.

How Lessons Arrive

Numbers reveal **how lessons arrive**, not whether they will.

Challenge, uncertainty, relationship, loss, and growth are universal features of human life. No Life Path exempts anyone from these experiences. What differs is **the channel through which they are delivered**—the language life uses to teach.

Numerology clarifies this channel. It explains *how* experience is processed, metabolized, and integrated by consciousness.

Different Frequencies, Different Classrooms

Each Life Path frequency learns through a distinct mode of engagement:

- **Some frequencies learn through action.**
  Life teaches through initiation, decision, risk, and consequence. Understanding emerges after movement—not before it. Action is the classroom.

- **Some learn through reflection.**
  Insight arises through observation, contemplation, and analysis. Silence, solitude, and inquiry become the teachers. Meaning is distilled inwardly.

- **Some learn through service.**
  Growth unfolds through responsibility, care, and relational commitment. Lessons arrive via what is asked of you by others and how you respond.

- **Some learn through disruption.**
  Change itself becomes the catalyst. Old structures dissolve so new awareness can emerge. Transformation is the teacher.

None of these classrooms are superior. Each is **necessary** for the evolution of human consciousness.

Life Speaks in Your Native Frequency

When life presents a lesson, it does so in the **language your frequency understands best**. A lesson meant for an action-oriented frequency will arrive as a decision that cannot be avoided. A lesson meant for a reflective frequency will arrive as a question that refuses to be answered superficially.

If the lesson is met consciously, it integrates.
If it is avoided or misunderstood, it repeats.

Repetition is not punishment.
It is **reinforcement**.

Why Lessons Intensify

When a lesson is ignored, life does not become cruel—it becomes **clearer**. The volume increases. The context shifts. The stakes rise. This is not judgment; it is feedback.

Just as a nervous system raises intensity when subtle signals are missed, life amplifies experience when awareness is absent.

This is why patterns often escalate:

- Relationships repeat with higher emotional charge

- Challenges return with greater consequence

- Decisions feel more urgent

The lesson has not changed. The **volume has**.

Integration Ends Repetition

When the lesson is integrated—when the frequency is honored—the pattern dissolves. Not because life becomes easy, but because the curriculum has been **completed at that level**.

A new lesson emerges, often more complex and refined.

Understanding how lessons arrive transforms suffering into information. It shifts experience from something that happens *to* you into something that is working *with* you.

Numerology does not promise comfort.
It offers **comprehension**.

And comprehension restores agency.

When you learn the language your soul speaks in, life no longer has to shout. It can whisper—and still be heard.

Because growth does not require pain.
It requires **attunement**.

And once attuned, lessons stop feeling like obstacles and start revealing themselves as what they always were: **instructions for becoming**.

Agency Through Alignment

Seeing numbers as **frequency** restores agency.

When a frequency feels difficult, the solution is not avoidance—it is **alignment**. Difficulty is often the body's and psyche's way of signaling that energy is being used inefficiently. Resistance consumes more effort than alignment ever will. When individuals work *with* their Life Path frequency rather than against it, experience begins to integrate more cleanly. Insight deepens. Growth accelerates—not because life becomes simple, but because **effort produces return**.

Alignment turns friction into feedback.

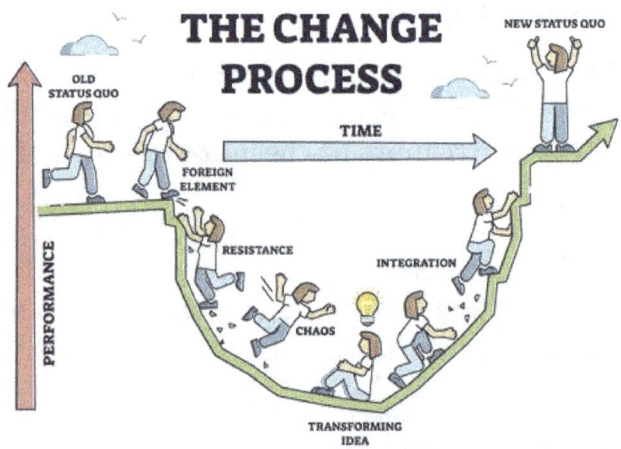

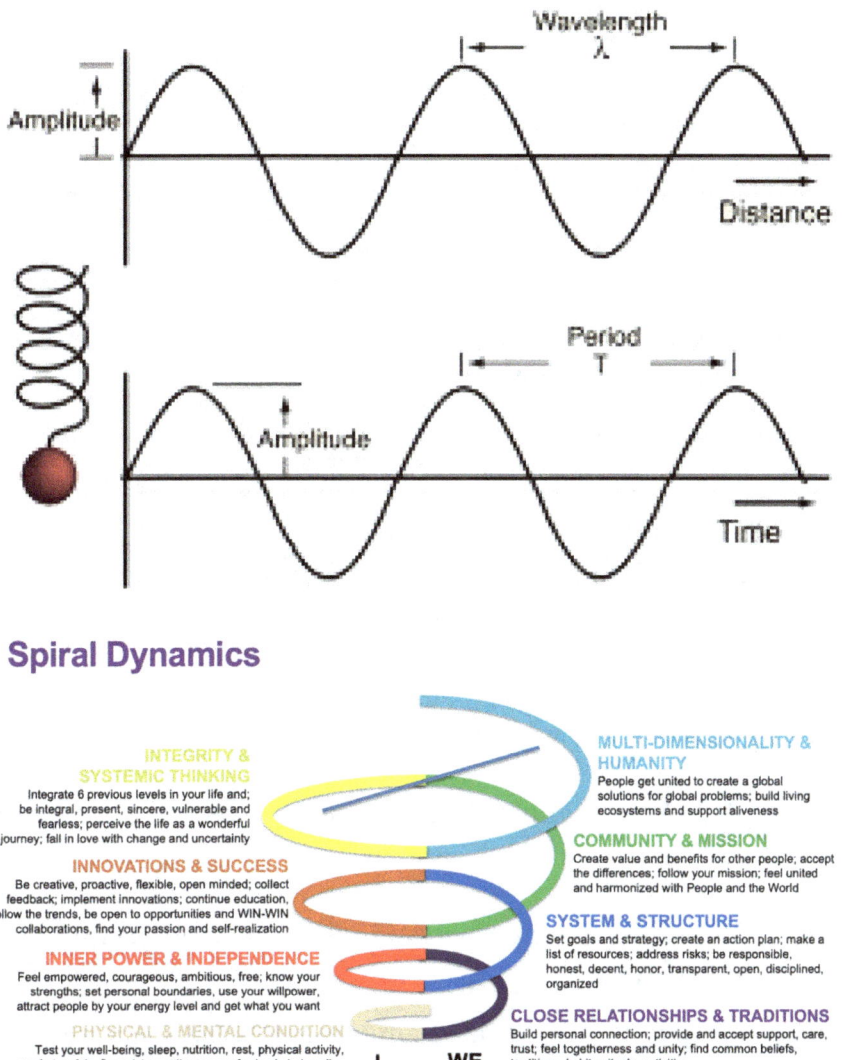

Spiral Dynamics

From Forcing to Functioning

Many people attempt to evolve by forcing change: pushing harder, staying longer, or trying to master lessons through methods that contradict their natural learning rhythm. This creates exhaustion without integration.

Alignment changes the equation.

When your strategies match your frequency:

- Challenges become intelligible rather than overwhelming

- Patterns resolve faster instead of repeating endlessly

- Energy stabilizes instead of fragmenting

You are no longer fighting your design.
You are **functioning within it**.

Clarity About Process

Numerology does not remove uncertainty. Life remains dynamic, relational, and unpredictable. What numerology *does* remove is confusion about **process**—the hidden rules by which learning unfolds for you.

With process clarity:

- You recognize why certain themes recur

- You know where to invest effort—and where to stop wasting it

- You discern when persistence is required and when a pivot is wiser

Uncertainty remains, but it becomes navigable.

A Better Question

Alignment shifts the internal dialogue.

You stop asking,
"Why does this keep happening to me?"
—a question rooted in confusion and self-blame—

and start asking,
"What is this frequency asking me to embody?"

This question restores authorship. It reframes experience as instruction rather than punishment. It invites embodiment rather than avoidance.

Agency, Refined

Agency through alignment is not about control. It is about **precision**. You learn to respond accurately to life's signals instead of reacting impulsively to discomfort.

Accuracy compounds over time.
Accuracy builds momentum.
Momentum builds trust—in yourself and in the process.

And with trust, alignment becomes sustainable.

You are not powerless in the face of your Life Path.
You are **empowered by understanding how it works**.

When frequency becomes conscious, growth stops being accidental.
It becomes intentional, embodied, and deeply human.

That is agency—not as force, but as **resonant choice**.

Destiny Without Determinism

When numbers are understood as **frequency rather than fate**, destiny becomes **dynamic**. You are not locked into outcomes, timelines, or roles. You are participating in **patterned evolution**—a living process in which choice, awareness, and timing interact with rhythm rather than submit to it.

Destiny, in this view, is not a verdict.
It is a **relationship**.

Training, Not Sentencing

Your Life Path does not sentence you.
It **trains you**.

Training implies repetition with purpose. It implies challenge calibrated for growth. It implies progression—where difficulty refines capacity rather than defines limitation. The same way an athlete trains specific muscle groups to build strength, your Life Path trains particular dimensions of consciousness.

What repeats is not punishment.
It is **conditioning for mastery**.

Each recurrence invites a more skillful response:

- More discernment where there was reactivity

- More presence where there was avoidance

- More integrity where there was compromise

The lesson remains until the skill is embodied.

From Adversarial to Instructional

When frequency becomes conscious, life stops feeling adversarial. Events no longer appear as random obstacles or personal attacks. They begin to read like **instructions**—clearer, more legible, and increasingly precise.

Pain may still occur. Loss may still arrive. Uncertainty remains part of the human experience. What changes is **access to meaning**.

Meaning does not erase pain.
It **contextualizes** it.

And context restores agency.

You stop bracing against life and start listening to it. You respond rather than react. You integrate rather than resist.

Illuminating the Pathway of Wisdom

Numbers do not control your future. They do not dictate success or failure. What they do is **illuminate the pathway through which wisdom is earned**.

They reveal:

- The tempo of your learning
- The arenas where growth concentrates
- The style through which insight integrates

With this illumination, choice becomes informed rather than frantic. You can move with intention even when outcomes are unknown.

Freedom Through Pattern Awareness

This is destiny without determinism—where structure exists without imprisonment, and pattern exists without inevitability.

You are free **within** rhythm, not constrained by it.

And when you learn the rhythm through which your soul metabolizes experience, growth stops feeling like resistance and starts feeling like participation. You are no longer being shaped *against* your will—you are shaping yourself *with* awareness.

That is not fate.
That is **frequency made conscious**.

And consciousness—once awakened—does not remove uncertainty.
It transforms uncertainty into **terrain you know how to navigate**.

Not because the map is fixed.
But because you finally understand **how you learn your way forward**.

Scientific Integration: Frequency, Form, and Pattern

Modern science increasingly supports numerology's core

premise: **frequency organizes form**. What ancient systems intuited symbolically, contemporary research now observes empirically—across physics, biology, and systems science.

Reality does not assemble itself through randomness.
It stabilizes through **patterned resonance**.

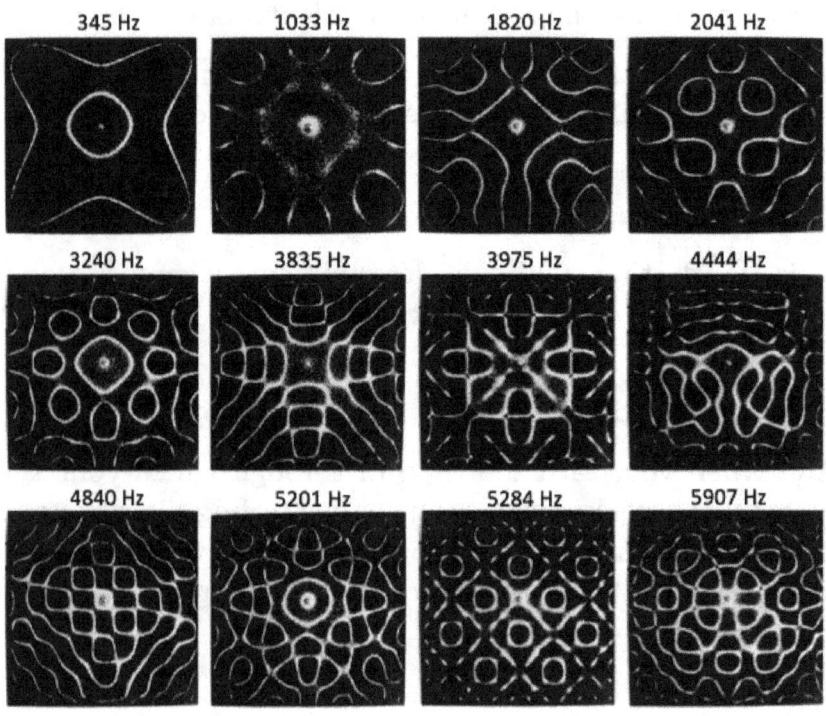

ENCODED IN THE STARS | 181

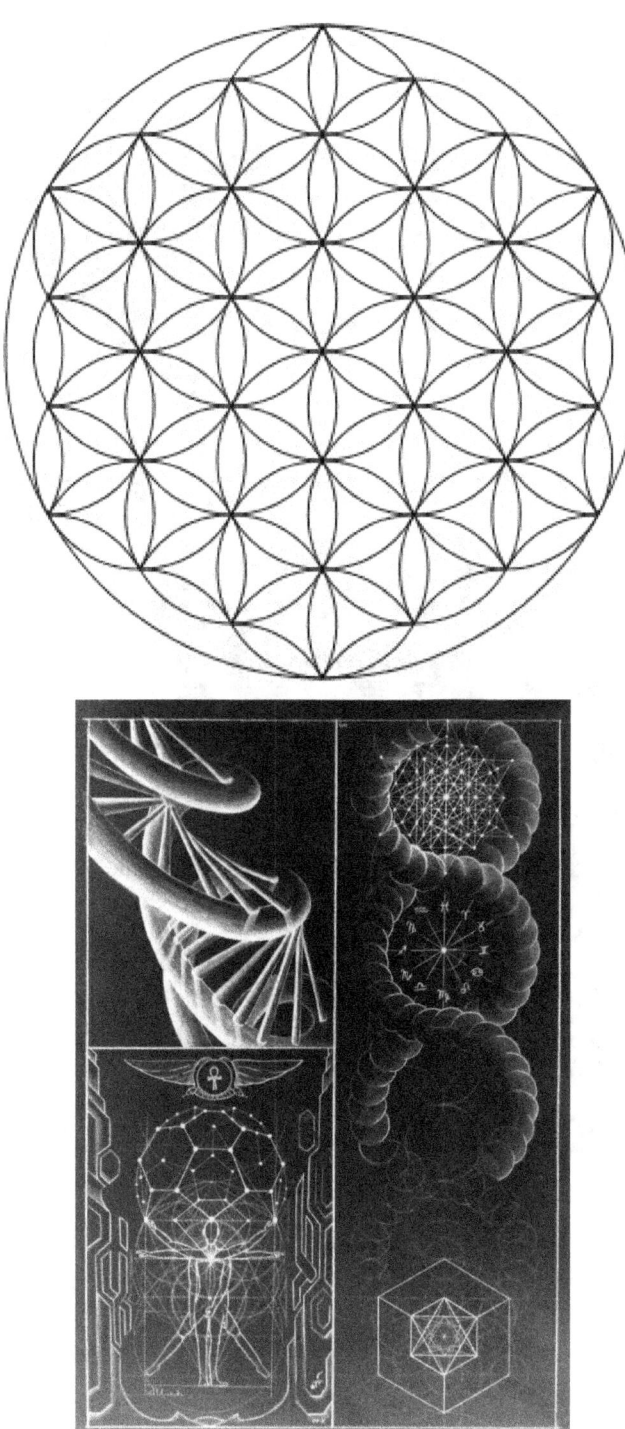

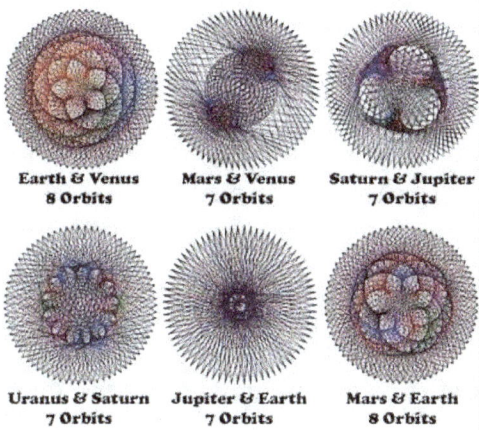

Earth & Venus
8 Orbits

Mars & Venus
7 Orbits

Saturn & Jupiter
7 Orbits

Uranus & Saturn
7 Orbits

Jupiter & Earth
7 Orbits

Mars & Earth
8 Orbits

Frequency as the Architect of Reality

At the most fundamental level, existence is vibrational. Matter, energy, light, sound, and even biological processes operate through oscillation and rhythm. Frequency determines how energy organizes into structure—how potential collapses into form.

This insight appears repeatedly across scientific disciplines, each using different language to describe the same underlying truth: **order emerges through resonance**.

Key Areas of Convergence

Pythagorean Harmonic Theory — Vibration as Foundation

Pythagorean harmonic theory proposed that reality is structured through numerical ratios and vibrational relationships. Modern physics mirrors this insight by demonstrating that particles, waves, and fields behave according to harmonic laws. Stability emerges not through force, but through **balanced ratios**.

What was once philosophical is now mathematical fact: vibration governs structure.

Cymatics — Sound Creating Visible Form

Cymatics provides one of the most visually compelling confirmations of frequency shaping form. When sound frequencies are applied to matter—such as sand, water, or liquid—distinct geometric patterns emerge. Change the frequency, and the pattern reorganizes instantly.

Nothing else is altered.
No structure is imposed.
Only **frequency shifts**, and form follows.

This demonstrates a foundational principle: **form is a response to vibration**, not its cause.

Sacred Geometry — Recurring Ratios in Nature

Sacred geometry reveals that certain mathematical ratios—such as the golden ratio and Fibonacci sequence—recur throughout nature. These ratios appear in:

- The spirals of galaxies

- The structure of DNA

- Flower petals and seed arrangements

- Shells, waves, and planetary orbits

These patterns are not decorative. They represent **efficient, stable solutions** to growth and movement within physical systems. Nature repeats what works.

Chaos and Systems Theory — Order from Complexity

Chaos theory and systems science demonstrate that complex order can emerge from simple rules applied repeatedly. Fractals, weather systems, ecosystems, and neural networks all exhibit **self-organizing intelligence**.

What appears chaotic on the surface often reveals deep mathematical consistency beneath it.

Order is not imposed from above.
It **emerges from patterned interaction**.

Numerology in Scientific Context

Numerology exists within this same framework—not as superstition, but as symbolic pattern recognition. Where science measures frequency, numerology interprets **meaning**. Where science models form, numerology contextualizes **experience**.

Both are observing the same phenomenon from different vantage points.

Numerology proposes that human lives—like all natural systems—organize through rhythm, repetition, and resonance. Life Path Numbers do not impose outcomes; they describe **how pattern unfolds through consciousness**.

Mathematical Elegance, Not Random Chance

Life is not random—it is **mathematically elegant**.

This does not mean life is predictable. It means it is **coherent**. Growth follows rhythm. Learning follows pattern. Wisdom emerges through repetition and integration.

Understanding this reframes destiny entirely. You are not navigating chaos; you are participating in a patterned universe that responds to awareness.

When frequency becomes conscious, form becomes flexible. When pattern is recognized, agency expands.

And in that recognition, numerology transforms from belief into **language**—a way of reading the mathematics already shaping existence.

Not to control life.
But to **move with its intelligence**.

INTERACTIVE ELEMENT: YOUR CORE NUMEROLOGICAL TRINITY

Calculating The Frequencies That Shape Your Becoming

Numerology becomes truly powerful when it is **applied**, not just understood. This interactive element invites you to calculate and reflect on your **Core Numerological Trinity**—three numbers that work together to describe *how you evolve, what motivates you from within*, and *how your energy meets the world*.

Think of this trinity as a **numerical blueprint**—not a script for what must happen, but a map of how frequency moves through your life.

V- The Blueprint of Your Soul Chart

Name:

From your Date of Birth

Date of Birth: Month Day Year
Calculation =
Calculation =

MAIN CORE NUMBERS:

From your Date of Birth

- Blueprint Destiny: ☐☐ = ☐
- Blueprint Birthday: ☐☐ = ☐
- Blueprint Attainments: 1) ☐ 2) ☐ 3) ☐ 4) ☐
- Blueprint Challenges: 1) ☐ 2) ☐ 3) ☐ 4) ☐

Age Timing of Blueprint Attainments & Blueprint Challenges:

- 1st phase begins at birth and ends at age ☐☐
- 2nd phase begins from age ☐☐ to ☐☐
- 3rd phase begins from age ☐☐ to ☐☐
- 4th phase begins at age ☐☐ until the end of life

Blueprint Journey's Cycle:

- Blueprint Influential Learning ☐☐ = ☐
  (Ends around age 27)
- Blueprint Personal Experiences ☐☐ = ☐
  (Ends around age 57)

© Joseph Ghabi & Free Spirit Centre Publishing
https://www.freespiritcentre.info & https://www.theblueprintofyoursoul.com
The Blueprint of Your Soul - Discover Yourself and Your Blueprint Destiny

1) Life Path Number — How You Evolve

What it reveals:
Your primary learning rhythm. The pathway through which growth, challenge, and wisdom are integrated over time.

How it functions:
This number describes *process*, not personality. It shows the style of evolution your soul uses to mature—through initiation, service, structure, inquiry, freedom, or transformation.

Reflection prompts:

- Which lessons seem to repeat until they are embodied?

- Where does growth feel most efficient when you lean into it?

2) Soul Urge Number — What Your Inner Self Desires

What it reveals:
Your inner motivation—the quiet pull beneath decisions, longings, and emotional needs.

How it functions:
Calculated from the vowels in your full birth name, the Soul Urge reflects *why* you do what you do when no one is watching. It points to what nourishes you emotionally and spiritually, even if it isn't always visible outwardly.

Reflection prompts:

- What consistently brings a sense of fulfillment or depletion?

- Where do you feel most authentically satisfied, regardless of outcome?

3) Expression Number — How Your Energy

Is Expressed Outwardly

What it reveals:
Your natural mode of expression—the talents, communication style, and behavioral tendencies others most readily perceive.

How it functions:
Derived from all the letters in your full birth name, the Expression Number shows *how* your energy moves into the world. It reflects skills, strengths, and the manner in which your inner frequency becomes visible through action.

Reflection prompts:

- How do others tend to describe your strengths?

- Where does expression feel effortless versus forced?

How the Trinity Works Together

These three numbers do not compete; they **collaborate**.

- The **Life Path** sets the rhythm of growth

- The **Soul Urge** fuels motivation and meaning

- The **Expression** shapes how energy is delivered

When aligned, life feels coherent. When misaligned, effort increases while fulfillment decreases.

Together, this trinity describes **motivation, behavior, and destiny as frequency rather than fate**. It explains why you may *want* one thing (Soul Urge), *grow* through another (Life Path), and *appear* a third way (Expression)

Integration Exercise

Take a moment to write your three numbers below:

- **Life Path Number:** _____

- **Soul Urge Number:** _____

- **Expression Number:** _____

Now reflect:

- Where do these numbers support one another?

- Where might tension be asking for integration rather than correction?

- What would alignment look like if all three were honored?

Your Core Numerological Trinity does not define you—it **reveals how your energy wants to move**.

When you honor all three—how you grow, what you desire, and how you express—you stop fragmenting yourself to meet expectations. You begin living from coherence.

And in coherence, destiny is no longer something you wait for. It becomes something you **participate in**, frequency by frequency, choice by choice.

Key Insight of This Chapter

You are not random.
You are **rhythmic**.

Your life unfolds in patterns not because it is predetermined or fixed, but because it is **encoded**. Just as music follows structure without losing creativity, your experiences follow rhythm without erasing choice. Numerology reveals that what often feels like chaos is, in truth, **mathematical poetry**—a living expression of order, timing, and resonance moving through consciousness.

Patterns are not prisons.
They are pathways.

When you understand your numbers, you begin to recognize *why* certain themes repeat, *how* challenges arrive, and *where* growth concentrates. What once felt like resistance starts to make sense as instruction. You stop fighting your nature and start **working with it**, allowing effort to become more efficient and insight to arrive more clearly.

Numbers do not tell you who to be.
They reveal **how your soul learns best**.

And in that revelation, limitation dissolves. Numerology does not shrink possibility—it expands it. By clarifying your rhythm, it frees you from comparison, self-judgment, and misalignment. You are no longer trying to evolve through methods that contradict your frequency. You are evolving through **coherence**.

This is liberation, not labeling.

When frequency becomes conscious, choice becomes accurate. When choice becomes accurate, momentum builds. And when momentum aligns with rhythm, life stops feeling like something you must force and starts feeling like something you **participate in with intelligence**.

You are not here to escape your design.
You are here to **become fluent in it**.

And when you do, destiny ceases to feel mysterious or overwhelming. It becomes a conversation—between number and intuition, pattern and choice, rhythm and expression.

Not fate.
But **frequency, lived consciously**.

CHAPTER 5

The Human Design Experiment

Where Destiny Meets Biology, Energy, and Choice

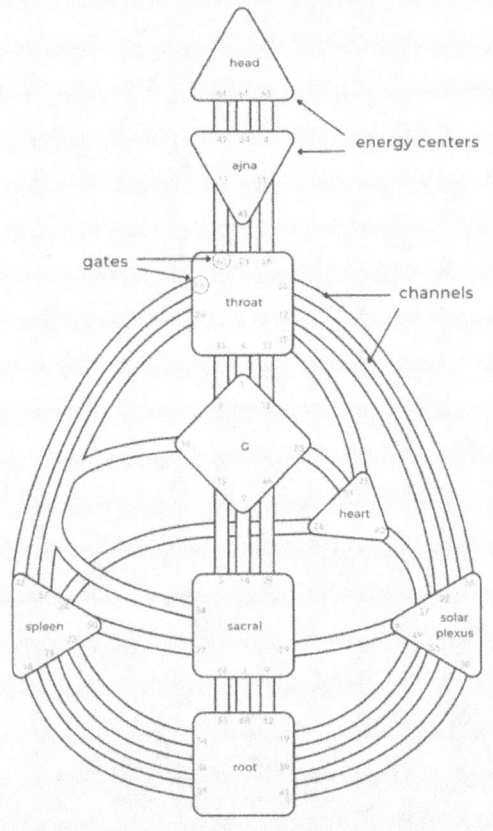

Human Design Type Guide

Type Name	Generator	Manifesting Generator	Manifestor	Projector	Reflector
Energy/Non-Energy	Energy Type	Energy Type	Energy Type	Non-Energy	Non-Energy
Sacral Life Force	Defined Type	Defined Sacral	Undefined	Undefined Sacral	Undefined Sacral
Definitions	Sacral and/or Motor Center(s) NOT defined to the Throat	Sacral and/or Motor Center(s) defined to the Throat	Motor Center(s) defined to the Throat	No Motor Center(s) defined to the Throat	No Centers defined
Natural State	Responsive/Active	Responsive/Clarity/Active	Directly Active	Attuning before involvement	Open to engage or not
Fulfilled or not	Satisfaction or Frustration	Clear in commitments or Leave a trail of devastation	Purposeful or Resentful/Resented	Guiding or ignored	Flowing/Overloaded
Habitually	Overworked	Overlybusy	Blocked/Annoyed	Under-appreciated	Overlooked
Needs	External stimulus	External stimulus & inner conviction	Right Timing & Circumstances	To have outer & inner recognitions	Time and space in synthesis
Purpose	Cross-pollination & effective action	Cross-pollination & deliberate expansion	Movement & catalysis	Providing Guidance	Developing wisdom
Key to success	Wait for sacral response before acting	Wait for sacral response, then "test" the action before commiting.	Inspire and include other to the right action	Wait for clear signal to provide guidance	Allow others to provide support

The Human Design System
Aura Types

 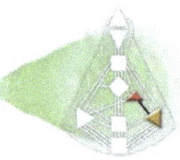 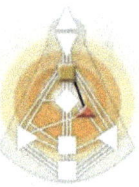 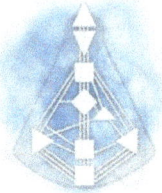

Human Design Is Not a Belief System. It Is an **Experiment.**

Human Design is not a philosophy you are asked to accept.
It is an **experiment** you are invited to run.

Unlike systems that require belief, devotion, or intellectual agreement, Human Design asks for something far more grounded: **observation**. It asks you to watch your body, your energy, your decision-making, and your lived experience over time—and to notice what actually works when you stop forcing yourself to operate like someone else.

The premise is simple, yet radical:
alignment is not about trying harder or becoming better.
It is about **operating correctly** according to your unique energetic design.

From Faith to Feedback

Most personal development systems are aspirational. They tell you who to become, how to improve, and what habits to adopt —often assuming that the same strategies should work for everyone. Human Design moves in the opposite direction. It does not prescribe ideals; it observes mechanics.

It asks:

- What happens in your body when you initiate versus when you wait?

- What shifts when you make decisions quickly versus giving them time?

- How does your energy respond when you push, versus when you respond?

The answers are not theoretical. They are **somatic**. You feel them as ease or resistance, clarity or confusion, vitality or exhaustion.

Human Design treats your body as the primary data source.

Alignment as Correct Operation

In this framework, alignment is not moral. It is **mechanical**.

Just as a machine functions optimally when used according to its design, the human system functions best when energy is applied in ways that match its configuration. When you operate correctly:

- Energy replenishes instead of depletes

- Decisions feel grounded rather than frantic

- Resistance from life decreases

- Effort produces meaningful return

When you operate incorrectly, the system compensates. Stress increases. Frustration accumulates. Burnout follows—not because you are weak, but because energy is being misapplied.

Human Design reframes struggle not as a personal failure, but as **feedback**.

The Body as Primary Intelligence

At its core, Human Design answers a question modern society rarely asks:

What if your body already knows how you are meant to move through life?

Neuroscience, somatic psychology, and bioenergetics increasingly support this idea. The body processes information faster than conscious thought. It registers coherence and misalignment long before the mind can justify them. Tension, fatigue, and emotional resistance are not inconveniences; they are **signals**.

Human Design proposes that much of human suffering does not come from lack of effort or discipline, but from **ignoring bodily intelligence** in favor of mental conditioning, social pressure, and comparison.

Suffering as Misalignment, Not Defect

This perspective is deeply compassionate. It suggests that suffering often arises not because something is wrong with you, but because you are operating in ways that contradict your design.

- Pushing when you are built to respond
- Sustaining output when you are built for bursts
- Initiating when you are built to guide
- Rushing when you are built to wait

Over time, these misapplications accumulate as exhaustion, bitterness, frustration, or disappointment—the very emotional signatures Human Design identifies as signals of misalignment.

These signals are not punishments.
They are **course corrections**.

The Experiment Itself

Human Design does not ask you to believe any of this.

It asks you to **test it**.

To experiment with:

- Following your Strategy instead of forcing timing

- Trusting your Authority instead of mental pressure

- Observing how your body responds when aligned versus when ignored

Over weeks and months, patterns emerge. Resistance lessens. Decision-making becomes cleaner. Energy stabilizes. The experiment becomes self-validating—not through belief, but through lived evidence.

A New Relationship with Yourself

Human Design ultimately offers a new relationship with the self—one rooted in respect rather than correction.

You are not here to override your body.
You are here to **partner with it**.

When you stop treating your body as something to discipline and start listening to it as an intelligent system, life shifts. Not because it becomes easy, but because it becomes **accurate**.

And accuracy—over time—creates freedom.

Human Design is not asking you to become someone else.
It is inviting you to finally operate as **yourself**.

Not by belief.
By experiment.

Origins of Human Design: A Synthesis System

Human Design was introduced in 1987 by **Ra Uru Hu**, who described it not as a new belief system, but as a **synthesis** —a unification of ancient wisdom traditions and modern scientific insight into a single, functional map of human energy.

This distinction matters. Human Design does not claim originality through invention; it claims coherence through **integration**. It weaves together multiple languages of intelligence—each describing the same underlying order from a different vantage point—and translates them into **mechanics you can test in daily life**.

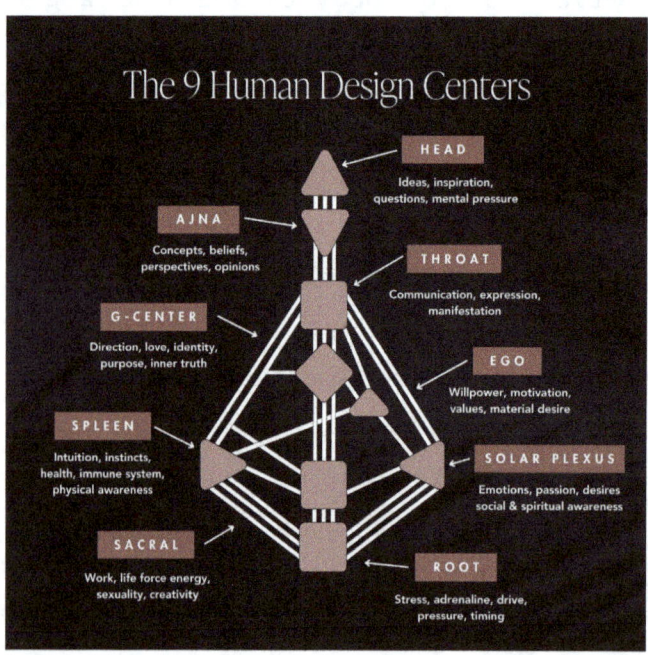

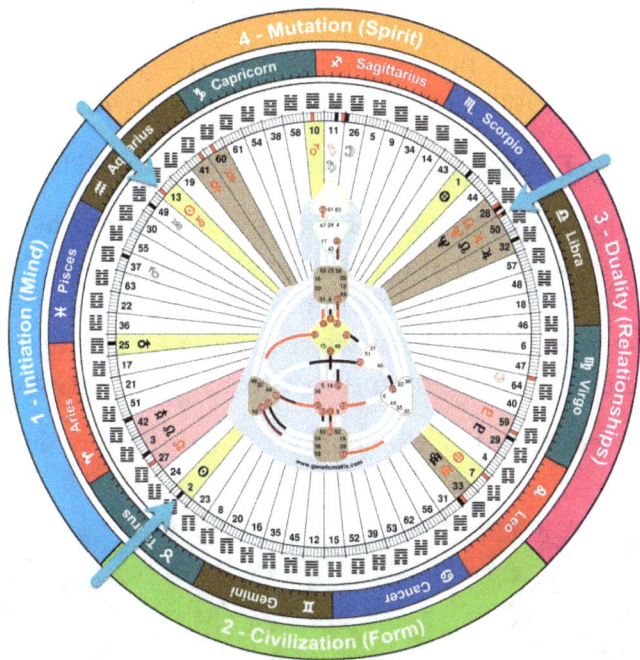

The Five Streams of the Synthesis

Astrology — Planetary Imprinting at Birth

Human Design begins with astrology's core insight: the moment of birth carries an informational imprint. Planetary positions are not viewed as causal forces, but as **timing markers**—indicators of the energetic environment into which consciousness emerges. In Human Design, these positions are mathematically mapped to define energetic activations within the bodygraph.

Astrology provides the *when* and *where* of imprinting.

I Ching — Binary Patterns of Change and Decision-Making

The I Ching contributes a binary logic of **yin and yang**, expressed through hexagrams—patterns that describe how change unfolds. These binary sequences parallel modern computing and genetic coding, offering a symbolic language for **decision-making pathways** and adaptive response.

In Human Design, the I Ching informs the gates and channels that describe **how energy moves and transforms**.

Kabbalah — Energetic Pathways and Life Force Flow

From Kabbalah comes the Tree of Life—a map of energetic pathways connecting states of consciousness. Human Design adapts this structure into channels that illustrate **how life force travels through the system**, linking centers and creating consistent themes of perception, motivation, and behavior.

Kabbalah contributes the *pathways* through which energy integrates.

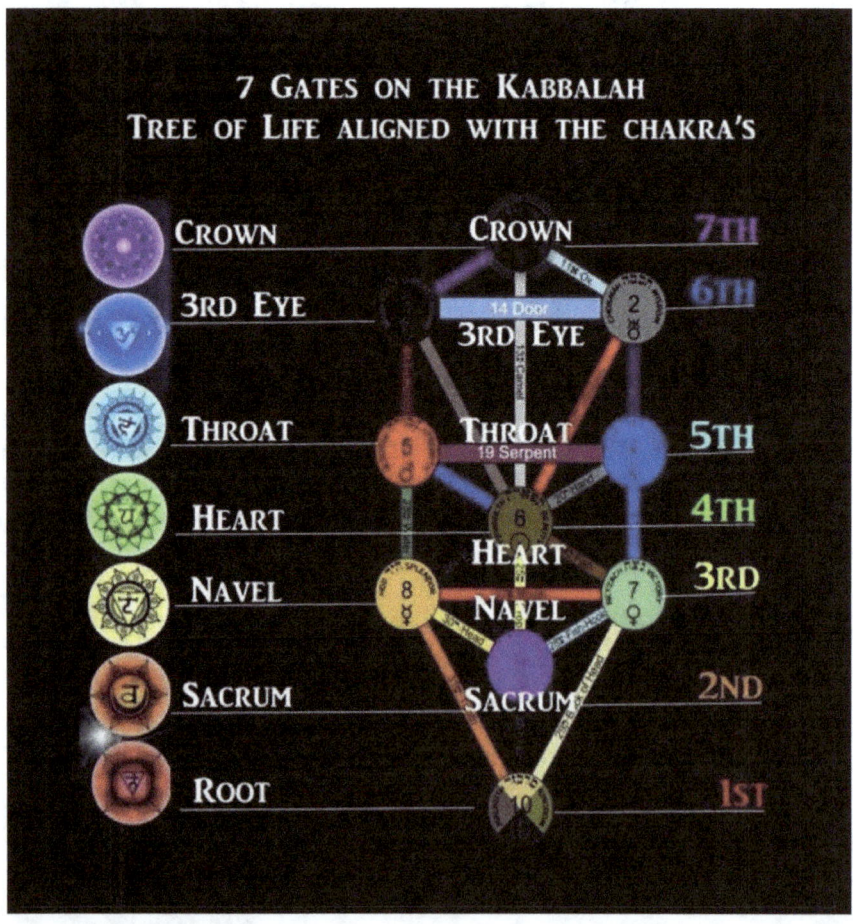

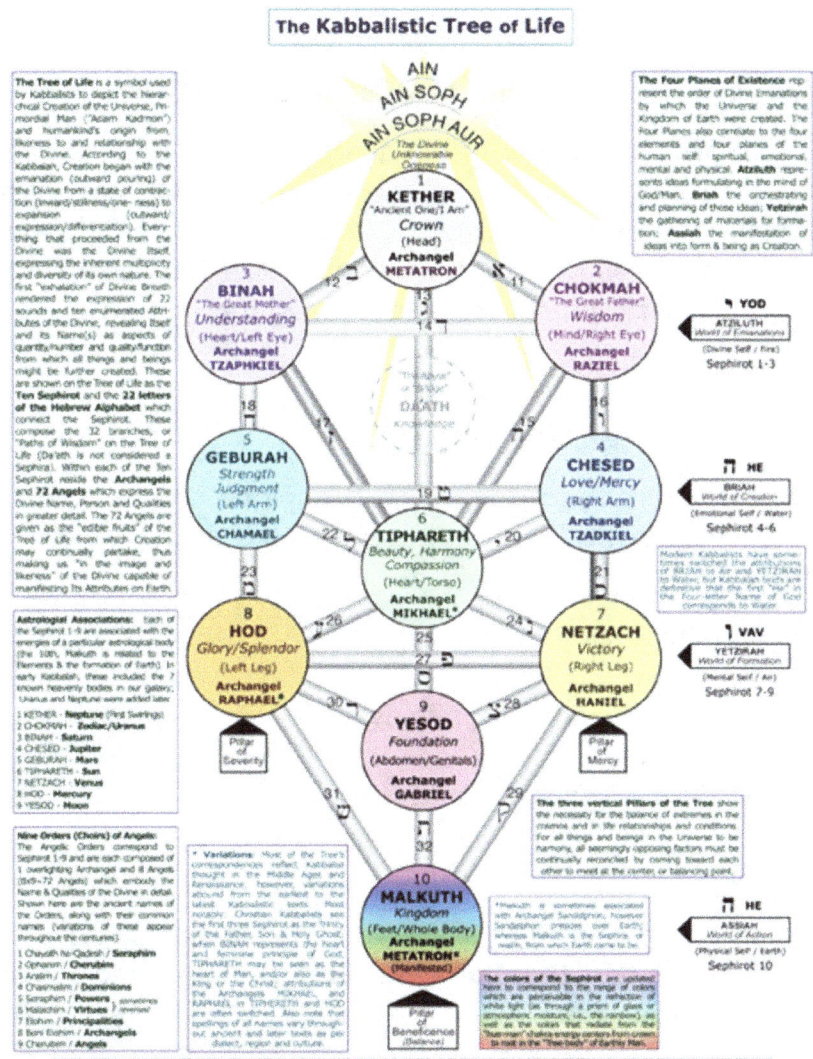

Chakra System — Centers of Energy Processing

Human Design modifies the traditional seven-chakra model into **nine energy centers**, reflecting both ancient insight and contemporary understanding of differentiation. These centers show **where information is processed**, whether energy is consistent or variable, and how conditioning occurs.

The chakra system contributes the *where* of energetic processing.

Genetics — Binary Coding, Differentiation, and Mutation

Modern genetics provides the scientific mirror. DNA operates through binary coding—on/off, active/dormant—governing differentiation and expression. Human Design aligns this with the I Ching's binary logic, suggesting a symbolic parallel between **genetic expression and energetic activation**.

Genetics contributes the *how* of differentiation.

One Intelligence, Many Languages

This synthesis reflects a deeper truth explored throughout this book: **the same intelligence expresses itself through multiple languages**.

- Symbolic (astrology, I Ching)
- Energetic (chakras, biofields)
- Structural (Kabbalah pathways)
- Biological (genetic coding)

Human Design does not argue which language is "right." It demonstrates that **they are describing the same order from different dimensions**.

From Theory to Mechanics

What makes Human Design distinct is its insistence on **practical mechanics**. It does not ask you to interpret meaning abstractly; it shows you *how energy operates*:

- How your aura interacts with others
- How decisions are meant to be made in your body

- How energy is replenished or depleted

- How conditioning takes root—and how it releases

This is where synthesis becomes usable.

Human Design translates ancient wisdom and modern science into **operational guidance**—not to control life, but to **navigate it accurately**.

Why This Matters

In a world saturated with advice, optimization strategies, and moralized productivity, Human Design offers something rare: **specificity without judgment**. It does not tell you how to be better. It shows you how to be **correct** for your design.

And correctness, over time, creates ease—not because life stops challenging you, but because your energy stops fighting itself.

Human Design is not asking you to believe in a system.
It is inviting you to **recognize the intelligence already moving through you**—expressed through stars, symbols, circuits, and cells.

One intelligence.
Many languages.
One body learning how to listen.

The Five Energy Types: How Energy Is Designed to Move

Human Design identifies **five primary energy types**, each with a distinct **aura, metabolic rhythm**, and **decision-making strategy**. These are not personality labels or behavioral stereotypes. They are **energetic mechanics**—describing *how life force is designed to move through you and meet the world.*

When a type operates according to its design, energy

replenishes, decisions clarify, and resistance decreases. When a type is pressured to operate like another, dysregulation follows—not because something is wrong, but because **energy is being misapplied.**

Manifestor — The Initiator

Designed to: Initiate and catalyze
Energy rhythm: Bursts, not sustained output
Aura quality: Impactful, directional

Manifestors are designed to **start things**—to open pathways where none existed before. Their energy moves in pulses, not marathons. When they attempt to sustain output like a Generator, resistance builds—internally and externally.

The key to Manifestor alignment is **informing before action**. Informing reduces resistance by preparing others for movement. When Manifestors initiate without informing, they often encounter pushback. When they inform, doors open.

Dysregulation shows up as: Anger, frustration, exhaustion
Alignment restores: Peace, momentum, clean initiation

Generator — The Builder

Designed to: Build, sustain, and master
Energy rhythm: Consistent life-force when engaged correctly
Aura quality: Open, magnetic

Generators carry sustainable energy—but only when they are **responding**, not forcing. Their power lies in engagement with what life presents, not in initiating from the mind. When Generators initiate prematurely, frustration emerges—not as failure, but as feedback.

Alignment comes through **waiting to respond**—to invitations, opportunities, questions, or internal gut signals. When response is honored, Generators access deep satisfaction and endurance.

Dysregulation shows up as: Frustration, burnout
Alignment restores: Satisfaction, mastery, vitality

Manifesting Generator — The Multidimensional Mover

Designed to: Build and initiate efficiently
Energy rhythm: Fast, nonlinear, responsive
Aura quality: Magnetic and impactful

Manifesting Generators are a **hybrid design**, combining Generator sustainability with Manifestor speed. They are wired for multi-passionate expression, rapid iteration, and course correction. Their learning style is experiential—**trial, error, adjust.**

Alignment comes through **responding first, then informing**. Skipping steps or trying to justify pivots creates resistance. Honoring their quick, responsive nature restores flow.

Dysregulation shows up as: Frustration, anger, impatience
Alignment restores: Flow, efficiency, creative momentum

Projector — The Guide

Designed to: Guide, optimize, and direct energy
Energy rhythm: Focused, non-sustainable output
Aura quality: Penetrating, attuned

Projectors are not designed for constant doing. Their intelligence lies in **seeing systems, people, and efficiencies** others miss. When they attempt to keep up with Generator output, bitterness and exhaustion follow.

Alignment comes through **recognition and invitation**. When Projectors are seen and invited, their guidance lands cleanly and powerfully. Waiting is not passivity—it is **energetic precision.**

Dysregulation shows up as: Bitterness, invisibility, burnout

Alignment restores: Recognition, influence, wisdom

Reflector — The Environmental Barometer

Designed to: Sample, reflect, and mirror
Energy rhythm: Cyclical, lunar-based
Aura quality: Resistant, receptive

Reflectors are highly sensitive to **environment and community health**. They do not carry consistent energy centers, which allows them to reflect the state of their surroundings with remarkable accuracy. Their clarity comes with **time**.

Alignment comes through honoring **lunar cycles**—giving decisions space to unfold over time. When rushed, Reflectors experience disappointment. When given time, they access profound objectivity.

Dysregulation shows up as: Disappointment, disorientation
Alignment restores: Clarity, perspective, discernment

Correctness, Not Comparison

Each type experiences dysregulation **not because something is wrong**, but because they are operating outside their energetic design—often due to societal pressure to be faster, louder, or more productive.

Alignment is not about doing more.
It is about doing **what is correct for your energy**.

When energy moves correctly:

- Decisions become cleaner

- Resistance decreases

- Effort produces return

- The body relaxes into trust

Human Design does not rank types. Each is essential. Initiation, building, guiding, and reflecting are all required for a healthy ecosystem.

The question is not *"What should I become?"*
It is *"How is my energy designed to move?"*

Answer that—and life stops demanding you be someone else. It invites you to operate **as yourself**, with accuracy, authority, and ease.

Aura Mechanics and Bioenergetics

Human Design proposes that each energy type emits a distinct **aura**—a bioenergetic field that shapes how you interact with others, how information reaches you, and how decisions settle in the body. This aura is not symbolic metaphor. It is **bioenergetic reality**.

Modern research increasingly supports this premise.

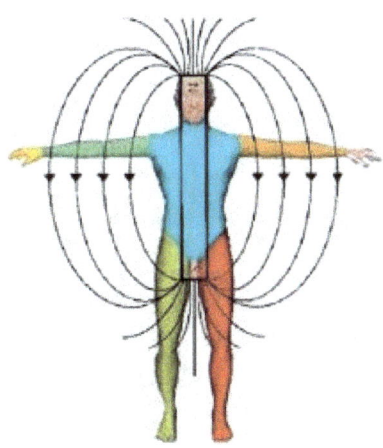

WHAT IS CO-REGULATION?
A Guide to Nervous System Harmony

The Role of Co-regulation

Co-regulation is a supportive process where one person helps another manage their emotions, behavior, and physical responses through warm, connected interactions.

This shared experience helps individuals gradually develop self-regulation skills, **making it easier to handle life's challenges on their own.**

The Science of Co-regulation

The autonomic nervous system is key in regulating our emotional responses.

Co-regulation helps balance our *sympathetic* ("fight or flight") and *parasympathetic* ("rest and digest") systems.

This helps us achieve a state of safety and calm.

Why It Matters

Co-regulation fosters a sense of **safety**, especially for people with attachment challenges or trauma backgrounds.

It provides tools to help us understand and regulate our emotions, which supports overall **emotional resilience**.

A regulated client is **better able to engage** in therapeutic activities and learning, and participate in daily life tasks.

Barriers to Co-regulation
and How to Avoid Them

Provider Dysregulation
Use grounding techniques to stay calm when a client is highly dysregulated.

Sensory Overload
Simplify the environment or use soothing sensory tools to ease co-regulation.

Emotional Escalation
Respond to aggressive behavior with empathy and clear boundaries to encourage calm.

Magnetic Field of the Heart

Our thoughts and emotions affect the heart's magnetic field, which energetically affects those in our environment whether or not we are conscious of it.

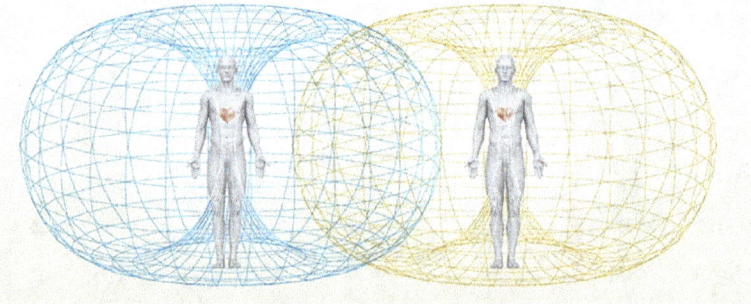

The Bioenergetic Field of the Human Body

The human body continuously emits electromagnetic signals generated by the heart, brain, nervous system, and cellular activity. These signals extend beyond the skin and interact with surrounding fields in real time.

Research demonstrates that:

- The heart produces the **strongest electromagnetic field** in the body

- Brain and cardiac rhythms influence nearby nervous systems

- Physiological states synchronize through proximity (co-regulation)

In other words, **we are not energetically sealed individuals**. We are interactive systems constantly influencing—and being influenced by—others.

Your aura is how that influence moves.

Co-Regulation: Why Energy Is Felt Before It's Understood

Long before language, interpretation, or conscious thought, **bodies are already communicating**.

Nervous systems are designed to **co-regulate automatically**. This means that when two or more people share space, their physiological systems exchange information instantly—below awareness, beyond intention, and prior to meaning-making. Before a word is spoken, the body answers a set of primal questions:

- *Is this safe or unsafe?*

- *Is this open or closed?*

- *Do I expand here or contract?*

This exchange happens through posture, breath rhythm, muscle tone, heart rate variability, and electromagnetic signaling. You feel it as a sensation before you understand it as a thought.

The Body Decides First

Modern neuroscience confirms what somatic and ancestral traditions have long known: **the body appraises the environment before the mind interprets it**. The nervous system is constantly scanning for cues of safety, threat, availability, and coherence.

This is why:

- Some people feel instantly calming without trying

- Others feel energizing or activating just by entering a room

- Some presences feel overwhelming, draining, or destabilizing

- Certain environments feel like home, while others exhaust you

These reactions are not emotional opinions. They are **physiological responses** to energetic information.

Your body knows before your story does.

Why Words Come Second

By the time language enters the picture, regulation has already occurred. The nervous system has either softened or braced, opened or closed, engaged or withdrawn. The mind then builds a narrative to explain what the body already decided.

This is why people often say:

- "I don't know why, but something feels off."

- "I felt safe there immediately."

- "I was exhausted for no clear reason."

The reason *is* clear—it just wasn't cognitive.

Co-Regulation Explains Emotional Contagion

Co-regulation also explains why emotions spread through groups so quickly. Calm, grounded nervous systems can stabilize others. Dysregulated systems can create unease without speaking a word. This is not personal—it is biological.

Your nervous system does not operate in isolation.
It is constantly adjusting to the **energetic field around it**.

Aura Mechanics as the Interface

Human Design names these differences **aura mechanics**.

Each energy type interacts with co-regulation differently:

- Some stabilize the field

- Some amplify momentum

- Some penetrate awareness

- Some mirror the state of the environment

These mechanics determine:

- How others feel around you

- How quickly regulation or dysregulation occurs

- How decisions settle in your body

- How much energy interaction requires

When aura mechanics are honored, co-regulation feels natural and supportive. When they are ignored, the nervous system compensates—often through fatigue, irritation, withdrawal, or overwhelm.

Why Alignment Changes Everything

Understanding co-regulation shifts self-perception profoundly. You stop blaming yourself for reactions that are **physiological**, not psychological. You stop forcing presence where your body signals misalignment. You begin trusting sensation as data rather than dismissing it as imagination.

Energy is felt before it is understood because **the body is designed to keep you alive**, not to explain itself politely.

Human Design does not invent this truth.
It simply gives language to it.

When you honor how your nervous system and aura interact with the world, relationships clarify, environments sort themselves, and decisions become less mental and more accurate.

Because regulation is not something you *think* your way into.
It is something you **allow**—through alignment, awareness, and respect for the intelligence already moving through your body.

How Different Auras Interact with the World

In Human Design, the aura is the **interface** between your internal system and the external world. It is how your energy meets people, environments, opportunities, and challenges—often before conscious intention or verbal exchange. Each design type carries a distinct **aura mechanic**, shaping how interaction unfolds and how energy moves through the system.

These mechanics are not behaviors you adopt.
They are **how energy naturally operates when left undistorted**.

Four Core Aura Mechanics

Auras That Push — Initiating Momentum

Some auras are designed to **initiate movement**. Their presence creates impact, direction, and forward motion. When these auras enter a space, energy shifts. Things begin. Pathways open.

- Interaction effect: Others feel activated or prompted to move

- Optimal use: Initiation, catalyzing change, opening new cycles

- When misaligned: Resistance increases because movement arrives without preparation

These auras function best when momentum is **signaled clearly**, not forced.

Auras That Draw — Magnetizing Response

Some auras are designed to **attract engagement**. Rather than pushing outward, they pull life toward them through availability and responsiveness. Energy flows in when the timing is correct.

- Interaction effect: Others feel invited to engage, respond, or contribute

- Optimal use: Building, sustaining, mastering, and refining

- When misaligned: Frustration emerges from initiating instead of responding

These auras thrive when life is allowed to come to them.

Auras That Penetrate — Focusing Awareness

Some auras are designed to **penetrate energy fields**, seeing deeply into systems, people, and patterns. Their presence brings clarity, insight, and optimization.

- Interaction effect: Others feel seen, understood, or analyzed

- Optimal use: Guidance, strategy, efficiency, and leadership through insight

- When misaligned: Bitterness arises from offering guidance without recognition

These auras are most effective when **invited**, not imposed.

Auras That Sample — Reflecting the Environment

Some auras are designed to **sample and mirror** what is present. Rather than projecting energy, they reflect the state of people and environments back to themselves.

- Interaction effect: Others see themselves more clearly

- Optimal use: Evaluation, reflection, community health assessment

- When misaligned: Disappointment arises when rushed or pressured

These auras require **time and spaciousness** to reach clarity.

How Aura Mechanics Shape Experience

Because aura mechanics operate automatically, they profoundly influence three key domains:

1. Decision-Making

Different aura types access clarity differently:
- Some know immediately
- Some need an external stimulus to respond to
- Some require recognition or invitation
- Some need time to cycle through perspectives

When decision-making honors aura mechanics, clarity arrives naturally. When it is rushed or mentally overridden, confusion follows.

2. Energy Sustainability

Aura mechanics determine whether energy:
- Replenishes through engagement
- Depletes through overextension
- Requires rest between bursts
- Depends on environment for vitality

Burnout is often not about capacity—it is about **energetic misuse**.

3. Resistance vs. Ease

Others respond unconsciously to aura mechanics. When energy moves correctly, interaction feels smooth and cooperative. When it doesn't, resistance appears—not as rejection, but as **energetic friction**.

Resistance is feedback, not failure.

Fluidity Through Correct Operation

When you operate according to your aura mechanics:

- Interaction feels fluid rather than forced
- Effort produces proportional return
- Relationships stabilize or self-select naturally
- The body relaxes into coherence

When you work against your aura:

- Resistance accumulates
- Energy leaks
- Decisions feel heavy or unclear
- The nervous system compensates through stress

This is not a moral issue.
It is a **mechanical one**.

Energetic Traffic, Correctly Routed

Think of aura mechanics like traffic patterns. When flow follows design, movement is efficient. When it doesn't, congestion builds. The solution is not more effort—it is **rerouting**.

Human Design does not ask you to change who you are.
It teaches you **how your energy already moves best**.

And when energetic traffic is correctly routed, life stops feeling like opposition and starts feeling like **participation**—a dynamic exchange where effort meets response, insight meets invitation, and presence meets ease.

Not because the world changed.
But because your energy finally moved **as designed**.

Strategy and Authority: The Science of Aligned Decision-Making

One of Human Design's most transformative insights is the **clear separation between mental decision-making and somatic authority**. This distinction restores accuracy to choice by relocating trust from conditioned thought to embodied intelligence.

Strategy refers to *how your energy is designed to engage with life*—the correct way opportunities, interactions, and momentum are meant to meet you.

Authority refers to *where reliable decisions originate within your body*—the internal signal that indicates alignment.

Together, Strategy and Authority form a **decision-making protocol** grounded in biology, not belief.

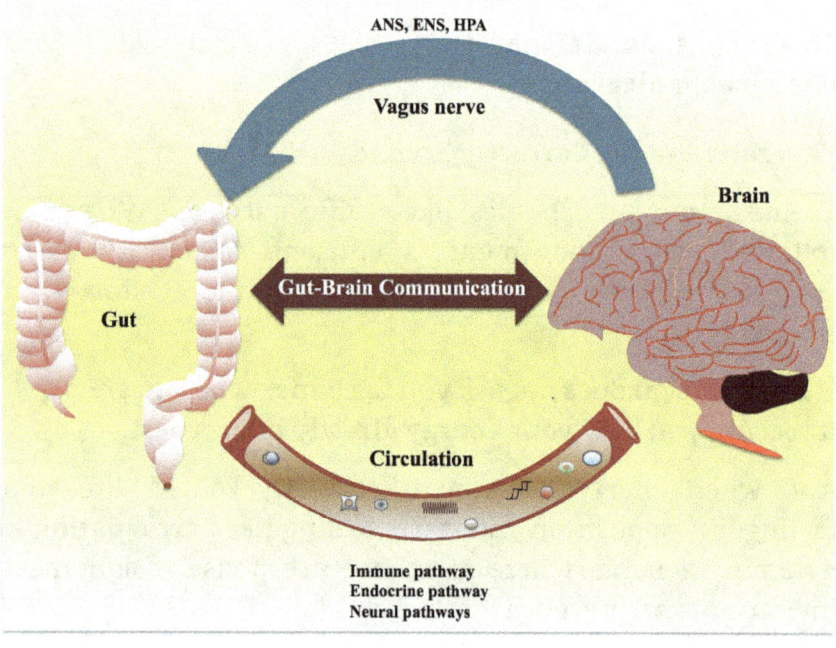

Heart Rhythms Directly Affect Physical and Mental Performance

Heart signals affect the brain centers involved in emotional perception, decision making, reaction times, social awareness and the ability to self-regulate.

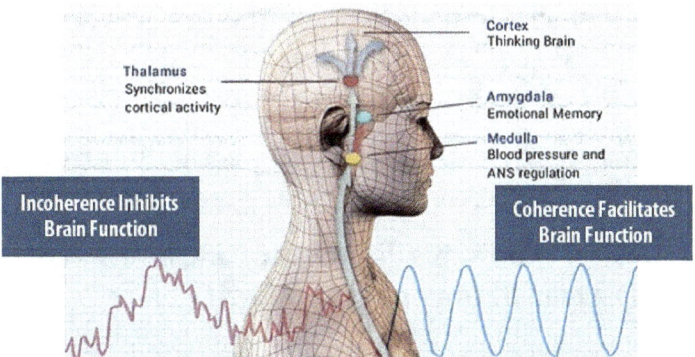

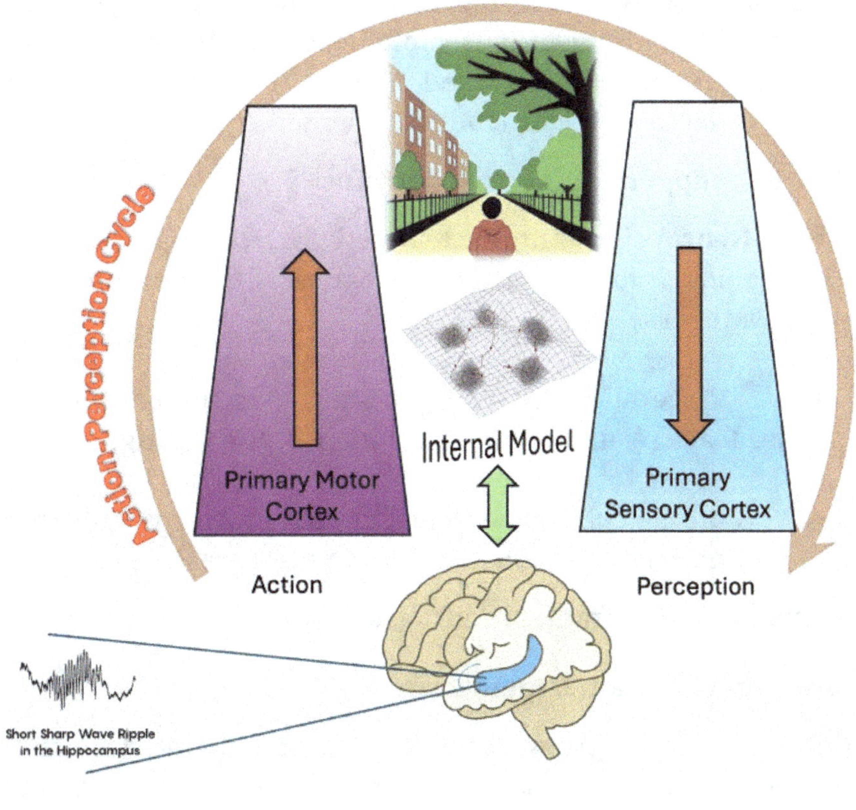

Why the Mind Is Not the Decision-Maker

Modern culture elevates cognition as the primary arbiter of choice. Yet neuroscience consistently demonstrates that the body processes information **faster and more comprehensively** than conscious thought. Sensory input, emotional salience, and threat/safety cues are integrated milliseconds before the mind constructs a narrative.

This means many "decisions" are actually **after-the-fact explanations** of what the body already registered.

Human Design names this discrepancy and offers a correction: **the mind is a translator, not the authority**.

Somatic Authority as Biological Intelligence

Intuition, in this framework, is not mystical guessing or emotional impulse. It is **biological intelligence**—signals emerging from neural, visceral, and electromagnetic systems that evolved to keep you alive and oriented.

Research supports this across domains:

- **Neural signaling**: Distributed processing across brain regions informs pattern recognition before conscious awareness.

- **Visceral input**: The gut-brain axis transmits rapid feedback related to safety, resonance, and timing.

- **Cardiac coherence**: Heart rhythm patterns influence emotional regulation and clarity under pressure.

Human Design reframes intuition as **data**, not drama.

Stress and Decision Degradation

Chronic stress impairs decision accuracy. Elevated cortisol narrows attention, biases perception toward threat, and reduces access to nuanced internal signals. Under pressure, the mind defaults to habit and conditioning rather than discernment.

This explains why rushed decisions often feel wrong *after* the fact.

Aligned decision-making requires **regulation first**, clarity second.

Strategy: Meeting Life Correctly

Strategy ensures that energy engages the world in ways that reduce resistance:

- Some designs must **wait to respond**

- Some must **inform before initiating**

- Some must **wait for recognition**

- Some must **allow time**

This is not passivity. It is **timing intelligence**.

When Strategy is honored, opportunities arrive with less friction. When it is ignored, resistance appears—not as punishment, but as feedback that energy is misaligned with engagement.

Authority: Trusting the Right Signal

Authority specifies **where clarity arises in the body**—not as a thought to be reasoned through, but as a signal to be *felt*. Human Design recognizes that decision-making is not a single mechanism shared by all humans. It is **differentiated**, rooted in how each nervous system processes information most reliably.

For some, clarity arrives as an **immediate visceral response**—a yes-or-no sensation that registers before words form.

For others, clarity **unfolds over time**, requiring emotional movement or cyclical perspective before certainty settles. For still others, clarity emerges through **environmental sampling**, observation, or reflection—understanding comes not from urgency, but from spaciousness.

The method differs.
The source does not.

Clarity is somatic, not cerebral.

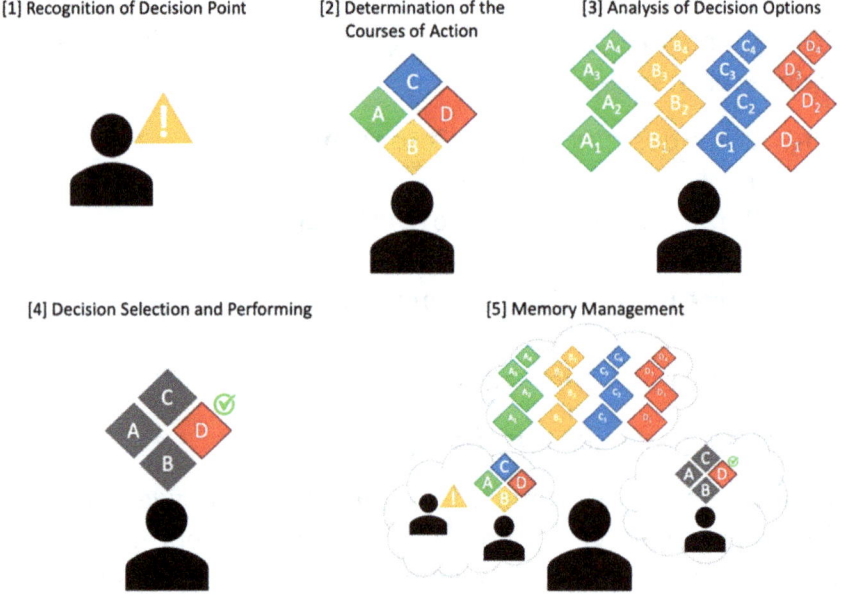

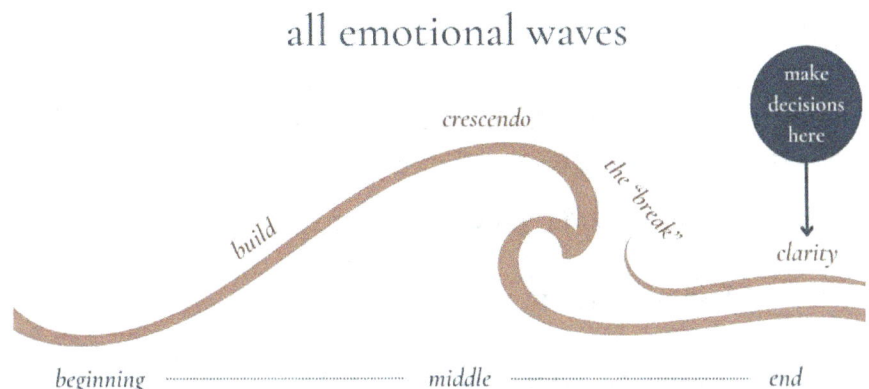

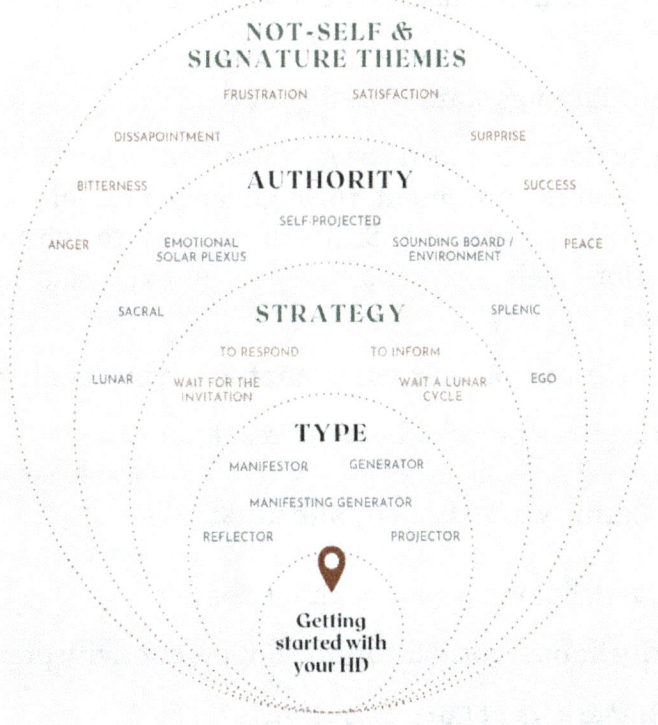

Why the Body Knows First

The body is continuously processing data the mind cannot track in real time: subtle shifts in safety, resonance, timing, and energetic cost. These signals arise through:

- Nervous system regulation
- Visceral sensation
- Emotional rhythm
- Energetic coherence

The mind, by contrast, is conditioned—shaped by fear, urgency, social expectation, and past outcomes. It is excellent at explaining decisions, but unreliable at *originating* them.

Authority returns trust to the system designed to keep you alive and oriented.

Different Timings, Same Intelligence

Authority does not mean speed. Some bodies know instantly. Others require movement through an emotional arc or a full cycle of perspective. Still others need to witness how a situation feels across different contexts before clarity stabilizes.

Trying to force one timing onto another creates confusion:

- Rushing a process that requires time
- Waiting when the body already knows
- Overthinking what is meant to be felt

Authority honors **correct timing**, not productivity pressure.

The Felt Markers of Correct Authority

When decisions are made from the correct authority, the body responds immediately—even if the outcome is challenging.

You will notice:

- **The body relaxes rather than tightens**
  There may be nervousness, but not internal resistance. The system does not brace against itself.

- **Commitment feels grounded rather than forced**
  You are not convincing yourself. You are agreeing with yourself.

- **Follow-through becomes sustainable**
  Energy holds. You don't burn out halfway through or resent the decision later.

These markers matter more than certainty. You do not need to know how everything will unfold. You need to know whether your body is **on board**.

Authority Builds Self-Trust

Each time you honor your authority, trust deepens. Not because every decision leads to comfort—but because your system recognizes integrity. Even when outcomes are difficult, regret diminishes. You may say, *"That was hard,"* but not *"I betrayed myself."*

Ignoring authority, on the other hand, often produces a specific pain: self-abandonment. The body knew. The signal was present. It was overridden.

Human Design teaches that wisdom is not the absence of difficulty.
It is **alignment during difficulty**.

From External Validation to Internal Accuracy

Authority shifts the reference point inward. You stop asking:

- "What should I do?"
- "What makes the most sense?"
- "What will others think?"

And begin asking:

- "Is my body relaxed or braced?"
- "Does this feel correct over time?"
- "Am I honoring my signal—or my fear?"

This is not impulsivity.
It is **discernment rooted in physiology**.

Authority as Embodied Integrity

Trusting the right signal is not about being perfect. It is about being **coherent**.

When your decisions originate from the correct authority:

- Energy stops leaking
- Resistance decreases
- Life responds with greater precision

Not because you controlled the outcome, but because you honored the intelligence that knows *how you move correctly through experience.*

Authority is not about certainty.
It is about **alignment**.

And alignment, over time, becomes the most reliable form of guidance there is.

Scientific Tie-Ins: Biology Meets Design

Human Design sits at a compelling intersection where **ancient pattern systems converge with modern biology**. What it describes symbolically—energy flow, authority, differentiation—modern science increasingly validates through physiology, neuroscience, and genetics. This convergence reframes Human Design not as mystical abstraction, but as a **functional map of embodied intelligence**.

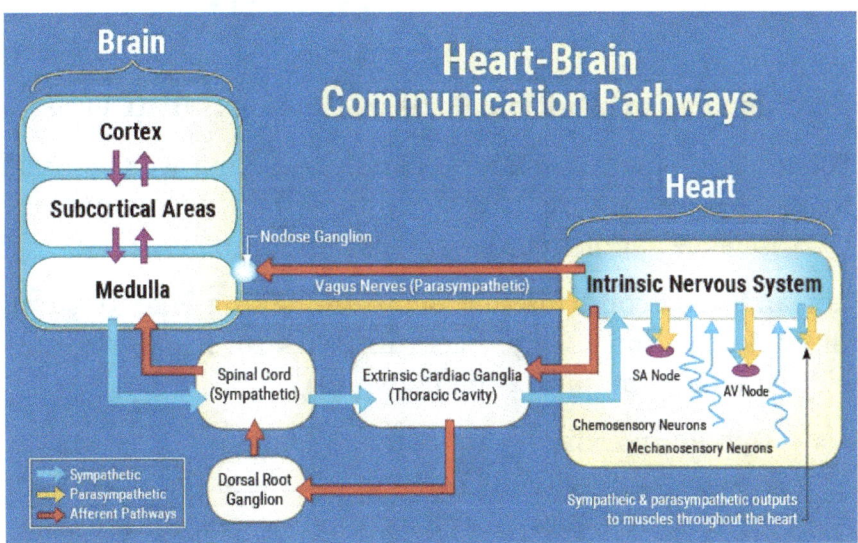

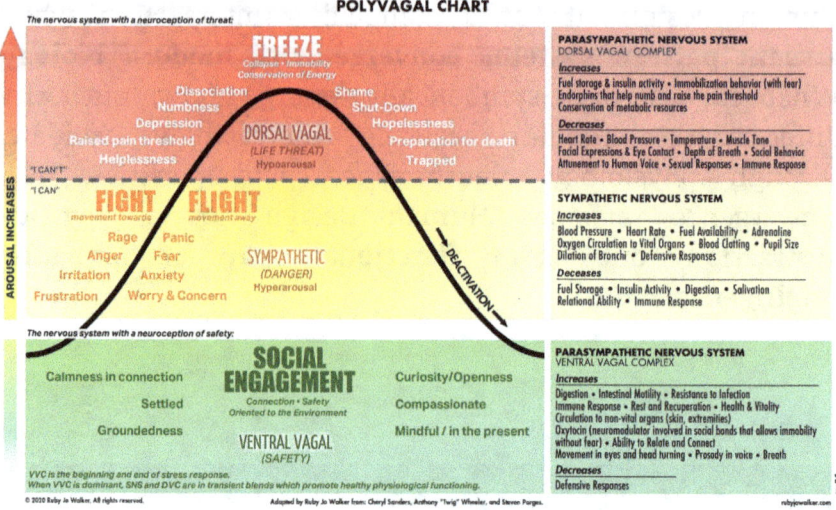

Neurobiology of Intuition: Decision-Making Is Distributed

For much of modern history, decision-making was believed to reside almost exclusively in the brain. Contemporary neuroscience has dismantled this assumption.

Research now confirms that **decision-making is distributed throughout the body**, coordinated through multiple bidirectional communication networks:

- **Gut–Brain Axis**
  The enteric nervous system contains hundreds of millions of neurons and communicates continuously with the brain. It processes threat, timing, and suitability rapidly—often registering "yes" or "no" responses before cognition catches up.

- **Heart–Brain Communication**
  The heart sends more signals to the brain than the brain sends to the heart. Heart rhythm coherence has been shown to influence emotional regulation, perception, and cognitive clarity, especially under pressure.

- **Vagal Signaling**
  The vagus nerve plays a central role in regulating safety, engagement, and withdrawal. It informs whether the system can expand into action or needs to pause and recalibrate.

Together, these systems support a central Human Design premise: **intuition is biological intelligence**, not imagination. Authority is not mystical—it is **physiological signal accuracy**.

Energy Metabolism and Differentiation: One Size Does Not Fit All

Human bodies do not process energy uniformly. Metabolic research shows clear variation in:

- Energy sustainability

- Recovery requirements

- Stress thresholds

- Cognitive versus physical expenditure

Human Design mirrors this reality by identifying designs optimized for **sustained output**, and others optimized for **precision, guidance, or sampling**.

Problems arise when social conditioning demands identical performance from fundamentally different systems.

Metabolic stress occurs when:

- A system built for bursts is forced into constant output

- A system built for guidance is pressured into nonstop production

- A system built for responsiveness is required to initiate constantly

This mismatch produces fatigue, burnout, inflammation, and emotional dysregulation—not because of weakness, but because **energy is being used against its design**.

Human Design reframes energy management as *alignment*, not discipline.

Genetic Coding and Binary Systems: Symbol and Biology Converge

One of the most striking parallels within Human Design is its use of the **I Ching's binary system**, which mirrors the structure of genetic coding.

- DNA operates through binary instructions: on/off, active/dormant

- Genes express differently depending on environment and signaling

- Differentiation—not uniformity—is fundamental to biological intelligence

The I Ching's hexagrams encode change through binary lines, describing how potential becomes form. Human Design overlays this logic onto the bodygraph, suggesting a **symbolic mirror of genetic differentiation**—not literal genetics, but an energetic language that reflects biological truth.

In both systems:

- Information is not static

- Expression depends on context

- Differentiation creates resilience

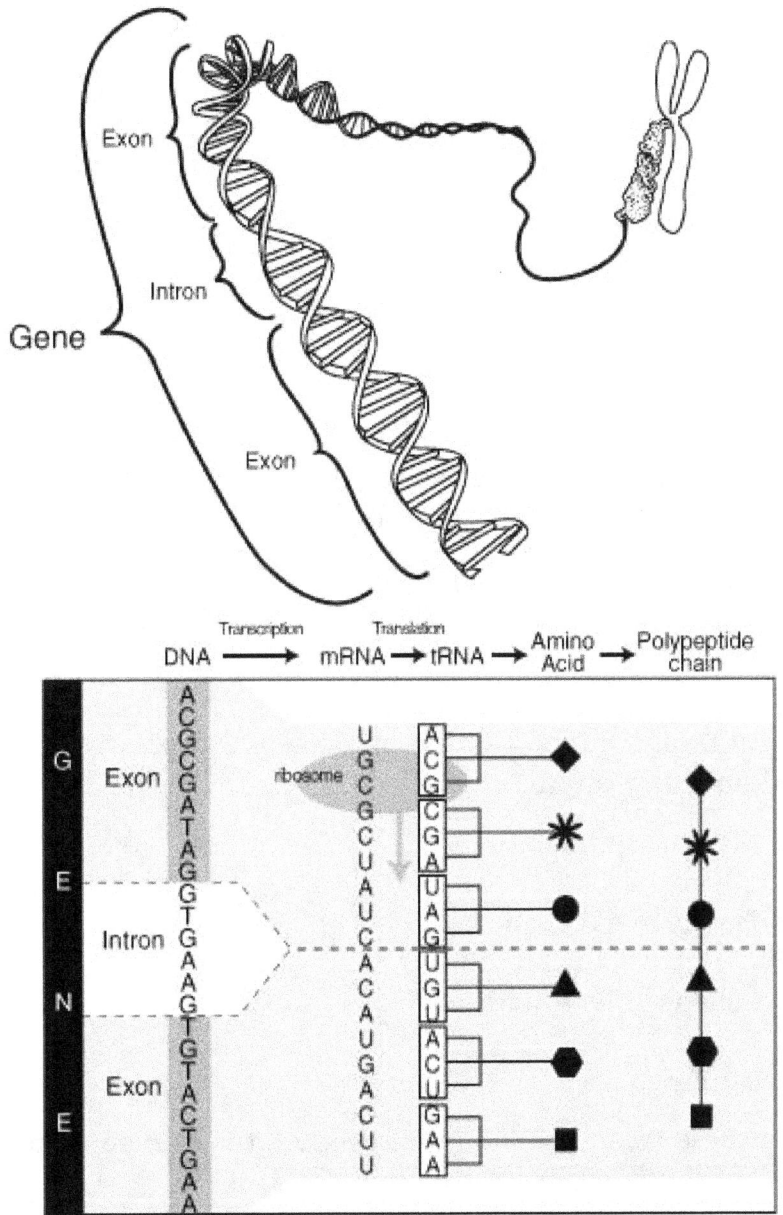

From Symbol to Systemic Coherence

Taken together, these scientific tie-ins support a powerful conclusion:

Human Design does not contradict biology—it **contextualizes it**.

It provides a symbolic framework that helps individuals understand:

- Why certain decisions feel right before they make sense
- Why energy depletes in some environments and flourishes in others
- Why timing matters as much as intention

This synthesis does not require belief. It invites **observation**—of regulation, energy, clarity, and outcome.

A New Model of Human Intelligence

Biology is not mechanical alone.
Symbol is not imaginary alone.

Human Design proposes that intelligence expresses itself **simultaneously** through:

- Nervous systems
- Energy metabolism
- Genetic differentiation
- Patterned decision-making

When these layers are honored together, the human system functions with greater coherence.

Not because life becomes predictable.
But because **the body stops fighting its own design**.

This is where science meets self-knowledge.
Where biology meets destiny—not as fate, but as **functional**

alignment.

Human Design as a Living Experiment

Human Design does not ask you to believe it.

It asks you to **test it**.

To observe:

- What happens when you follow your strategy
- What happens when you honor your authority
- How your body responds when aligned versus when forced

Over time, patterns become undeniable.

Reflection Prompt

When have you ignored your design—and how did your body respond?

Consider:

- Moments of exhaustion, frustration, bitterness, or disappointment
- Times when clarity followed patience rather than pressure
- Situations where your body knew before your mind did

Your body has always been giving feedback.
Human Design teaches you **how to listen**.

Key Insight of This Chapter

You were never meant to live by **generic rules**.

Much of modern struggle comes from a quiet but persistent

error: the assumption that the same strategies, timelines, and expectations should work for everyone. Human Design exposes the cost of this assumption. It shows that alignment is not a matter of willpower or discipline—it is a matter of **design**.

When you attempt to live outside your design, effort increases and results diminish. Energy leaks. Decisions feel heavy. Resistance appears—not as punishment, but as feedback that the system is being used incorrectly.

Suffering is not a failure.
It is often **misapplication**.

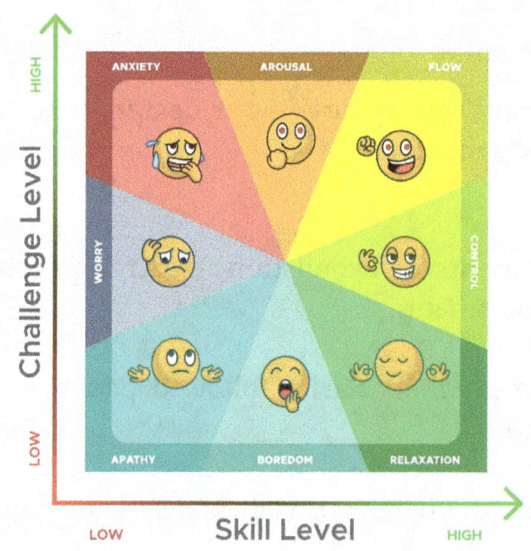

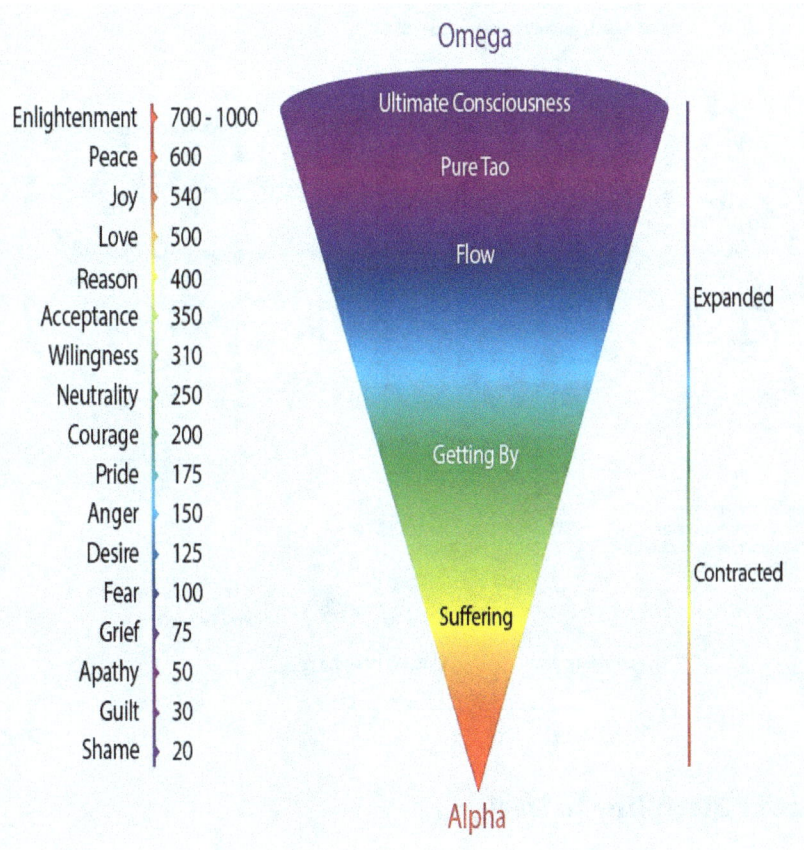

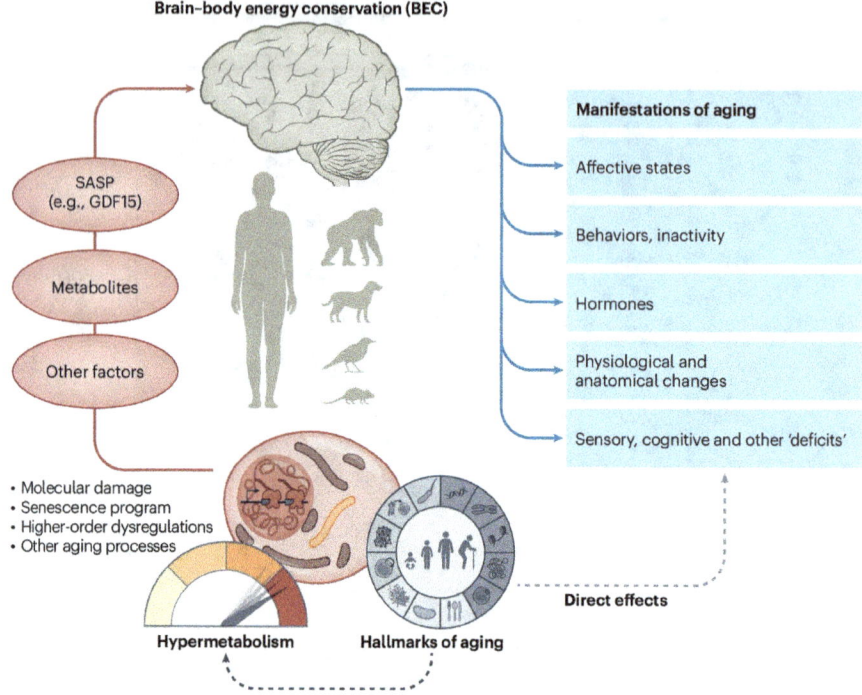

From Discipline to Design

Discipline asks you to override signals.
Design asks you to **listen to them**.

Human Design reframes growth away from self-correction and toward self-accuracy. Instead of asking, *"How do I push harder?"* it asks, *"How is my energy meant to move?"* This shift changes everything. You stop measuring success by exhaustion and start measuring it by **coherence**.

Coherence is when your body, decisions, and actions agree with each other.

Accurate Choice Restores Agency

Human Design does not remove choice. It refines it.

Generic advice multiplies options without improving

outcomes. Accurate choice does the opposite—it narrows the field to what actually works for *you*. Strategy and Authority do not tell you what to want; they tell you **how to decide** in a way your body can sustain.

This is freedom with precision.

When choices are accurate:

- Commitment feels clean, not forced

- Follow-through is natural, not draining

- Regret decreases, even when outcomes are challenging

You may still face difficulty. You simply stop fighting yourself while you do.

Flow Is Correctness, Not Ease

Flow is often misunderstood as ease. In Human Design, flow means **correctness**. It means energy is routed properly. It means the nervous system is not bracing against its own decisions.

Life can be demanding and still feel right.
Challenges can arise without internal resistance.

This is the difference between effort that depletes and effort that **builds capacity**.

Living by Design

When you align with your design:

- Resistance becomes information, not opposition

- Energy stabilizes instead of scattering

- Decisions feel embodied rather than mental

- Life responds with less friction

Not because the world changed—
but because **your energy finally did**.

Human Design does not promise comfort.
It offers **correctness**.

And correctness, over time, produces a form of ease that discipline alone never could: the relief of no longer trying to be someone you were never designed to be.

That is the true insight of this chapter.
Not how to improve yourself—
but how to **operate as yourself**, with accuracy, integrity, and flow.

CHAPTER 6
Lineage, Karma, and Genetic Memory
The Past Living Inside the Present

You did not arrive in this life empty.

You arrived **carrying memory**.

Before personality formed, before language developed, before conscious choice emerged, your body already held information —encoded through lineage, biology, and ancestral experience. Chapter 6 explores one of the most profound and often misunderstood truths of destiny work:

Your life purpose does not begin with you alone. It emerges from a lineage.

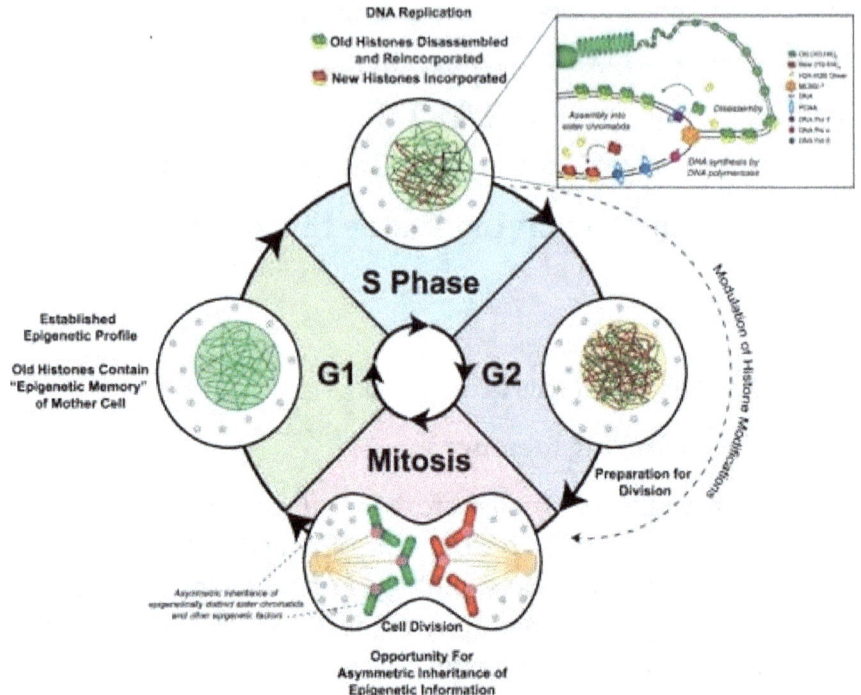

Lineage is not merely genetic—it is **informational**.

Your DNA is not a static codebook limited to physical traits like eye color, height, or metabolism. It is a living archive, carrying layered instructions shaped by **experience across generations**. Embedded within your biology are adaptive responses developed long before you were born—responses that once ensured survival, connection, and continuity.

Your DNA carries:

- **Survival strategies** forged in times of threat, migration, scarcity, or resistance

- **Stress responses** calibrated by what previous generations endured and overcame

- **Emotional patterning** shaped by attachment, loss, love, and protection

- **Relational imprints** reflecting how safety, trust, and power were navigated

- **Latent gifts and talents** refined through repetition—skills, sensitivities, and intelligences that proved useful over time

These inheritances are not abstract ideas. They live in the nervous system, the endocrine system, and cellular signaling—guiding perception and response often before conscious choice arises.

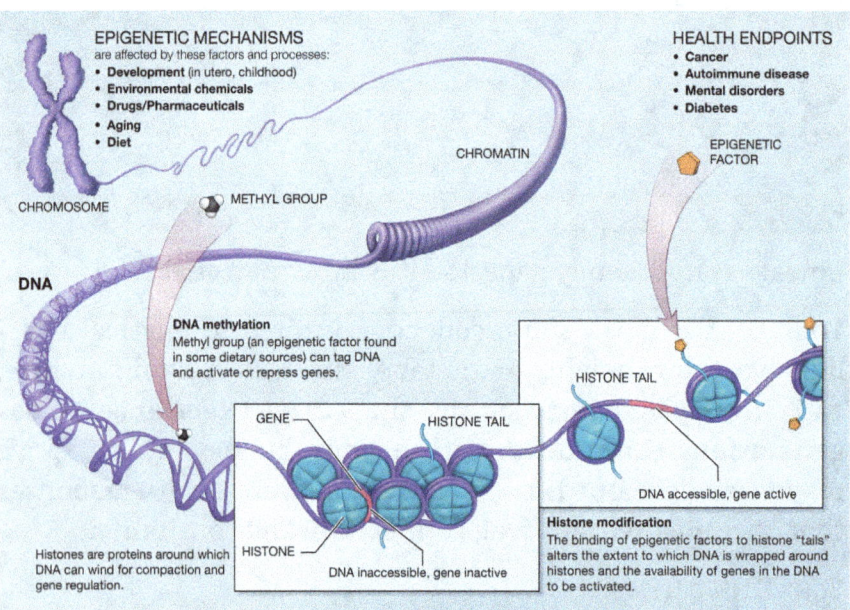

Ancient Knowing, Modern Confirmation

Ancient cultures understood this intuitively. Across African, Indigenous, Eastern, and diasporic traditions, ancestors were never considered "gone." They were understood as **present within the living**—speaking through intuition, dreams, bodily sensations, and recurring life themes.

Ancestral remembrance was not nostalgia.
It was **navigation**.

Rituals, prayers, libations, and storytelling were methods of maintaining communication with the intelligence carried forward through blood and spirit. Destiny was seen not as an individual pursuit, but as a **continuation of a lineage story** seeking resolution, expression, or restoration.

Modern science now confirms what these traditions preserved: **experience leaves biological residue**.

The Body as a Keeper of Memory

Trauma, resilience, innovation, and mastery do not disappear when a generation passes. They are **encoded forward**, influencing how descendants respond to stress, bond in relationships, and access creativity or leadership.

This is why:

- Some fears arise without personal origin

- Some strengths feel instinctive rather than learned

- Some callings feel ancient, as if remembered rather than chosen

Your body may react to situations that resemble ancestral conditions—not because you are broken, but because **your system recognizes familiar terrain**.

Memory is not only cognitive.
It is **cellular**.

Endurance and Mastery Are Also Inherited

It is important to name this fully: lineage does not pass down pain alone.

Your ancestors also mastered:

- Survival under impossible conditions
- Creativity amid constraint
- Community building in fractured worlds
- Spiritual technologies for endurance and meaning
- Innovation born from necessity

These capacities live within you as **dormant competencies**, waiting for conditions where they can be safely expressed.

You are not only the descendant of what was endured.
You are the descendant of what was **mastered**.

Inheritance as Invitation, Not Burden

Ancestral DNA as spiritual inheritance reframes responsibility with compassion. You are not asked to carry the past as a burden. You are invited to **relate to it consciously**.

What remains unconscious repeats.
What becomes conscious can evolve.

Your body remembers what your ancestors endured—and what they mastered—not to trap you in history, but to **equip you with wisdom** refined through time.

You are not starting from zero.
You are continuing a story that already learned how to survive.

Your task is not to relive that survival.
It is to decide **what becomes possible now that survival is no longer the only goal**.

That decision—made with awareness—is where lineage becomes destiny transformed.

Epigenetics: How Memory Crosses Generations

Epigenetics has radically reshaped our understanding of inheritance by revealing a truth long held in ancestral traditions: **memory does not end at the individual**. Genes are not rigid blueprints dictating destiny; they are **responsive systems**, dynamically shaped by environment, stress, nutrition, relationships, and emotional experience.

Rather than altering the DNA sequence itself, epigenetic mechanisms—such as DNA methylation and histone modification—adjust **how genes are expressed**. In simple terms, life experience can turn certain genetic pathways *up* or *down*, amplifying or quieting specific responses. These adjustments can persist—and be passed forward.

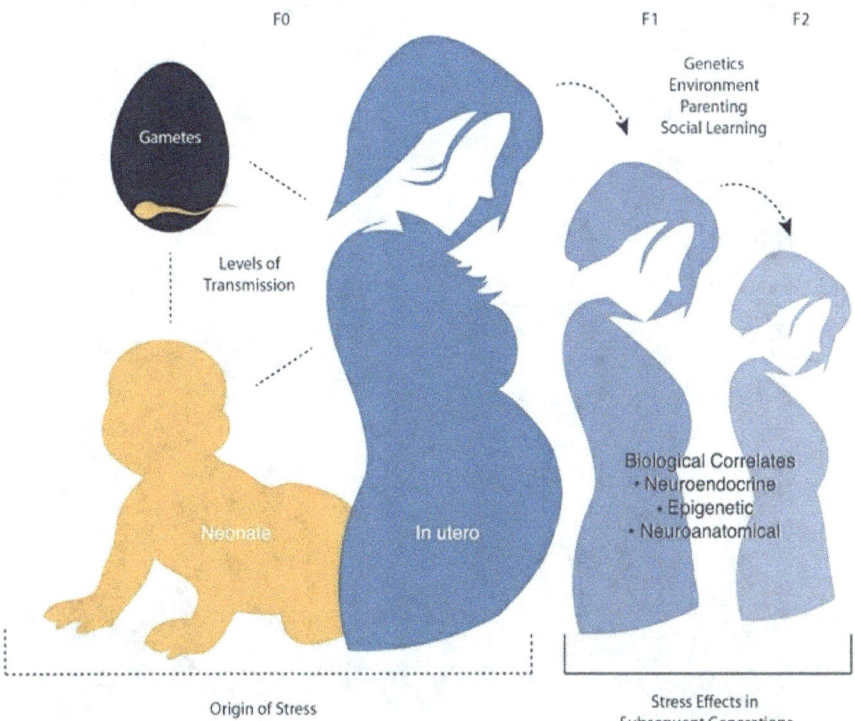

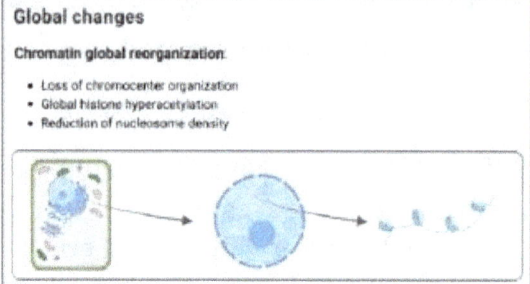
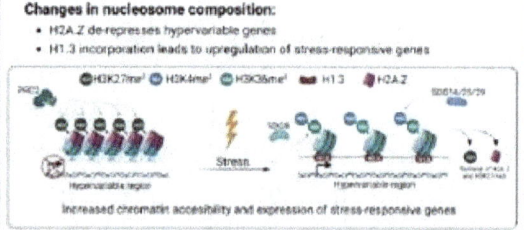

Trauma, Adaptation, and Biological Messaging

Groundbreaking research by **Rachel Yehuda** and others has demonstrated that trauma experienced by one generation can influence gene expression in subsequent generations. Studies involving descendants of individuals exposed to extreme stress—such as war, genocide, or chronic violence—show measurable differences in genes related to:

- Stress hormone regulation (e.g., cortisol sensitivity)
- Fear and threat detection
- Emotional reactivity and recovery
- Nervous system regulation

These changes do **not** rewrite DNA. They modify *how DNA responds*—particularly in systems designed to keep humans alive under threat. What gets passed forward is not trauma itself, but a **preparedness profile**: the body's expectation of the world.

Why Some Experiences Feel "Older Than You"

Epigenetics helps explain phenomena that psychology alone cannot fully account for:

- **Fears without personal origin**
  Anxiety, hypervigilance, or avoidance may arise in the absence of direct experience because the body inherited a heightened sensitivity shaped by ancestral survival conditions.

- **Struggles that feel ancient**
  Repeating patterns—scarcity thinking, relational mistrust, or over-responsibility—can reflect adaptive strategies that once ensured survival but are now

outdated.

- **Strengths that emerge effortlessly**
  Resilience, intuition, leadership, creativity, or spiritual attunement may surface naturally—not because they were taught, but because they were **encoded through repetition across generations**.

This inheritance is not mysterious when viewed biologically. It is **efficient**. Evolution favors systems that remember what kept the lineage alive.

Inheritance Is Neutral Information

Crucially, epigenetic inheritance is not pathology.

It is **information**.

The body does not judge experience; it records it. It does not distinguish between past and present; it responds to cues it recognizes. What was once adaptive can become maladaptive if the environment changes—but the original imprint was protective, not defective.

Seen this way, inherited patterns are **messages**, not malfunctions.

Awareness as Biological Intervention

The most empowering insight of epigenetics is this: **expression is not fixed**. While ancestral experiences influence baseline sensitivity, awareness, safety, nourishment, and regulation can reshape expression over time.

When environments change, biology updates.

Practices that promote regulation—such as trauma-informed therapy, somatic work, ritual, stable relationships, and conscious meaning-making—act as **epigenetic interventions**, signaling to the body that the conditions requiring hyper-survival are no longer present.

From Burden to Belonging

Understanding epigenetics reframes inheritance with compassion. You are not "carrying trauma" because something is wrong with you. You are carrying **memory because your lineage learned how to survive**.

This knowledge invites a powerful shift:

- From self-blame to self-understanding
- From repetition to resolution
- From unconscious inheritance to conscious stewardship

This is not pathology.
It is inheritance.

And inheritance, when understood, becomes **choice**.

You cannot change what your ancestors endured—but you can change how that memory lives forward. Through awareness, regulation, and intention, inherited patterns can soften, transform, and even become sources of wisdom.

The past lives on in you not to trap you—
but to be **met, integrated, and evolved**.

Karma as Biological and Energetic Momentum

Karma is often misunderstood as punishment or reward—a moral accounting system imposed from outside. In its original sense, however, **karma simply means action and consequence carried forward**. It describes **momentum**: what continues moving because it has not yet been completed, integrated, or resolved.

Seen this way, karma is not judgment.
It is **continuity**.

Karma Through a Scientific Lens

From biology and neuroscience, karma closely resembles **biological and energetic momentum**—the way systems conserve and repeat what once worked.

- **Repeated adaptations become default responses.**
  When an adaptation successfully protected life—hypervigilance, emotional restraint, over-responsibility—the nervous system encodes it as "safe." Over time, the response becomes automatic, even when conditions change.

- **Learned survival strategies are passed forward.**
  Through epigenetic inheritance, stress regulation patterns, threat sensitivity, and relational defenses can transmit across generations—not as memories, but as *preparedness*.

- **Unresolved trauma loops until integrated.**
  What is not metabolized by one generation often resurfaces in another—not to punish, but to be processed under safer conditions. Biology seeks completion.

In this view, karma is not mystical debt.
It is **unfinished physiological learning**.

Karma Through a Spiritual Lens

Spiritually, karma has always been understood as **unfinished learning seeking resolution**. Patterns repeat because awareness has not yet reached the point where a different response becomes possible.

This repetition is not cruelty.
It is **instruction**.

The same lesson appears in different forms until consciousness can:

- Recognize the pattern

- Regulate the response

- Choose differently

When learning completes, momentum dissolves. The cycle ends—not through effort, but through **integration**.

Where Science And Spirit Converge

Biology and spirituality meet at a shared truth:

> **What remains unconscious repeats.**
> **What becomes conscious can transform.**

Neural pathways change through awareness and repetition. Epigenetic expression shifts with safety and regulation. Energetic patterns soften when met with presence instead of resistance.

Karma, then, is neither fate nor failure.
It is **movement awaiting coherence**.

From Burden to Trust

This understanding reframes lineage entirely.

You are not burdened by your lineage—
you are **entrusted with it**.

Entrustment implies capacity. It suggests that the generation receiving the pattern also carries the resources to resolve it. You may be the one with:

- Greater safety

- More awareness

- Better tools

- Expanded consciousness

That is not coincidence. It is timing.

Why Patterns Choose You

Karmic patterns do not attach randomly. They move toward environments where **completion is possible**. When conditions are safer, learning can finally finish.

This is why many people feel they are:

- The cycle breaker

- The healer

- The one who "woke up"

- The one who questioned what was normalized

You did not attract this work because you are defective. You encountered it because **you could hold it**.

Momentum Can Change Direction

Momentum only continues when left unexamined. Once awareness enters the system, energy reorganizes. New responses become available. Biology updates. Spirit integrates.

Karma does not demand suffering.
It asks for **presence**.

And presence—over time—creates choice.

The Deeper Truth

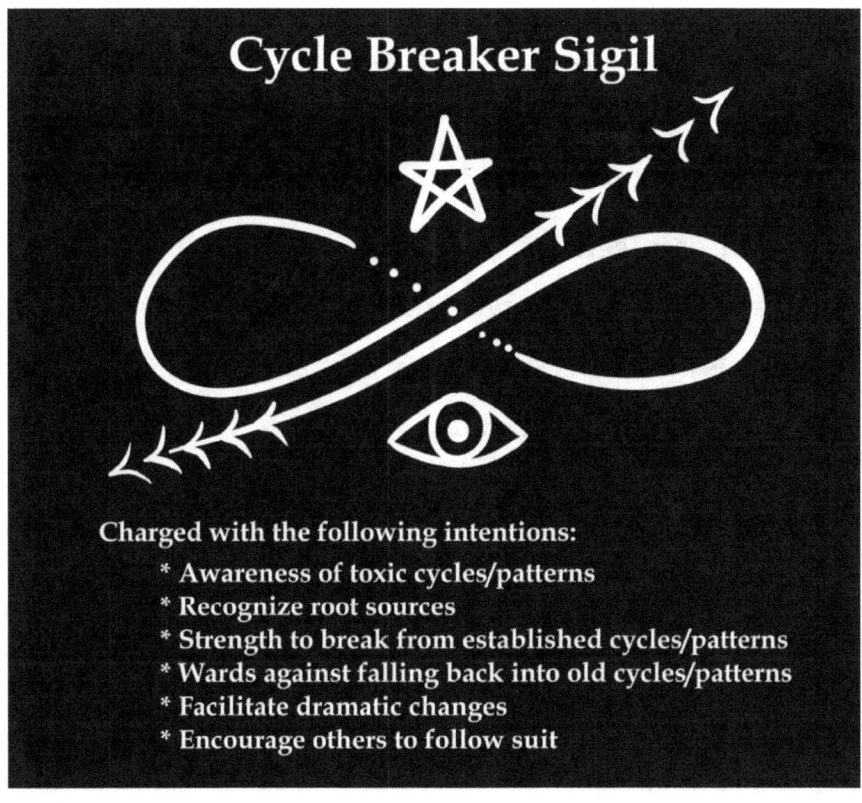

You are not here to **pay** for the past.
You are here to **complete** it.

Completion is not repetition. It is resolution.

To pay implies debt, punishment, or moral judgment. Completion implies learning brought to coherence. It means the pattern has finally reached a point where a different response is possible—because the conditions have changed, the awareness has expanded, and the body can now choose regulation over survival reflex.

This is the distinction that changes everything.

Completion Is a New Response, Not a New Story

You do not complete the past by reliving it.
You complete it by **responding differently**.

Where ancestors braced, you regulate.
Where silence protected, you speak.
Where hypervigilance was necessary, you rest.
Where love was unsafe, you build it slowly and consciously.

Nothing is erased.
Everything is integrated.

Completion honors what was endured without recreating it.

Freedom Is a Nervous System State

Freedom is not philosophical.
It is physiological.

A regulated nervous system can perceive choice. A dysregulated one cannot. When the body is no longer operating from inherited threat, it gains access to curiosity, creativity, and discernment. This is why healing lineage is not about blaming the past—it is about **changing the present conditions** under which memory expresses.

More conscious.
More regulated.
More free.

That is not avoidance.
That is evolution.

Momentum Transformed

Karma, understood as momentum, only continues while it remains unconscious. Once awareness enters the system, direction becomes adjustable. Energy that once looped now flows forward.

This is karma transformed—not by force, but by **completion**.

Not punishment.
Not destiny.

But **inheritance meeting awareness**.

The Moment the Lineage Turns

There is always a moment in a lineage when repetition gives way to choice. It happens quietly—often in the body before the mind understands it. A pause where reaction used to be. A breath where urgency once lived. A decision that feels unfamiliar because it is no longer driven by fear.

That moment matters more than any story about the past.

It is the moment the lineage turns.

Moving Forward Without Forgetting

Completion does not mean forgetting where you came from. It means carrying forward **only what is still needed**—the wisdom, the strength, the discernment—and releasing what no longer serves.

You are not betraying your ancestors by living differently.
You are honoring them by **finishing what they could not**.

This is how the past becomes a foundation instead of a weight.

The Truth That Liberates

You are not here to suffer in loyalty to history.
You are here to **resolve it through presence**.

That is the deeper truth.

Not fate imposed.
Not karma owed.

But consciousness arriving at the exact point where the pattern can finally end—and something new can begin.

That is not escape.
That is **completion**.

And completion is how the future opens—

not by forgetting the past,
but by **meeting it with enough awareness to let it move on**.

Generational Cycles and Purpose

Every lineage carries patterns—not as curses, but as **unfinished stories seeking completion**.

These patterns are not mistakes in the family line. They are adaptive responses formed under specific historical, social, and emotional conditions. When circumstances made full integration impossible—because of danger, oppression, loss, or instability—the learning did not end. It **paused**, carrying its momentum forward to the next generation.

Across generations, families transmit recurring themes that shape:

- How life is approached

- How safety is negotiated

- How connection, power, and worth are understood

- How meaning is constructed

These themes surface as **cycles**, repeating not to punish descendants, but to find a moment in time where awareness, safety, and capacity finally allow resolution.

ENCODED IN THE STARS | 257

Abandonment or Resilience

Some lineages carry repeated experiences of abandonment—loss through death, separation, migration, incarceration, or emotional absence. Descendants may inherit hyper-independence, fear of closeness, or over-responsibility.

Other lineages respond to the same conditions with extraordinary resilience—developing endurance, adaptability, and the ability to survive against impossible odds.

Both patterns originate from the same question: *How do we stay alive when connection is uncertain?*

The cycle repeats until safety allows the nervous system to learn that **connection no longer equals danger**.

Displacement or Leadership

Histories of displacement—whether through colonization, enslavement, forced migration, or exile—often give rise to a later emergence of leadership. What began as survival under marginalization evolves into a calling to organize, protect, guide, or advocate.

Leadership here is not ambition—it is **compensatory wisdom**.

The lineage learned how to navigate instability. Later generations inherit the capacity to:

- Read systems quickly

- Anticipate threat or opportunity

- Hold groups together under pressure

The pattern repeats until leadership is no longer reactive, but **intentional and grounded**.

Silence or Voice

Many families carry generations of silence—where speaking truth was unsafe, costly, or forbidden. Emotional suppression became protection. Endurance replaced expression.

In later generations, this silence often gives rise to a descendant who cannot remain quiet. The voice emerges—not out of rebellion, but out of **necessity**.

Truth-telling becomes the medicine where silence once kept people alive.

The pattern pauses only when expression is no longer punished—when the system can tolerate honesty without collapse.

Scarcity or Innovation

Lineages shaped by scarcity often pass down vigilance around resources, security, and survival. Anxiety about loss may coexist with remarkable creativity.

Scarcity sharpens ingenuity.

From deprivation emerges:

- Innovation
- Resourcefulness
- Problem-solving ability
- Creative adaptation

The cycle resolves when abundance becomes regulated—not hoarded or feared, but **trusted**.

Why These Patterns Repeat

These patterns are not random repetitions. They are **signals of where learning paused**—where circumstances made integration impossible at the time.

When survival was the priority, there was no space for:

- Emotional processing
- Meaning-making
- Nervous system regulation
- Conscious choice

So the lesson waited.

It moved forward in time until a generation arrived with:

- More safety
- More awareness
- More resources
- More permission to feel and choose

That generation is often **you**.

Completion Requires Capacity

Completion does not happen because someone tries harder. It happens because the conditions finally allow the system to process what was once too overwhelming.

This is why lineage work often surfaces in people who feel:

- More sensitive than their family

- More aware of patterns

- More uncomfortable with "how it's always been"

- More compelled to change things

Sensitivity is not weakness.
It is **capacity**.

From Repetition to Resolution

When patterns are seen clearly, they begin to loosen. Awareness interrupts momentum. Choice enters where reaction once ruled.

You are not repeating history because you are broken.
You are meeting it because **you are equipped to finish the learning**.

These stories are not asking to be relived.
They are asking to be **completed**.

And completion does not erase the past—it transforms it into wisdom that no longer needs to repeat itself to be remembered.

Where Purpose Emerges

Purpose rarely appears in the most comfortable places of

lineage.

It emerges **where something stalled**—where history paused learning because survival demanded all available resources.

Purpose is born at the **threshold**.

The Edge Where Capacity Arrives

Where there was **no safety to grieve**, someone is born with the capacity to feel—deeply, honestly, without shutting down. The nervous system that once had to harden gives way to one that can soften. Tears become information. Grief becomes integration. Feeling becomes the medicine that survival postponed.

Where there was **no permission to speak**, someone arrives with a voice that refuses to stay silent. Truth-telling surfaces not as defiance, but as restoration. Silence protected life once; now expression restores wholeness. The voice emerges because the system can finally tolerate honesty without collapse.

Where survival demanded **conformity**, someone emerges with the courage to innovate. Creativity appears where rules once kept people alive. New pathways open because the risk of imagining something different is no longer fatal. Innovation becomes the next evolutionary step, not a threat.

Not Rebellion—Readiness

This is not rebellion for its own sake.
It is **evolution responding to readiness**.

Purpose does not ask you to reject your lineage. It asks you to continue it **with more options available**. When conditions change—when safety increases, when awareness expands—the system naturally seeks completion. What once had to be endured can now be transformed.

This is why purpose often feels both personal and ancestral. It carries urgency without aggression, conviction without contempt. It is not trying to prove anything; it is trying to **finish something**.

The Physics of Transformation

Transformation requires contrast. Purpose forms where tension once lived—between restraint and expression, fear and curiosity, endurance and choice. At that edge, energy gathers. Insight sharpens. Direction clarifies.

Purpose is not found by escaping the past.
It is found by **standing at its edge** and responding differently.

From Endurance to Expression

What your lineage endured created the conditions for what you can now express. The very places where history tightened its grip are where release becomes possible. Purpose, then, is not a job title or a role—it is a **movement**:

- From numbness to feeling

- From silence to voice

- From conformity to creativity

Each movement completes a chapter that could not be finished before.

The Invitation

Purpose asks a simple, demanding question: *What can be transformed now that could not be transformed then?*
Your answer is not theoretical. It is lived—in how you grieve, speak, create, lead, and choose.

Purpose forms at the edge between **what was endured** and **what can now be transformed**.
Stand there long enough, with awareness and courage, and direction emerges—not as pressure, but as clarity.

That clarity is not rebellion.
It is readiness made visible.

The Callings That Repeat Across Lineages

Across generations, certain callings surface again and again—not as trends, but as **responses**. Many people feel an unshakable pull toward roles that seem larger than personal ambition, as if something ancient is asking to be completed through their life.

These callings are not chosen lightly.
They are **remembered**.

The Cycle Breaker

The cycle breaker is the one who interrupts harmful repetition—not by force, but by awareness. They notice patterns others normalize. They question what was never questioned. They choose differently where the default once ruled.

This role is often lonely at first. It requires courage to stand between "how it's always been" and "what must change." Yet the cycle breaker does not reject the lineage; they **protect its future** by refusing to perpetuate what no longer serves.

The Healer

The healer carries a nervous system attuned to regulation, compassion, and repair. Where chaos or numbness once dominated, the healer brings presence. Where pain was ignored, they bring care. Where survival demanded hardness, they bring gentleness without fragility.

Healing here is not limited to profession. It is a **quality of engagement**—the ability to soothe, to listen, to hold complexity without collapsing. This calling emerges because the lineage finally has the safety to feel.

The Truth Teller

Truth tellers name what was hidden, denied, or unspeakable. They speak into silence not to provoke, but to restore coherence. Their words often disrupt—not because they are harsh, but because they are accurate.

This calling arises in lineages where silence once preserved safety. The truth teller appears when honesty is no longer lethal—when the system can finally survive clarity.

The Restorer of Lost Knowledge

Some are called to reclaim what was taken, buried, or suppressed: culture, wisdom, language, ritual, spirituality, craft. They feel drawn to ancestral practices, forgotten histories, or intuitive knowings that feel older than memory.

This restoration is not nostalgia. It is **repair**. It brings back what was lost so the lineage can stand whole again.

Why These Callings Feel So Personal

These roles often feel instinctive, urgent, and deeply personal—because they move through the body as impulse, curiosity, and conviction. Yet they are rarely *only* personal.

They are **lineage intelligence expressing through you**.

The lineage carries unfinished work. When conditions allow—when awareness, safety, and capacity converge—that work seeks a vessel. Not the strongest. Not the loudest. The one who can hold it **without becoming it**.

Responsibility Without Burden

Being called does not mean being condemned to struggle. It means being trusted with **choice**. These roles are invitations, not sentences. They ask for presence, not perfection.

When you honor the calling:

- Patterns loosen

- Energy clarifies

- Purpose feels grounded rather than pressured

You are not meant to carry the past on your back.
You are meant to **carry it forward with discernment**.

The Through-Line

Each of these callings shares a single aim: **completion**. They bring cycles to rest, wounds to regulation, silence to speech, and loss to remembrance.

This is not destiny imposed.
It is intelligence continuing itself.

And when you answer the call—not to prove, but to participate—you do not disappear into lineage. You become the place where lineage **evolves**.

Not by erasing what was.
But by allowing what is now possible to finally arrive.

Why You, and Why Now

Lineage does not pass responsibility blindly.
Patterns do not land at random.

They move—intelligently—toward generations that have the **capacity to hold them differently**.

Across time, unresolved patterns wait for conditions that make completion possible. Those conditions include:

- **Greater safety** — physical, emotional, relational, or social

- **More resources** — access to education, stability, and support

- **Expanded awareness** — language for trauma, regulation, and meaning

- **Access to healing tools** — therapeutic, somatic, spiritual, and cultural

When these conditions converge, momentum shifts. What once had to be endured can finally be examined. What once demanded silence can be spoken. What once required numbness can now be felt.

This is not coincidence.

It is **timing**.

Capacity Changes the Assignment

You may be the first generation with the nervous system capacity to:

- **Pause instead of react**

- **Feel instead of numb**

- **Choose instead of comply**

This capacity is not accidental. It reflects an evolutionary threshold—where survival is no longer the sole objective, and integration becomes possible.

Previous generations were not weak. They were **occupied with staying alive**. They did not lack insight; they lacked safety. They did not avoid healing; they lacked permission.

Now, the conditions are different.

Why the Work Arrives Through You

Patterns seek resolution where regulation exists. Healing does not move toward chaos—it moves toward **containment**. When a generation develops enough stability to stay present with discomfort, the lineage recognizes an opportunity.

You are not being asked to suffer more.
You are being asked to **respond differently**.

That difference—pausing, naming, choosing—is the intervention.

Strength Is Not the Point

This is not about being stronger, braver, or more virtuous than those who came before you. It is about **readiness**.

You carry:

- More context

- More choice

- More tools

- More support

That makes transformation feasible.

The lineage does not ask you to fix the past.
It asks you to **stop repeating it**.

The Privilege and Responsibility of Timing

Being born into a moment of greater awareness is both privilege and responsibility. Privilege, because you have options that did not exist before. Responsibility, because awareness makes choice unavoidable.

Once you can see the pattern, you cannot unknow it.

But this responsibility is not a burden. It is an **invitation to**

evolve with integrity.

The Quiet Truth

You are not here because you are exceptional.
You are here because the **conditions are finally right**.

Right for truth.
Right for regulation.
Right for completion.

And when you meet that timing—not with pressure, but with presence—you become the place where lineage stops bracing for survival and starts learning how to live.

That is why you.
That is why now.

Evolution, Not Erasure

Evolving lineage does not mean rejecting where you came from.
It means **continuing the story with more options available**.

Erasure denies the past. Evolution **integrates** it.

Your ancestors' lives were shaped by constraints—social, political, economic, and emotional—that limited what could be expressed, chosen, or even imagined. Survival required sacrifice. Adaptation required silence. Endurance often replaced joy. None of this was failure. It was necessity.

Evolution begins when necessity loosens its grip.

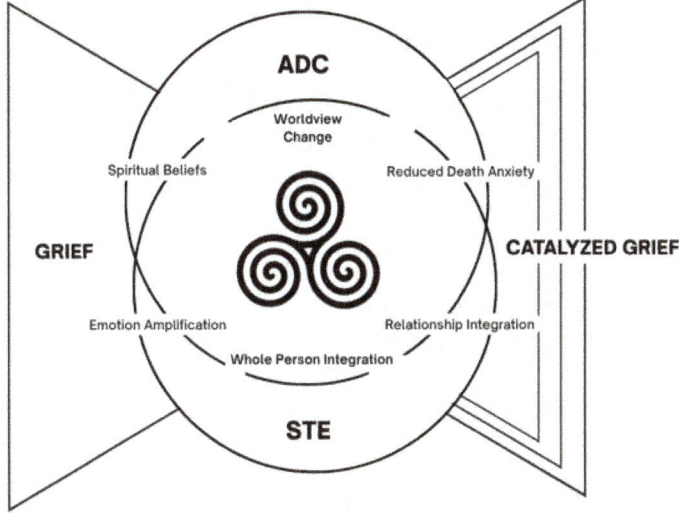

Honoring Without Repeating

You do not honor your ancestors by recreating their suffering. You honor them by allowing the story to **move beyond survival**.

You honor them by:

- **Living the freedom they could not access**
  Choosing rest where exhaustion was normalized. Choosing safety where vigilance was required. Choosing

authenticity where conformity protected life.

- **Expressing the gifts they had to hide**
  Creativity, leadership, spirituality, intellect, sensuality, or voice that once carried risk can now be embodied openly. What was suppressed becomes contribution.

- **Creating outcomes they were never allowed to imagine**
  Stability without fear. Success without self-erasure. Love without abandonment. Joy without punishment.

These choices are not betrayals of the past.
They are its **fulfillment**.

Why Repetition Is Not Loyalty

There is a quiet myth embedded in many lineages: that suffering proves loyalty. That struggle validates belonging. That ease somehow dishonors those who endured hardship.

This is a misunderstanding.

Repetition is not remembrance.
Pain is not proof of respect.

True honoring does not require reenactment. It requires **completion**.

Carrying Wisdom, Not Wounds

Evolution allows you to carry forward what was learned—strength, resilience, discernment—without carrying forward what was harmful. You are not asked to forget history. You are asked to **extract wisdom from it**.

Wisdom knows when a pattern has served its purpose.
Wisdom knows when it is time to choose differently.

This discernment is what separates evolution from erasure.

Healing Forward

Lineage does not heal backward.
It heals **forward**.

Each generation adds a layer of choice. When you choose regulation over reactivity, expression over silence, creativity over constraint, the entire system updates. The future inherits something lighter—not because the past was denied, but because it was finally integrated.

This is how lineage heals forward:

- Not by rewriting history

- But by **changing what history produces next**

The Living Tribute

Your life is not meant to be a monument to what was endured. It is meant to be a **living tribute to what was possible but postponed**.

When you allow yourself to live with more freedom, clarity, and wholeness, you do not abandon your ancestors. You stand on their endurance and take the next step they could not.

That step matters.

Because evolution is not forgetting where you came from.
It is ensuring that where you came from does not remain the only place the story can go.

The Role of Purpose

Purpose, in this context, is not a job title, a résumé line, or a singular achievement to be reached and checked off. Purpose is a **direction of energy**—a consistent movement toward integration where fragmentation once lived. It is how life organizes itself through you when awareness meets readiness.

Purpose is not something you chase.
It is something that **moves when you do**.

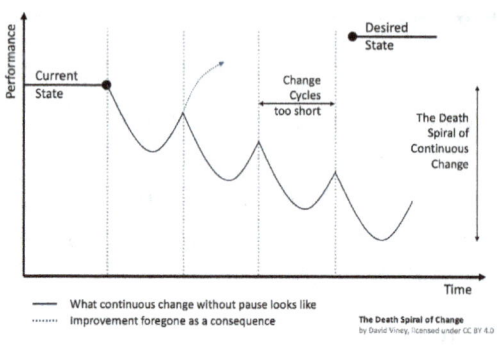

The Death Spiral of Change
by David Viney, licensed under CC BY 4.0

Purpose as Integration

Fragmentation occurs when parts of experience cannot be felt, named, or metabolized—when survival requires splitting, silencing, or suppressing. Purpose emerges as the counterforce to that fragmentation. It draws energy toward wholeness, coherence, and continuity.

This is why purpose often shows up as:

- A pull toward healing what was avoided
- A compulsion to tell truths that were hidden

- A desire to build what was missing

- A need to restore what was lost

Purpose is the psyche's and lineage's **organizing principle**—the way unfinished material finds a path toward completion.

Evolution, Not Reenactment

You are not here to relive the past.
You are here to **evolve it**.

Evolution does not require perfection. It requires **presence**—the capacity to stay with discomfort without defaulting to old responses. It requires **awareness**—the ability to recognize when a pattern is appearing. And it requires **choice**—the willingness to respond differently when it does.

No grand gesture is needed.
Just a different response, made consistently.

That response—again and again—is how cycles close.

How Cycles Actually End

Cycles do not end through confrontation alone. They end through **integration**. When the nervous system learns it no longer needs the old strategy, repetition loses its momentum. What once demanded attention no longer needs to repeat itself to be seen.

This is why destiny work is subtle and cumulative:

- A pause where there used to be reaction

- A boundary where there used to be silence

- A choice where there used to be inevitability

Each moment of presence rewrites what the future will

inherit.

Liberation After Completion

When a cycle closes, purpose does not disappear.
It **liberates**.

Energy that once had to manage survival becomes available for:

- Creativity

- Joy

- Play

- Exploration

- Love that is not transactional

Expression no longer has to justify itself by being useful or protective. It becomes **generative**—creating simply because life has room to breathe.

This is not the end of purpose.
It is the **expansion of it**.

The Deeper Function of Destiny Work

The deeper function of destiny work is not to bind you to history, to identity, or to obligation. It is to position you at the exact point where history can finally move.

You become the generation where:

- Awareness interrupts momentum

- Choice replaces compulsion

- Meaning replaces repetition

Not because you are exceptional, but because the conditions are finally right.

Purpose, then, is not a burden to carry.
It is a **current to align with**.

And when you align with it—patiently, imperfectly, consciously—you do not erase the past. You **complete it**.

That completion does not trap you in responsibility.
It frees you into expression.

This is how destiny stops being inherited and starts being **embodied**—
not as obligation,
but as a life that finally has the space to move forward.

Cultural Memory and Ancestral Remembrance

Across cultures and throughout history, ancestral memory has never been treated as symbolic nostalgia or abstract belief. It has been understood as **living intelligence**—a presence that continues to inform identity, ethics, destiny, and healing across generations.

Long before modern science named epigenetics or intergenerational trauma, cultures around the world already knew: **the past does not disappear; it participates**.

African Traditions: Ancestors as Active Participants

In many African cosmologies, ancestors are not relegated to memory or mythology. They are **active, conscious participants** in the lives of the living—present, responsive, and relational. Death does not sever relationship; it **changes its mode**.

Ancestors are often described as *the living-dead*: those who have crossed from physical embodiment but remain engaged in the moral, spiritual, and energetic life of the community.

They are neither distant nor abstract. They are **accessible**.

A Permeable Boundary Between Worlds

Unlike Western frameworks that sharply divide life and death, many African traditions understand existence as a **continuum**. The boundary between the seen and unseen worlds is permeable and dynamic, maintained through:

- **Ritual** – intentional acts that open communication

- **Prayer** – dialogue, not supplication

- **Libation** – offerings acknowledging presence and relationship

- **Remembrance** – naming, honoring, and storytelling

These practices do not "summon" ancestors as outsiders. They **recognize** them as already present.

The ancestors are not watching passively. They are:

- Observing ethical alignment
- Supporting communal balance
- Warning when harmony is threatened
- Reinforcing values that sustained the lineage

Ancestors as Guides, Not Gods

Ancestors are not worshipped as deities. They are **respected elders**—holders of lived wisdom who understand both human limitation and spiritual law.

Their role includes:

- **Guidance** – offering direction through intuition, dreams, signs, or divination
- **Witnessing** – holding the moral memory of the lineage
- **Protection** – guarding descendants who walk in alignment
- **Correction** – signaling when imbalance or neglect arises

Correction is not punishment. It is **course adjustment**.

Right Relationship as the Foundation of Health

To remember ancestors is to remain in **right relationship** with the forces that ensured survival—through colonization, enslavement, displacement, famine, and systemic violence. Ancestors are honored because they endured what descendants did not have to.

Health, in this worldview, is not merely physical. It is **relational and spiritual**.

When illness, misfortune, or persistent imbalance appears, it is often understood not as random suffering, but as a **communication**:

- Something has been forgotten
- A relationship has been neglected
- A value has been violated
- A responsibility has been deferred

The question is not "What is wrong with me?"
It is "**What is out of alignment?**"

Illness as Information, Not Failure

In many African healing traditions, illness is not immediately medicalized. It is first **interpreted**. The body is understood as a messenger, carrying signals from the ancestral, spiritual, and communal field.

Illness may indicate:

- Suppressed grief that was never mourned
- Disconnection from lineage or land
- A calling being ignored
- An ancestral story seeking acknowledgment

Healing, therefore, may require:

- Ritual acknowledgment
- Ancestral offerings
- Community witnessing

- Behavioral or ethical realignment

This does not reject medicine—it **contextualizes** it.

Survival Wisdom Lives in the Ancestors

Ancestral wisdom is practical, not romantic. It includes:

- How to survive oppression
- How to adapt under threat
- How to preserve identity under erasure
- How to protect community cohesion

To honor ancestors is to honor **strategy, resilience, and intelligence**—not just spirit.

This is why forgetting ancestors is considered dangerous in many traditions. Forgetting severs access to **earned wisdom**.

Restoration, Not Guilt

Ancestral accountability is not about guilt or obligation. It is about **restoration**. When something is out of harmony, the response is not shame—it is repair.

Restoration may involve:

- Naming the forgotten
- Speaking the silenced
- Reclaiming practices that were outlawed or shamed
- Living in ways ancestors were denied

The living are not punished for ancestral wounds. They are **entrusted** with healing them when conditions allow.

Why This Matters Now

Many people of African descent today experience spiritual disorientation not because they lack belief—but because ancestral relationships were **systematically disrupted** through slavery, colonialism, and forced religious conversion.

Ancestral remembrance becomes an act of:

- Healing identity fragmentation
- Restoring continuity
- Reclaiming spiritual authority

It is not about returning to the past.
It is about **re-establishing relationship** with wisdom that was never meant to be lost.

The Living Agreement

In African cosmologies, there is an unspoken agreement between ancestors and descendants:

> *We endured so you could live.*
> *You live so we can be remembered.*

When remembrance is restored, protection strengthens. When relationship is honored, guidance returns. When harmony is reestablished, illness and imbalance lose their hold.

Ancestors are not haunting the living.
They are **standing with them**.

And when descendants listen—not with fear, but with respect—the lineage does not repeat pain.
It **transforms it into wisdom**.

This is not superstition.

It is an ancient relational science—one modern systems theory and epigenetics are only beginning to understand.

The ancestors were never gone.
They were waiting for remembrance to become conscious again.

Indigenous Cosmologies: Land, Blood, and Story as One

Across Indigenous cosmologies worldwide, identity is not housed solely within the individual. It is **relational**—formed through an unbroken bond between **land, blood, and story**. These are not separate domains. They are expressions of the same living system.

In this worldview, land is not property.
It is **ancestor, archive, and teacher**.

Land as Living Memory

Indigenous traditions understand land as alive and conscious

—capable of holding memory, transmitting wisdom, and responding to human relationship. Rivers remember who was baptized, buried, or crossed through them. Mountains hold the prayers, ceremonies, and initiations that occurred upon them. Forests carry the footsteps of generations who learned how to survive, gather, and listen within them.

Memory does not live only in DNA.
It lives in **place**.

This is why sacred sites matter. Burial grounds, ceremonial spaces, and migration routes are not symbolic—they are **energetic repositories** of ancestral experience. To walk these lands is to enter a conversation already in progress.

Blood Carries the Map, Land Holds the Key

Indigenous knowledge systems often teach that the body recognizes land instinctively. Certain places evoke familiarity without explanation. This is not imagination—it is **somatic recognition**. Blood remembers what land once taught.

To know who you are is to know:

- Where your people lived

- How they related to land

- Which waters sustained them

- Which stories shaped their ethics and survival

Identity emerges from **relationship**, not isolation.

Story As Instruction, Not Entertainment

Oral traditions are not folklore. They are **instructional technologies**—methods of transmitting ecological knowledge, moral law, cosmology, and survival strategy across generations.

Stories encode:

- How to live in balance with the land
- How to respond to crisis
- How to maintain communal cohesion
- How to honor ancestors and descendants

When stories are interrupted, identity fragments.

Displacement as Spiritual and Biological Trauma

From an Indigenous perspective, displacement is not merely geographic—it is **existential**.

Colonization, forced relocation, land theft, and cultural erasure severed:

- Access to sacred sites
- Transmission of ancestral knowledge
- Continuity of ceremony and language

This rupture created not only political injustice, but **spiritual and biological disruption**. The nervous system, evolved to regulate in relationship with specific environments, was forced to adapt rapidly to unfamiliar terrain and imposed systems.

Trauma, here, is not just historical—it is **ecological**.

Healing Requires Reconnection

In Indigenous cosmologies, healing cannot occur in isolation. It requires reconnection:

- To **land** — returning physically, symbolically, or ceremonially

- To **ceremony** — restoring rhythm, meaning, and communal regulation

- To **communal memory** — remembering stories that contextualize suffering

Healing is not about "moving on."
It is about **coming back into relationship**.

Even when physical return is impossible, remembrance, ritual, and land acknowledgment re-establish continuity.

The Land Remembers

One of the most profound Indigenous teachings is this:
The land remembers when people are forced to forget.

When language is banned, the land still holds its names.
When ceremony is outlawed, the land still remembers the rhythm.
When people are displaced, the land still waits.

This memory is not passive. It calls—through dreams, longings, grief without clear origin, and a sense of incompleteness that modern explanations cannot satisfy.

Why This Matters Today

Many people feel disconnected not because they lack purpose, but because they lack **place-based continuity**. Urbanization, globalization, and forced assimilation have created identities untethered from land and lineage.

Indigenous cosmologies offer a corrective:
You are not meant to exist abstractly.
You are meant to belong **somewhere**—to a story larger than

yourself.

Restoring the Triad

Land. Blood. Story.

When these are reunited—even symbolically—coherence returns. The nervous system settles. Identity stabilizes. Purpose clarifies.

You do not heal by forgetting where you come from.
You heal by **remembering in relationship**.

This is not nostalgia.
It is **restoration of orientation**.

Indigenous wisdom teaches that when humans lose relationship with land, they lose themselves. And when that relationship is restored—through reverence, responsibility, and remembrance—healing ripples forward through generations.

The land is not silent.
It has been holding the story until people were ready to listen again.

Eastern Philosophies: Karma as Collective and Cyclical

Eastern philosophical systems—particularly within Hindu, Buddhist, Taoist, and Yogic traditions—understand karma not as individual moral bookkeeping, but as **collective, cyclical movement**. Karma is not about reward and punishment assigned to a single life. It is about **cause and consequence unfolding across time**, often far beyond the lifespan of any one person.

In this framework, life is not linear.
It is **recursive**.

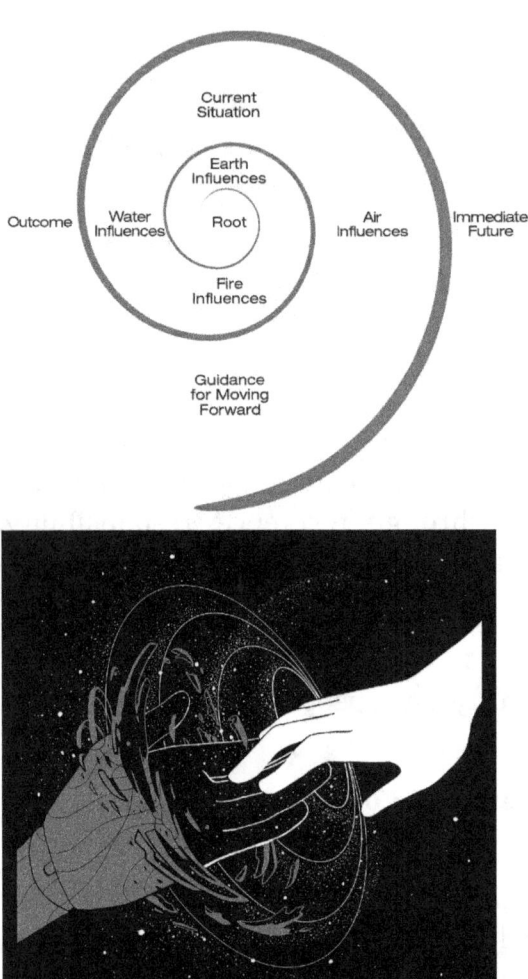

Karma as Motion, Not Judgment

The original meaning of karma is *action*. Action sets energy into motion. That motion continues until it is met with awareness sufficient to redirect it. Karma, therefore, is not moral condemnation—it is **momentum**.

When actions arise from fear, scarcity, or ignorance, they generate conditions that echo forward. When actions arise from clarity, compassion, and wisdom, they generate different conditions. Neither is judged. Both are **instructive**.

Karma is not punishment.
It is **unfinished consequence seeking resolution**.

Why Karma Is Inherently Collective

Eastern philosophies recognize that no action exists in isolation. Every choice is embedded within family systems, social structures, ecological conditions, and historical contexts. What one generation does shapes the terrain the next must walk upon.

This is why karma is understood as:

- **Familial** — passed through bloodlines and household systems

- **Communal** — shaped by cultural norms and collective behavior

- **Societal** — reinforced by institutions, power structures, and economies

- **Generational** — carried forward until consciously transformed

A single life does not create karma alone.
A single life does not resolve it alone.

Ancestry as Karmic Context

From this perspective, ancestry is not an add-on to karma —it is **central**. One generation's unresolved actions create the conditions another must inhabit. This does not mean descendants are guilty of past actions. It means they are **born** into momentum.

You do not inherit blame.
You inherit **context**.

That context influences:

- Access to resources

- Patterns of safety or threat

- Emotional regulation norms

- Beliefs about worth, duty, and belonging

Liberation, then, is not escape from history. It is **engagement with it**, skillfully and consciously.

Liberation as Integration, Not Escape

Western interpretations often frame liberation as transcendence—rising above suffering, leaving the world behind, or detaching from responsibility. Eastern philosophies emphasize something different: **integration**.

Liberation occurs not when karma is denied, but when it is **understood and metabolized**.

This includes:

- Seeing how patterns repeat

- Recognizing where reaction replaces choice

- Responding differently within familiar conditions

Enlightenment is not separation from the cycle.
It is **clarity within it**.

The Bodhisattva Principle: Collective Awakening

In Mahayana Buddhism, the Bodhisattva ideal embodies this truth. A Bodhisattva delays personal liberation in order to assist collective awakening. This is not sacrifice—it is recognition that **no one is free until the conditions that bind many are addressed**.

Healing, therefore, is relational.

Freedom expands as systems integrate wisdom. Individual awakening contributes to collective resolution. Each regulated nervous system reduces collective reactivity. Each conscious choice alters the karmic field.

Cycles Close Through Awareness

Karma continues until it is met with sufficient awareness to change its trajectory. This awareness may arrive as:

- Insight
- Compassion
- Boundary-setting
- Ethical realignment
- Collective reckoning

When awareness enters the system, repetition loosens. The cycle does not disappear—it **completes**.

What This Means for Purpose

From an Eastern perspective, purpose is not self-actualization alone. It is **participation in resolution**. A life well-lived does not escape karma; it **transforms it**.

This is why purpose often feels heavier than personal preference. It carries gravity because it is **shared**.

And this is why liberation is never solitary.

The Deeper Teaching

You are not paying for the past.
You are **responding to it**.

You are not trapped in cycles.
You are **standing at a point of choice within them**.

Karma is not fate.
It is **movement awaiting direction**.

And when a generation gains enough awareness to respond rather than react, karma does what it was always meant to do:
it **teaches**,
it **integrates**,
and then—quietly—it **releases**.

This is not moral accounting.
It is **evolution through relationship**.

And in that evolution, liberation is not a private victory.
It is a **collective unfolding**, carried forward one conscious response at a time.

Mythological Systems: Inherited Quests, Curses, and Blessings

Across mythological systems worldwide, destiny is never born in isolation. From epic cycles to oral traditions, heroes step into lives already shaped by what came before them. They inherit **unfinished quests**, **unresolved curses**, and **latent blessings**—threads left dangling by ancestors who lacked the safety, time, or awareness to complete them.

These stories are not warnings against ancestry.
They are teachings about **continuity**.

Inheritance as Narrative Momentum

In myth, inheritance is rarely about guilt. It is about **momentum**. Something set in motion continues until it encounters the one capable of finishing it. A curse persists not because it is malicious, but because its lesson has not yet been integrated. A blessing lies dormant not because it is absent, but because the conditions for its expression have not arrived.

Myths understand what modern psychology and systems theory now echo:
what is unresolved does not disappear—it waits.

Curses as Unintegrated Knowledge

Mythic curses are often misunderstood as moral punishments. In their deeper meaning, they represent **unintegrated knowledge**—truths that were denied, suppressed, or mishandled.

A family cursed with betrayal may actually be grappling with a legacy of broken trust that was never repaired. A lineage marked by exile may be carrying wisdom about belonging that has not yet found its voice. The "curse" repeats until the hero responds differently—by naming the truth, setting a boundary, or choosing compassion where fear once ruled.

In myth, curses lift not through force, but through **right action**.

Blessings as Dormant Potential

Blessings in myth often skip generations. A gift promised long ago finally awakens in a descendant who can carry it responsibly. This reflects a crucial truth: **capacity matters.**

Power, insight, leadership, healing—these qualities require maturity, regulation, and context. When earlier generations could not safely embody them, the blessing waited. When the hero arrives with the necessary awareness, the gift activates.

Blessings are not rewards.
They are **responsibilities entrusted to readiness**.

The Hero as Threshold Figure

The mythic hero is rarely the strongest or most favored. They are the one who stands at the **threshold**—between what was endured and what can now be transformed. Their task is not to erase the past, but to **carry it forward with consciousness**.

This is why the hero's journey is marked by:

- Trials that mirror ancestral wounds
- Encounters with guides or elders
- Tests of integrity rather than strength
- A return that brings wisdom back to the community

The journey completes not when the hero escapes suffering, but when the **lineage gains resolution**.

Myth as Psychological and Spiritual Map

These stories were never meant to be read as literal history alone. They are **maps of the psyche and the lineage**, encoding truths about how patterns repeat and how they can be transformed.

They teach that:

- Destiny is shaped by inheritance
- Awareness interrupts repetition
- Courage opens new outcomes
- Right relationship heals what force cannot

In this way, myth anticipates both depth psychology and ancestral healing.

Ancestral Work, Not Personal Glory

The hero's triumph is rarely personal glory. It is **restoration**. The land heals. The kingdom stabilizes. The curse ends. The blessing flows onward. The hero becomes a conduit through which the past finally completes itself.

This is why the hero's journey is rarely just personal.
It is **ancestral work carried forward**.

The Living Myth

You do not need to slay monsters or cross oceans to live this story. In modern life, the inherited quest appears as:

- Choosing truth where silence was safer
- Creating stability where chaos once ruled
- Loving where fear once closed the heart
- Building futures ancestors could not imagine

These are mythic acts in ordinary form.

And when you respond with awareness, courage, and integrity, you do not escape inheritance—you **transform it**.

Myth teaches us this enduring truth:
Destiny is not what you inherit.
Destiny is **what you do with what you inherit**.

And when the story finally changes through you, it does not end.
It **evolves**—freeing the generations that follow to begin their journeys without carrying what was never theirs to hold.

What These Traditions Share

Despite vast differences in language, geography, and cosmology, these traditions converge on a single, unwavering truth:

Healing is not only personal—it is generational.

Across African ancestral cosmologies, Indigenous land-based wisdoms, Eastern philosophies of karma, and mythological systems of inheritance, well-being is never confined to the individual. A life is understood as a **node within a living continuum**, shaped by what came before and shaping what comes next.

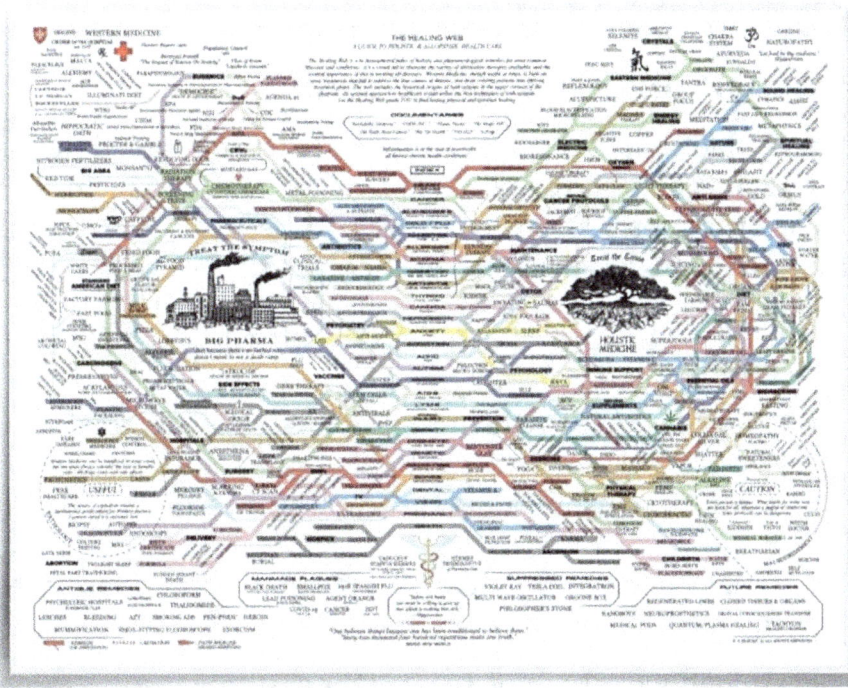

Health as Relational Coherence

In these traditions, health is not defined by symptom absence or personal achievement alone. It is measured by **relational coherence**—within the self, the family, the community, the land, and the ancestral field.

A person is considered well when:

- Their nervous system is regulated enough to choose rather than react

- Their relationships do not require fragmentation to survive

- Their actions do not perpetuate unresolved harm

- Their life adds continuity rather than rupture to the lineage

Well-being, therefore, is a **systemic state**, not a solitary one.

The Individual as a Transmission Point

These traditions recognize that each person functions as a **transmission point**. What you metabolize, integrate, and transform does not end with you. It becomes part of the informational field inherited by those who follow.

This is why a single person's healing matters far beyond their own relief:

- When one person regulates, relational chaos decreases

- When one person names the truth, silence loosens its grip

- When one person chooses differently, repetition loses momentum

A healed individual subtly **updates the system**.

Success Redefined

Modern culture often defines success as personal fulfillment, independence, or upward mobility. These traditions offer a deeper metric:

Does this life reduce inherited suffering—or pass it forward unchanged?

Success is not measured only by what one acquires, but by **what no longer needs to be carried**. A lineage moving toward balance, continuity, and coherence is the truest indicator of well-being.

Healing as Field Change

When one person heals, they do not heal in isolation. They alter the **relational field**:

- Children inherit more nervous system safety

- Descendants inherit fewer unresolved adaptations

- Future choices are made from clarity rather than compulsion

This is why ancestral healing is often quiet but profound. It may not announce itself, but it **changes what becomes possible**.

Continuity Over Perfection

None of these traditions demand perfection. They emphasize **continuity**—the steady movement toward greater awareness, regulation, and ethical alignment over time.

Healing is not about erasing pain or rewriting history.
It is about ensuring that pain does not remain the primary teacher.

The Shared Ethical Core

At their core, these traditions agree on this principle:

What you resolve within yourself becomes a gift to those who come after you.

And conversely:

What you avoid does not disappear—it waits.

This is not a threat. It is an invitation to participate consciously in the unfolding of time.

The Quiet Power of One Life

A single life lived with awareness can shift generations. Not through grand gestures, but through **pattern interruption**:

- Responding where others reacted

- Feeling where others numbed

- Choosing where others complied

These micro-choices accumulate. Over time, they become **legacy**.

The Convergence Made Clear

Different languages.
Different rituals.
Different metaphors.

One shared truth:

Healing is not the end of the story.
It is how the story learns to move forward.

And when one person heals, the lineage does not just survive.
It **evolves**—with more balance, more coherence, and more freedom than it had before.

That is the inheritance these traditions point toward.
Not perfection.
But **progress made conscious**.

Science Catching Up to Memory

Modern science is now arriving—through careful measurement and decades of research—at insights that ancestral cultures have preserved for millennia through lived observation. Fields such as epigenetics, neurobiology, and systems theory increasingly confirm a foundational truth: **memory is not confined to the individual mind, nor limited to conscious recall**. It is relational, embodied, and transmissible.

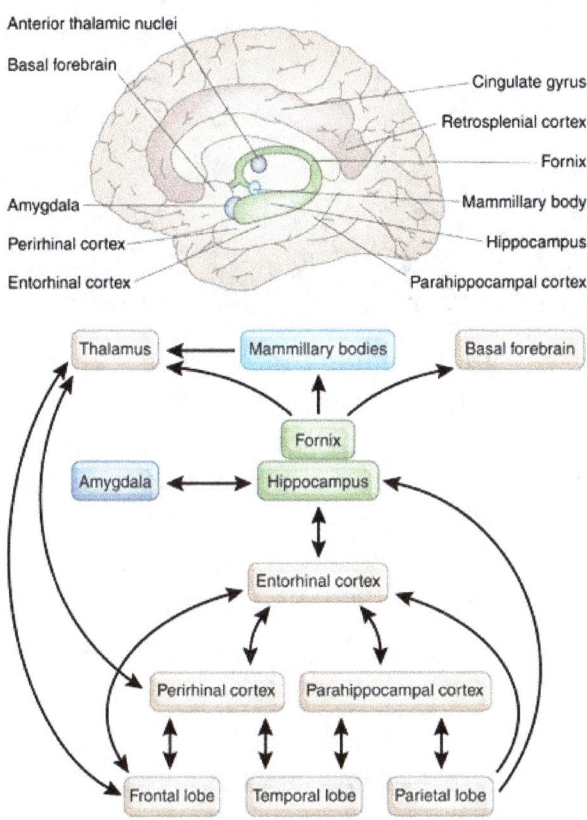

Epigenetic research demonstrates that experience leaves biological traces. Stress, trauma, nourishment, and emotional environments influence how genes express themselves—not only within a single lifetime, but across generations. These changes do not alter DNA sequences; they modify how DNA responds. In this way, bodies carry histories. What was once adaptive for survival can quietly shape physiology, emotional regulation, and behavior long after the original threat has passed.

Neurobiology adds further depth. The nervous system is not an isolated processor—it is relational and predictive. Patterns of safety and threat are learned through repeated experience and passed forward through caregiving behaviors, attachment styles, and stress responses. Infants inherit not only genes, but **regulated or dysregulated nervous systems** shaped by their caregivers' unresolved experiences. Memory, here, is not stored as narrative alone; it is stored as tone, posture, reactivity, and expectation.

Systems theory completes the picture by revealing how patterns persist within interconnected systems until something changes the conditions. Families, communities, and cultures operate as living systems governed by feedback loops. When a pattern is adaptive, it stabilizes. When it becomes maladaptive but remains unexamined, it repeats. Repetition is not pathology—it is information waiting for awareness. Once awareness enters the system, the pattern can reorganize.

This convergence of science reframes what many cultures have always known: **stories live in bodies**, not as metaphor, but as measurable reality. Grief unexpressed becomes tension. Silence becomes hypervigilance. Survival strategies become inherited defaults. Patterns repeat not because people fail to move on, but because systems move toward coherence using the tools they already know.

Seen through this lens, cultural remembrance was never superstition. It was **applied wisdom**—a practical understanding of how memory, meaning, and survival transmit through time. Ritual, storytelling, ceremony, and ancestor veneration were not symbolic indulgences. They were technologies of regulation, integration, and continuity.

Science is not disproving ancestral knowledge.
It is finally learning how to name it.

What was once spoken through myth, ritual, and land-based knowing is now echoed through data and diagrams. Both are pointing to the same conclusion: **healing requires relationship, awareness, and time**. And when awareness becomes conscious—within a person, a family, or a generation—memory stops repeating itself as fate and begins transforming itself into wisdom.

This is not new knowledge.
It is remembered knowledge—now spoken in a language

modern science is finally able to understand.

Remembrance as Responsibility, Not Burden

Ancestral remembrance is often misunderstood as something heavy—an inheritance of guilt, obligation, or emotional debt owed to the past. In truth, remembrance is not about carrying what was suffered. It is about **entering relationship** with what is still speaking. Relationship implies dialogue, discernment, and choice—not submission.

To remember ancestors is not to live inside their pain. It is to listen for the wisdom embedded within it and decide —consciously—how that wisdom will move forward through your life.

Remembrance does not demand loyalty through suffering. It invites **participation through awareness**.

When the past is ignored, it continues to speak through pattern. When it is acknowledged, it begins to speak through insight. This is the difference between repetition and responsibility. Responsibility does not mean fixing everything or atoning for what came before. It means recognizing that you stand at a point in time where awareness makes response possible.

To remember is not to be trapped.
It is to be **informed**.

Information changes how systems behave. When you understand why a pattern exists—where it came from, what it once protected—you no longer have to fight it blindly. You can decide whether it still serves. Awareness creates space between impulse and action, inheritance and choice.

This is where agency returns.

When remembrance is paired with awareness, **choice emerges naturally**. Not forced choice, not moral pressure—but clarity. You begin to see when a reaction belongs to history rather than the present moment. You recognize when a fear is inherited rather than immediate. You notice when a silence is protective rather than truthful.

In that noticing, you gain options.

Responsibility, then, is not about carrying weight. It is about **carrying understanding**. Understanding allows you to choose what continues and what completes. It allows you to honor the past without reenacting it. It allows you to transform inheritance into intention.

This is the quiet power of remembrance done well. It does not bind you to what was. It positions you to decide what will be.

And in that decision—made again and again with awareness—the lineage does not remain stuck in memory.

It moves forward, informed, lighter, and more free.

The Living Continuum

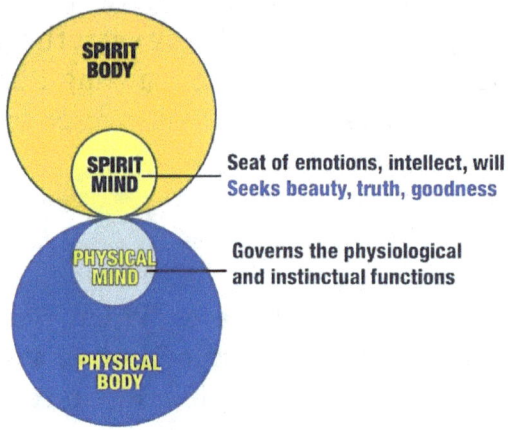

Spiral Dynamics

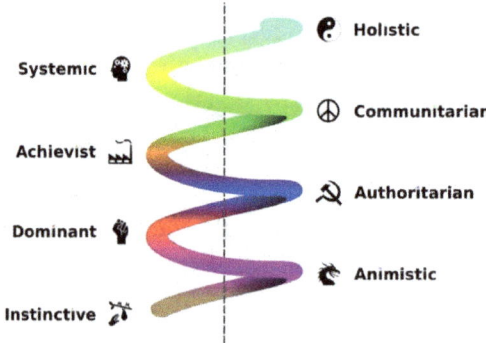

You are not separate from those who came before you, and you are not overshadowed by them. You are not living in their shadow—you are living **through** a continuum they helped carry forward. Lineage is not a hierarchy of past over present; it is a **flow of becoming**, where each generation inherits not only history, but possibility.

In this living continuum, memory, biology, spirit, and story converge. What your ancestors experienced shaped the terrain you were born into—physiologically, emotionally, culturally, and spiritually. What you experience now reshapes that terrain for those who follow. The continuum is not static. It is responsive, adaptive, and alive.

These traditions understood something essential: **consciousness changes inheritance**. When one generation becomes aware—of patterns, of wounds, of strengths—the entire lineage benefits. Healing does not remain contained within one body or one lifetime. It ripples outward, altering relational dynamics, stress responses, and expectations about what is possible. Wisdom accumulates not as abstract knowledge, but as embodied choice.

This is why ancestral healing has such quiet power. It may not announce itself with dramatic events, yet it **lightens the future**. Children inherit calmer nervous systems. Descendants inherit fewer unspoken rules. Choices expand where once there were only reactions. The continuum becomes more spacious.

This is not romanticism.
It is **inheritance made conscious**.

When inheritance remains unconscious, it governs behavior from behind the scenes—through repetition, compulsion, and unexplained pull. When it becomes conscious, it transforms into guidance. Patterns become information. History becomes context rather than constraint.

In that consciousness, ancestral memory stops being a weight to carry and becomes a **ground to stand on**. It offers orientation rather than obligation, belonging rather than burden. You begin to feel connected without being confined, rooted without being restricted.

Belonging, here, is not about sameness. It is about **continuity with integrity**—the knowing that you are part of something larger that supports your growth rather than competes with it. You do not have to disappear to honor the past. You do not have to suffer to prove loyalty.

You are the place where memory becomes choice, where biology meets meaning, where story turns forward. The living continuum does not ask you to be perfect. It asks you to be present.

And when you are—when awareness enters the stream—the lineage does not just remember.
It **evolves**.

Reclaiming Lineage Blessings and Talents

Lineage carries brilliance as well as pain. While much attention is rightly given to inherited wounds, an equally powerful truth often goes unnamed: **your ancestors also passed down extraordinary capacities**. These are not abstract ideals. They are embodied intelligences—ways of seeing, creating, leading, healing, adapting, and enduring that once ensured survival and continuity.

Across generations, lineage transmits **creativity**—the ability to imagine solutions where none appear to exist. It transmits **leadership**—the instinct to organize, protect, and guide in moments of uncertainty. It transmits **spiritual sensitivity**—attunement to subtle cues, intuition, and meaning beyond the visible. It carries **healing capacity**—the ability to soothe, restore, and regulate within relationships and communities. It carries **innovation**—the courage to adapt under pressure—and **endurance**—the stamina to persist when conditions are harsh.

Many of these gifts went unused or unrecognized—not because they were absent, but because the environments in which your ancestors lived were **hostile to their expression**. Creativity may have been dangerous. Leadership may have invited punishment. Spiritual insight may have been outlawed or ridiculed. Healing gifts may have been necessary for others' survival, leaving no space for the healer's own flourishing. Innovation may have been constrained by rigid systems. Endurance became the priority because survival demanded it.

What could not be expressed did not disappear.
It **waited**.

Gifts, like wounds, follow conditions. They emerge where

there is safety, recognition, and permission. You may be the generation where those conditions finally exist— where creative expression does not threaten survival, where leadership can be ethical and visible, where spiritual insight can be explored without fear, where healing can be reciprocal rather than sacrificial.

Reclaiming lineage blessings is not about claiming superiority or romanticizing the past. It is about **recovering wholeness**. When only pain is acknowledged, the lineage remains incomplete. When gifts are named and embodied, balance returns. Strength is no longer defined only by endurance; it includes joy, expression, and contribution.

This reclamation often feels like remembrance rather than acquisition. Talents may surface as a sense of familiarity— an ease with certain skills, a pull toward particular forms of expression, a knowing that feels older than personal experience. These are not coincidences. They are **continuities**.

When you allow these gifts to emerge, you are not taking anything away from the past. You are **fulfilling it**. You become a safe vessel for what was once suppressed, completing a circuit that could not close before.

Lineage healing is not only about resolving pain.
It is about **liberating brilliance**.

And when ancestral talents are finally expressed in conditions of safety and awareness, the lineage does more than heal. It **flourishes forward**—passing down not just survival strategies, but living proof that what was once hidden can now thrive.

You are not inventing these gifts.
You are giving them a future.

What To Take Away From This Chapter

This chapter reframes destiny through a wider, more honest

lens—one that extends beyond individual identity and into the living architecture of lineage. You are not only becoming yourself. You are also completing, correcting, and continuing a story that began long before you arrived. Your life is both personal and participatory, shaped by inheritance and shaped again by choice.

In this framework, purpose is not self-centered. It is **ancestrally informed**. The impulses, callings, sensitivities, and talents that feel deeply "yours" are often responses to what was unfinished or unexpressed in the lineage. This does not diminish individuality; it deepens it. You are not losing yourself to history—you are discovering yourself **within context**.

When you heal yourself, you are not only changing your own future. You are altering the **trajectory of memory** that will move forward through children, communities, and generations yet to come. Regulation replaces reactivity. Awareness interrupts repetition. Choice enters where compulsion once ruled. The future inherits something lighter, more spacious, and more coherent because of decisions you make now.

This chapter is not about blame. It does not ask you to carry guilt for what your ancestors endured, nor does it suggest that suffering was deserved or necessary. It is about **responsibility held with compassion**—the responsibility that naturally arises when awareness becomes available. Responsibility here does not mean fixing everything. It means recognizing that you stand at a point in time where different responses are possible.

You are not responsible for the wounds of the past.
But you are uniquely positioned to decide **what continues**.

That decision does not require perfection. It requires presence. Each time you pause instead of react, speak instead of silence, choose instead of comply, you participate in destiny as an active force rather than a passive inheritance.

And that choice—made consciously, repeatedly, and with care—is one of the most powerful expressions of destiny there is.

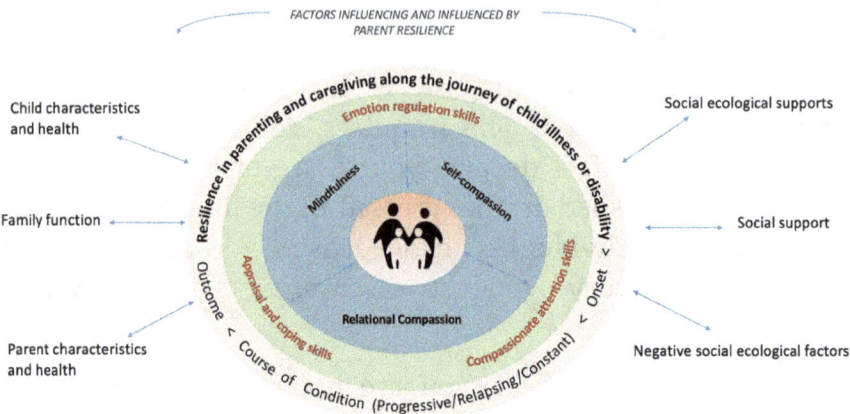

Reflection Prompt

What patterns in your life feel older than you are—and what gifts might be waiting beneath them?

CHAPTER 7

Activation Points: Destiny Through Experience

This chapter explores a truth that is both confronting and liberating: **destiny does not awaken through comfort alone**. While stability can support integration, it rarely initiates transformation. Destiny activates through **experience**—particularly experiences that interrupt the familiar and require a reorganization of perception, identity, and response.

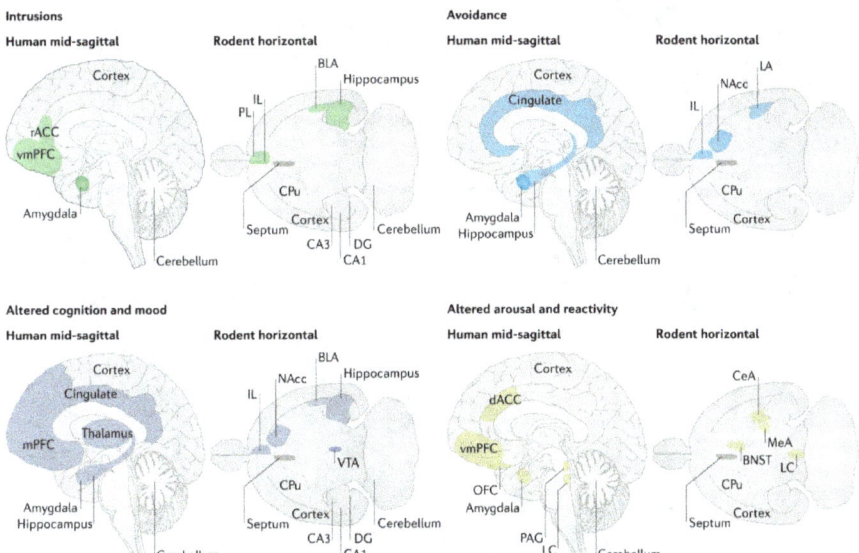

This does not mean that suffering is necessary or virtuous. It means that **experience is the medium through which consciousness evolves**. When life unfolds predictably, the nervous system relies on existing strategies. When rupture occurs—through loss, challenge, transition, or uncertainty—those strategies are tested. If they fail, something new must emerge. That emergence is awakening.

Challenge acts as a signal, not a sentence. It communicates that a previous level of functioning is no longer sufficient for what life is asking next. In this way, disruption is not opposition to destiny—it is **its delivery mechanism**. Transition creates the conditions in which latent capacities are forced into expression, not by choice, but by necessity.

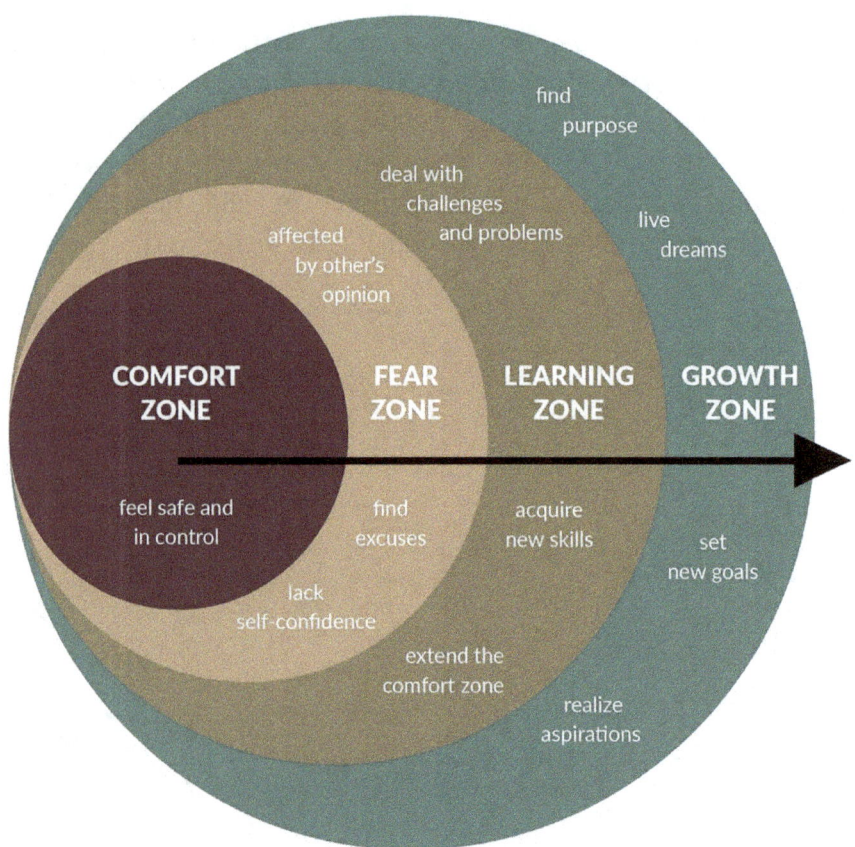

Experience is the language through which consciousness reorganizes itself because it engages the whole system. Insight alone does not rewire neural pathways. Intention alone does not reshape identity. **Embodied experience—** what is felt, navigated, endured, and integrated—is what transforms the brain, the nervous system, and the sense of self. Growth happens not because something is understood intellectually, but because something has been *lived through* and metabolized.

Here, destiny is no longer abstract or philosophical. It is not a future concept or a theoretical path waiting to be discovered. It is **immediate and embodied**, emerging through the way you respond to what life places in front of you. Destiny reveals itself in real time—through the choices you make under pressure, the truths you acknowledge in transition, and the capacities you discover when the old way no longer holds.

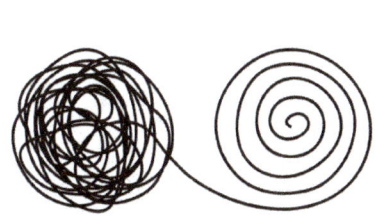 

When destiny is lived, it stops feeling distant or mysterious. It becomes recognizable as the **through-line** that connects experience to meaning. Not everything that happens is chosen —but how you engage with what happens determines what it activates. In this sense, destiny is not found by seeking certainty. It is revealed through **participation**.

This chapter invites a reframing: challenges are not detours from destiny; they are often its thresholds. And when you meet experience with awareness, curiosity, and presence, destiny stops waiting for the "right time" and begins unfolding **now**, in the life you are already living.

Challenges as Coded Awakenings

12 Sacred Buddhist Spiritual Symbols

 Lotus Flower: Rising from adversity, Spiritual purity

 Treasure Vase: Spiritual and material abundance

 Bodhi Tree: Enlightenment, Buddha's awakening

 Banner of Victory: Overcoming obstacles, spiritual triumph

 Fig Tree: Wisdom, Abundance, Success

 Symbol of Buddha: Enlightenment, inner peace.

 Dharma Wheel: Buddha's teachings, Path to enlightenment

 Third Eye: Intuition, spiritual insight

 Conch Shell: Spiritual awakening, Spread of dharma

 Infinity Knot: Endless cycles, eternal continuity.

 Golden Fish: Happiness, freedom from suffering.

 Begging Bowl: Simplicity, spiritual rather than material

MEANINGFUL SYMBOLS

Lotus
A symbol of purity and spiritual awakening, rising above challenges.

Om
The sacred sound of the universe, representing inner peace and unity.

Tree of Life
A symbol of growth, strength, and interconnectedness.

Mandala
A symbol of wholeness, meditation, and cosmic unity.

Hamsa
A protective symbol of blessings, strength, and good fortune.

Dharma Wheel
A guide to wisdom, truth, and the path to enlightenment.

Yin Yang
The balance of opposites, reminding us of harmony in life.

Endless Knot
A symbol of eternity, connection, and the flow of life.

Triskel
A sign of motion and progress, symbolizing life's cycles.

Buddha Groove
Sterling Silver Ring

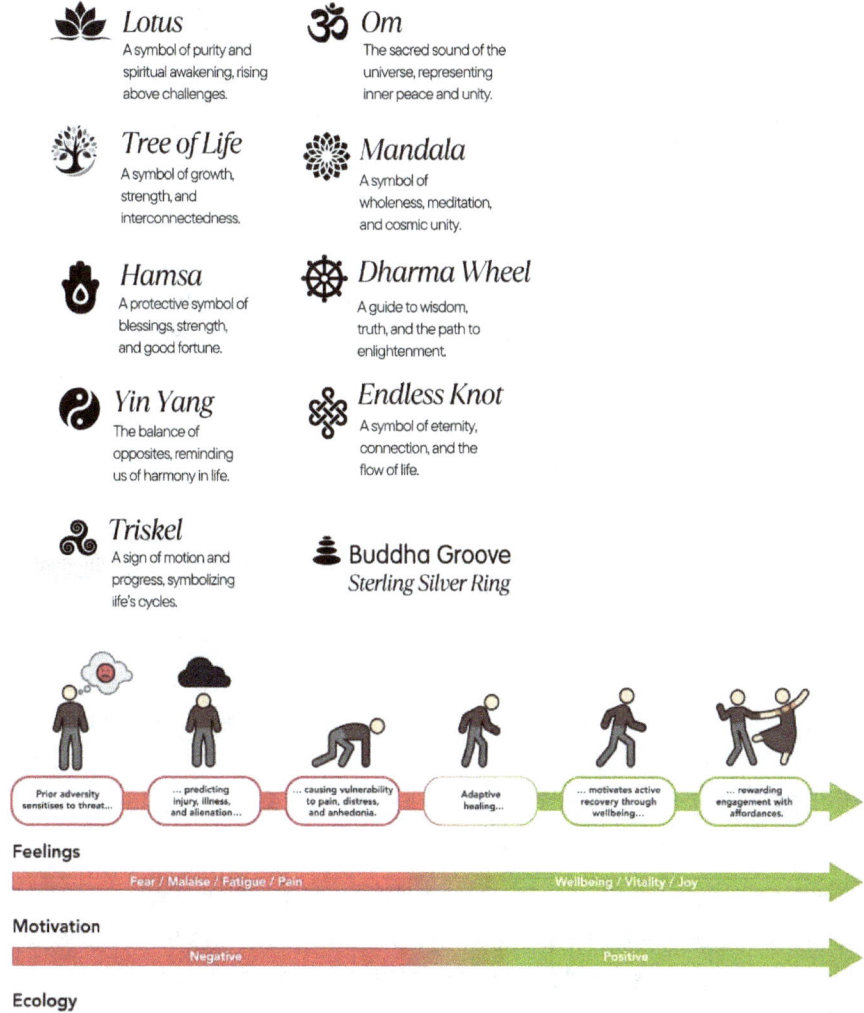

Life challenges are not random disruptions to an otherwise orderly path. They are **activation points**—precise moments where life applies pressure in order to reveal what has not yet been fully expressed. While challenges often feel destabilizing, their deeper function is organizational. They rearrange priorities, expose misalignments, and force the system to confront its own limits.

When the nervous system encounters conditions it cannot meet with familiar strategies, it is compelled to adapt. Old coping mechanisms—avoidance, compliance, control, or dissociation—no longer provide resolution. In that moment, the system either collapses or **evolves**. Adaptation is not a sign of weakness. It is intelligence responding to new demand. That adaptive response—when supported by awareness—is awakening.

Every major challenge carries **encoded information**. It reveals what no longer works by exhausting it. Patterns that once maintained safety begin to fail, signaling that their usefulness has expired. Challenges also illuminate what must be released —relationships, environments, beliefs, or identities that once fit but now restrict growth. Just as importantly, difficulty exposes latent strengths that comfort never required you to access: resilience, discernment, courage, clarity, and self-trust.

Awakening does not arrive as sudden enlightenment. It emerges through **forced honesty**. Challenge strips away illusion by making incongruence unbearable. You can no longer pretend something is working when it is not. This clarity, while uncomfortable, is liberating. It marks the moment where choice becomes unavoidable.

Destiny does not unfold when life goes according to plan. Plans preserve existing identity. Destiny unfolds when reality demands an **upgrade**—in perception, in behavior, and in how you understand who you are. Challenges do not appear to derail destiny. They appear to **initiate it**, calling forth capacities that were always present but never required until now.

Seen this way, difficulty is not evidence that you are off path. It is often evidence that you are standing at a threshold. When challenges are met consciously—rather than resisted or personalized—they become gateways. And through those gateways, destiny moves from abstraction into lived embodiment, one adaptive response at a time.

Karmic Relationships as Catalysts, Not Destinations

Some of the most powerful activation points in a life arrive through **relationships**. Not all connections are designed for longevity. Karmic relationships—romantic, familial, professional, or spiritual—enter at precise moments to **accelerate transformation**, not to guarantee permanence. Their intensity is not an accident; it is the mechanism through which insight becomes unavoidable.

These relationships act as mirrors. They **expose unconscious patterns** by pulling them into the foreground—attachment styles, boundary habits, conflict responses, and unexamined beliefs about worth and safety. What remains hidden in solitude becomes visible in connection. Through proximity, the psyche reveals itself.

Karmic relationships also **trigger unresolved wounds**. This is not cruelty; it is efficiency. When a relationship reliably activates old pain, it highlights exactly where integration is still needed. The nervous system reacts because the lesson is active. The body responds before the mind can rationalize. In this way, the relationship becomes a diagnostic tool—showing where healing has stalled and where attention is required.

Equally important, these connections **mirror disowned aspects of the self**. Traits you admire, resent, fear, or idealize in another often point to qualities you have not fully claimed or integrated. The relationship brings these aspects into view so they can be reclaimed, regulated, or expressed with maturity rather than projection.

Because they compress learning, karmic relationships **accelerate emotional and spiritual growth**. Growth that might take years in isolation can unfold rapidly within relational intensity. This acceleration often feels destabilizing, but it is purposeful. The system is being asked to reorganize at a higher level of coherence.

Their purpose, however, is not comfort. It is **revelation**. Comfort stabilizes; revelation transforms. When the lesson embedded in the connection is integrated—when boundaries are learned, self-trust is restored, or truth is spoken—the relationship frequently **changes form or ends**. This is not failure. It is completion.

Endings in this context are not losses; they are **closures of curriculum**. The relationship fulfilled its role by activating growth. Staying beyond that point can recreate pain without producing new insight. Leaving honors the learning rather than repeating the wound.

Seen clearly, karmic relationships are not punishments or mistakes. They are **initiations**—arriving when you are capable of learning what they came to teach. When you release the expectation that every meaningful relationship must be permanent, you gain the freedom to receive its wisdom fully.

And when a karmic relationship completes, it does not disappear from your life story. It becomes integrated as understanding—quietly reshaping how you relate, choose, and love going forward. That is its gift.

Why You Cannot Grow Where You Were Hurt

The saying *"you cannot grow in the same space where you were hurt"* is not a metaphor meant only for emotional encouragement. It reflects a **neurobiological reality** about how the brain and nervous system encode experience. Trauma does not live solely in memory; it lives in **context**. The brain records not just what happened, but where it happened, with whom, and under what conditions.

ENCODED IN THE STARS | 321

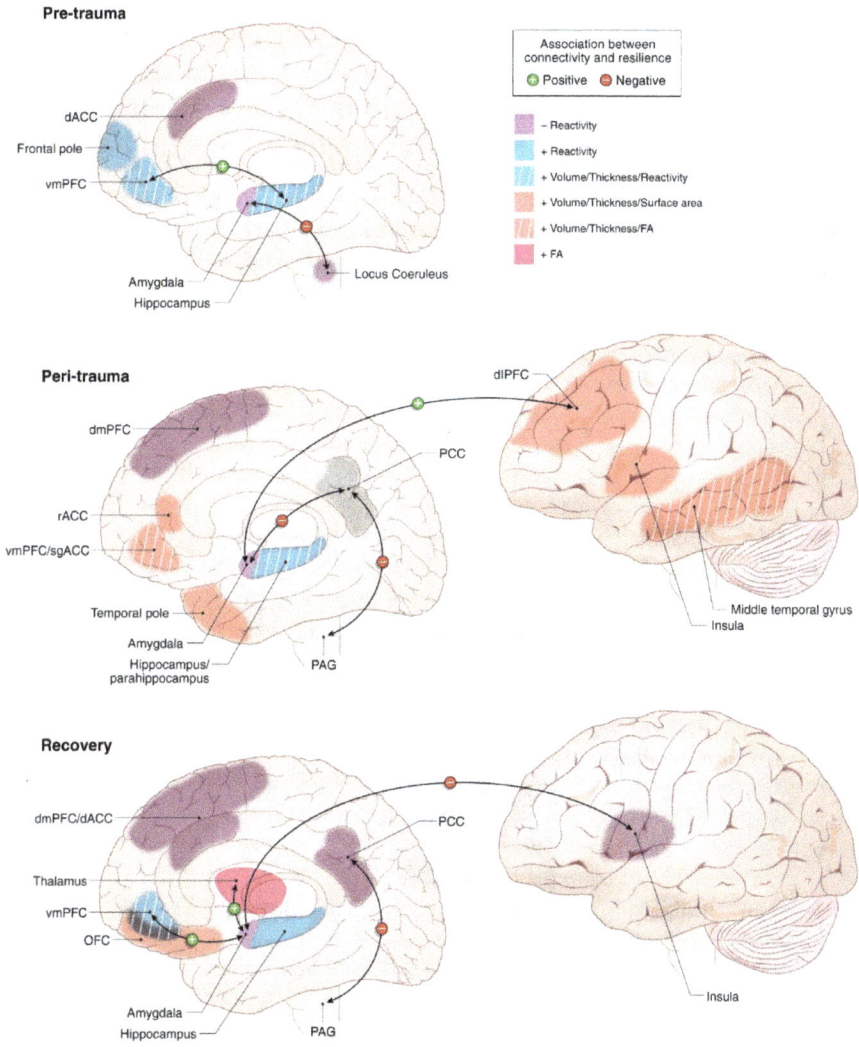

When harm occurs, the nervous system links threat to environment. Places, people, routines, and even sensory cues —lighting, smells, sounds, time of day—become encoded as signals of danger. This is an adaptive survival mechanism. The brain's priority becomes vigilance, not expansion. It scans for threat, conserves energy, and limits risk. In such a state, growth is biologically deprioritized.

Remaining in an environment associated with trauma forces the nervous system to stay in **protective mode**. Even if conscious understanding has shifted, the body continues to react to familiar cues. This is why people can intellectually "know" they are safe yet still feel anxious, frozen, or depleted. The body remembers the context before the mind can intervene.

1. **Evolution of social cooperation** – benefits to reproductive fitness from cooperative behavior

2. **Motivational drivers of social cooperation** – emotional distress in response to anticipated or experienced social exclusion

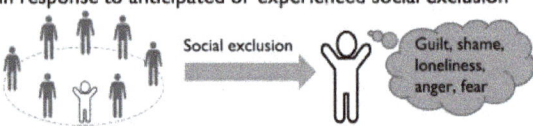

3. **Alleviation of distress and social reintegration** – empathy, emotional contagion, compassion, and consoling behaviors reduce distress and restore social connections

4. **Use of symbolic healing to alleviate distress and restore social connection** – cultural evolution components of symbolism, language, and symbolic group identity used in specific healer roles

Ultimate-level explanations (1–2)
Proximate-level explanations (3–4)

Conditions where psychological healing is less likely.
a. Not a member of social group, or a perceived threat to social group
b. Difference in life experience or social class
c. Professional cultural symbols that are not shared
d. Lack of belief in abilities of the healer
e. Healing lacks social inclusion component
f. Discriminatory healing institution
g. Healing techniques or technologies impede empathy
h. Lack of touch or physical movement
i. Emotional distress of healer (e.g., burnout)

Conditions where psychological healing is more likely.
a. Perceived group membership
b. Shared life experience
c. Shared cultural symbols
d. Belief in abilities of the healer
e. Healing involves social inclusion
f. Healing institution is welcoming to all group members
g. Healing techniques or technologies promote empathy
h. Use of touch or physical movement
i. Emotional well-being of healer (e.g., healer's ability for emotion regulation)

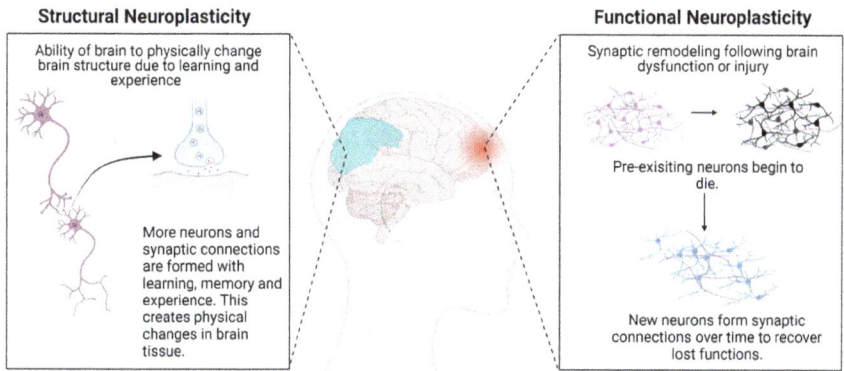

Healing, therefore, requires **novelty**. New sensory input gives the brain information it has never associated with harm. New relational patterns demonstrate that connection can occur without threat. New spatial contexts—different cities, homes, routines, or even redesigned personal spaces—send a powerful signal: *this is not the same environment where danger occurred.* That signal allows the nervous system to downshift from survival into learning.

Leaving a harmful environment is not avoidance. It is **biological wisdom**.

Avoidance is reactive and fear-driven. Wisdom is responsive and restorative. Choosing distance from harm creates the conditions for regulation. Once the nervous system settles, neuroplasticity increases. The brain becomes more flexible. New neural pathways form. Identity expands beyond survival adaptations.

In new environments, the brain can **re-map safety**. Experiences that were once impossible—rest, curiosity, trust, creativity—become accessible. Regulation replaces hypervigilance. Learning replaces bracing. Growth becomes not only possible, but natural.

This does not mean the past is erased. It means the body is finally given the opportunity to update its expectations.

Healing does not happen because you leave; it happens because leaving creates the conditions where healing can occur.

Growth requires space—neural, emotional, and physical. And when the environment supports safety, the system no longer has to defend itself against the past. It can invest energy in the future.

This is not weakness.
It is the intelligence of a nervous system choosing **life beyond survival**.

The Neuroscience of Transformation and Post-Traumatic Growth

Neuroscience has fundamentally overturned the old belief that the brain is static after childhood. Research on **neuroplasticity** demonstrates that the brain is continually reorganizing itself in response to experience, environment, and meaning. Neural pathways strengthen with use, weaken with disuse, and reconfigure when circumstances demand new strategies for survival or adaptation.

Trauma disrupts neural networks by forcing the brain into prolonged states of threat detection. Circuits related to fear, vigilance, and stress response become overactive, while systems responsible for integration, reflection, and emotional regulation may go offline. This disruption is not damage in a moral or permanent sense—it is **adaptation under pressure**. The brain reorganizes itself to survive.

What neuroscience now confirms is that disruption does not have to be the end of the story. When the nervous system is given safety, support, and new experiences, the brain can **rewire itself again**—this time toward integration rather than protection. Growth does not happen by suppressing trauma, but by allowing the system to reorganize around new information that contradicts the original threat.

This is where the concept of **post-traumatic growth** emerges. Longitudinal studies have shown that many individuals, following significant adversity, experience measurable psychological and neurological shifts—not despite trauma, but through the process of integrating it. These shifts often include increased resilience, as the nervous system learns it can survive and adapt. They include deeper meaning-making, as the brain searches for coherence after disruption. Empathy expands as lived experience deepens relational understanding. Purpose clarifies because life is no longer taken for granted.

Importantly, post-traumatic growth does not mean trauma was "worth it," nor does it imply that pain disappears. Growth does not erase pain. It **recontextualizes** it. The brain reframes chaotic, overwhelming experience into structured understanding. What once felt senseless becomes informative. What once hijacked the nervous system becomes part of an integrated narrative.

From a neurological perspective, this reframing is profound. When meaning is established, stress responses decrease. Memory networks become less reactive. The brain no longer treats the past as an ongoing emergency. Chaos becomes **information**, and information becomes guidance.

Transformation, then, is not a return to who you were before trauma. It is the emergence of a more complex, adaptive, and conscious system than existed prior. The brain does not simply recover—it **evolves**.

This is why destiny so often unfolds after disruption. Trauma shakes the system out of rigid patterns. Growth emerges when that disruption is met with support, awareness, and new experience. In this way, neuroscience confirms a deep truth echoed across spiritual traditions: breakdown can become breakthrough—not by accident, but by **reorganization guided by meaning**.

Post-traumatic growth is not about glorifying suffering.
It is about recognizing the brain's extraordinary capacity to transform experience into wisdom when the conditions for healing are finally present.

Why Chaos Activates the Next Level

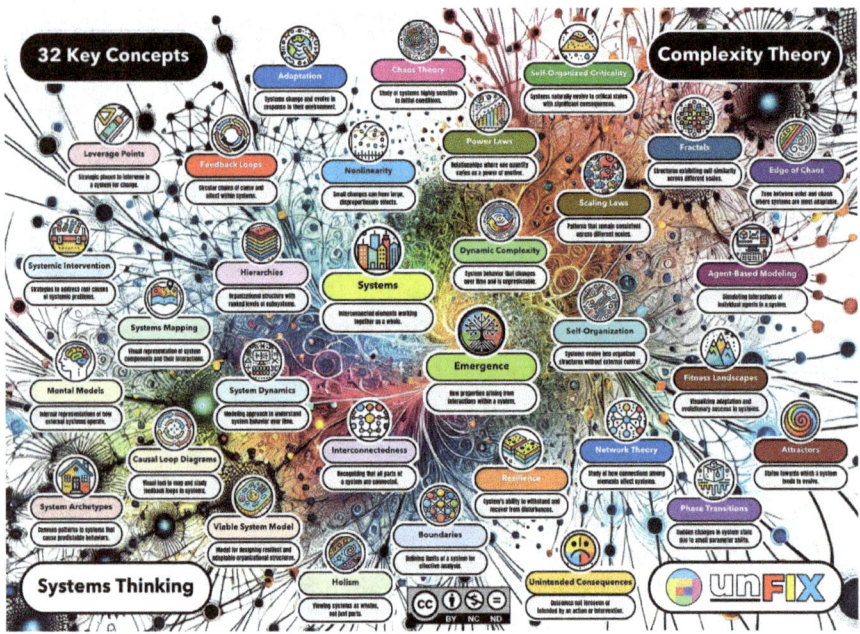

From the lens of **chaos theory**, living systems do not evolve by remaining stable. They evolve when they are pushed **far from equilibrium**—to a point where existing structures can no longer maintain coherence. In stability, a system repeats itself efficiently. In disruption, it must reorganize or collapse. Evolution chooses reorganization.

This principle applies to ecosystems, weather patterns, economies—and human lives.

When conditions are familiar and predictable, the nervous system conserves energy by relying on established patterns. Identity stabilizes around what works well enough. Beliefs, behaviors, and relationships settle into grooves. This is not a failure; it is efficiency. **Comfort preserves identity** by reducing the need for adaptation.

But preservation is not expansion.

Disruption—loss, transition, conflict, uncertainty—pushes the system beyond what its current organization can handle. Old strategies no longer regulate emotion. Old identities no longer explain experience. The familiar frame cracks. In chaos theory, this moment is called a **bifurcation point**—a threshold where the system must either regress or reorganize at a higher level of complexity.

Spiritually and neurologically, this is initiation.

Chaos activates new capacities because it **demands new information processing**. The brain forms new neural pathways. The psyche integrates previously split-off aspects. Meaning-making deepens. Identity expands to include complexity that comfort never required. This is not linear growth; it is **phase change**—a shift in how the system is organized.

Disruption transforms identity not by destroying it, but by **outgrowing its container**. What once fit no longer does. What once defined you becomes insufficient. This can feel like disorientation, grief, or fear—but it is also the birthplace of insight, courage, and coherence at a higher order.

Destiny activates precisely here—when the familiar can no longer contain who you are becoming. The old life may still exist, but it no longer matches your internal frequency. The system senses mismatch and seeks alignment. Chaos is the signal that expansion is overdue.

Seen this way, chaos is not the enemy of destiny. It is **its catalyst**.

It clears space where stagnation once lived. It interrupts loops that could not end on their own. It creates the instability required for reorganization—neurologically, psychologically, and spiritually. Without disruption, the next level remains inaccessible because the current level is sufficient.

Chaos does not promise ease. It promises **possibility**.

And when met with presence rather than resistance, it becomes the gateway through which destiny moves from potential into embodiment—reorganizing your life not back into what was, but forward into what can finally hold who you are becoming.

Leaving the Comfort Zone as a Biological Upgrade

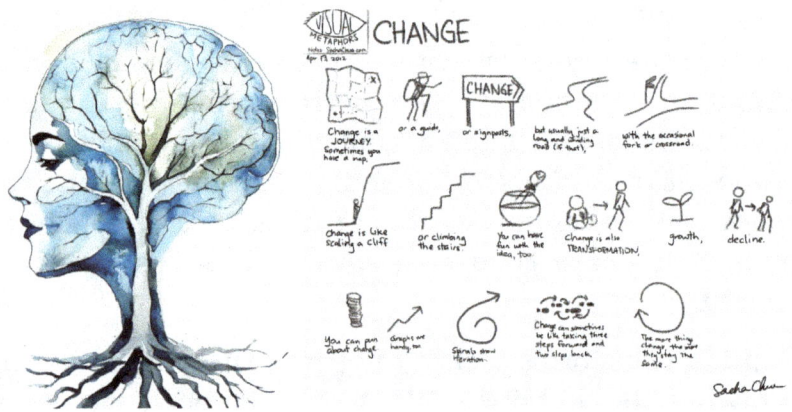

Stepping beyond the known is not reckless—it is **developmental**. From a biological perspective, growth requires exposure to novelty. The brain evolves by encountering conditions it has not yet mastered. When experience stretches beyond familiar parameters, neural circuits are forced to reorganize. New challenges stimulate new pathways; new demands recruit latent capacities; new environments invite the nervous system to update its expectations about what is possible.

Comfort zones are efficient, but efficiency is not evolution. Within the familiar, the brain relies on established routes that conserve energy. Identity stabilizes around what has already been learned. This is useful for maintenance—but insufficient for transformation. Expansion begins when familiarity can no longer meet the complexity of lived experience.

New risks demand new capacities. Courage, discernment, adaptability, and self-trust do not develop in theory; they develop in response to uncertainty. When the system encounters situations that cannot be navigated by old strategies, it must innovate. This innovation is not psychological bravado—it is **biological upgrading**. The nervous system learns to regulate under new conditions, and the brain integrates information it previously had no reason to process.

New environments require new versions of the self. A change in context—geographic, relational, professional, or internal—alters sensory input and relational dynamics. This shift signals the brain that prior assumptions may no longer apply. As a result, identity loosens its grip on outdated roles and reorganizes around present reality. What once defined you becomes a starting point rather than a boundary.

This is why transitions often feel destabilizing. What feels like loss is often **initiation**—the shedding of identities that cannot accompany you forward. Grief arises not only from what ends, but from the nervous system releasing a structure that once ensured safety. That release is necessary for something larger to take shape.

What feels like chaos is often **recalibration**. The system is not failing; it is adjusting. During recalibration, uncertainty increases because new reference points have not yet stabilized. With time, support, and awareness, coherence returns—at a higher level of integration than before.

Leaving the comfort zone does not mean abandoning discernment. It means recognizing when safety has become stagnation. Growth asks for calculated exposure, not reckless overwhelm. When expansion is met gradually and consciously, the nervous system adapts without collapse.

Biologically, this is how evolution occurs. Psychologically, this is how identity matures. Spiritually, this is how destiny moves from potential into form.

You are not betraying yourself by leaving what once worked. You are responding to the intelligence that knows **what worked before cannot carry you where you are going**.

And when you step beyond the familiar—not to prove strength, but to answer readiness—you do not lose yourself. You **upgrade**.

The Core Teaching of This Chapter

The core teaching of this chapter is both simple and profound: **experience is the mechanism of awakening**. Life does not reveal destiny through comfort, certainty, or avoidance of pain. It reveals destiny through **engagement**—through moments that challenge the familiar and demand a deeper level of presence, honesty, and adaptability.

Every challenge is a **code of awakening**. It arrives carrying information about what is outdated, what is misaligned, and what is ready to evolve. Challenges do not appear to punish or derail; they surface when existing structures—internal or external—can no longer support the next stage of growth. What feels disruptive is often the system alerting you that expansion is required.

Every disruption carries **instruction**. When routines break, relationships shift, or identities dissolve, something essential is being communicated. Disruption strips away automatic behavior and reveals where consciousness has been operating on habit rather than intention. It forces attention. It asks for awareness. And in doing so, it creates the conditions for insight that stability rarely provides.

Every ending creates a **threshold**. Endings are not voids; they are passages. They mark the point where the old configuration releases its hold and a new one begins to form. Thresholds are uncomfortable because reference points disappear. Yet it is precisely within this uncertainty that choice becomes available. What you step into next is shaped by how consciously you move through the ending.

Destiny does not unfold by avoiding difficulty. Avoidance preserves what already exists. Destiny unfolds by **meeting experience consciously**—by staying present with what is happening without collapsing into blame, fear, or resignation. Conscious engagement transforms experience from something endured into something integrated.

This chapter invites a shift in orientation. Rather than asking, *"Why is this happening to me?"*—a question that centers powerlessness—it invites you to ask, *"What is this experience activating in me?"* This question restores agency. It recognizes that even when circumstances are not chosen, **response remains available**.

When experience is met with awareness, destiny stops being something that happens to you. It becomes something that **moves through you**—expressed through the way you adapt, choose, and embody growth. Destiny, then, is not a fixed endpoint or predetermined script. It is the unfolding intelligence revealed through conscious participation in life as it actually occurs.

The challenges you face are not interruptions of destiny. They are its **language**.

And when you learn to listen—not with fear, but with curiosity and presence—life begins to speak with clarity. What once felt chaotic becomes instructive. What once felt random reveals pattern. And destiny, no longer distant or abstract, becomes something you live—moment by moment, through the courage to meet experience as it is and allow it to transform you.

CHAPTER 8

Synchronicity and The Language of the Universe

The Universe Speaks in Pattern

This chapter explores one of the most quietly powerful dimensions of destiny: **the way the universe communicates through pattern, timing, and meaningful coincidence**. Long before formal language, before science named probability, and before philosophy systematized thought, humans learned to orient themselves by reading the world as a living text. The seasons taught rhythm. The moon taught timing. The stars taught cycles. Animals, weather, dreams, and repetition taught meaning.

These early forms of knowing were not naïve. They were **relational**.

Humans learned that certain moments carried weight—not because they were dramatic, but because they *aligned*. A birth during a particular season, a chance encounter at a crossroads, a repeated symbol appearing at a moment of decision—these experiences felt too precise to dismiss as random. They did not demand belief. They demanded **attention**.

Synchronicity names this experience: the moment when **inner experience and outer events mirror one another** in ways that feel purposeful rather than accidental. It is not about predicting the future or assigning magical explanations to everything that happens. It is about recognizing when probability organizes itself around meaning. The event itself may be ordinary. The *timing* is what makes it extraordinary.

This is why synchronicity is not superstition. It is **pattern recognition with context**. It requires discernment, not blind faith. The meaning does not live in the symbol alone—it lives in the relationship between the symbol and the moment in which it appears. A repeated number means nothing in isolation. A repeated number appearing at a moment of uncertainty, decision, or transition becomes information.

In synchronicity, the universe does not shout. It **reflects**. It mirrors what is already stirring within you—questions you are asking, thresholds you are approaching, alignments you are testing. The signal is subtle because it respects agency. It offers feedback, not instruction.

Here, destiny speaks softly—but clearly.

It does not override choice. It refines it. It does not remove uncertainty. It provides orientation within it. When you learn to listen to pattern without projecting meaning, to timing without forcing interpretation, and to coincidence without dismissing curiosity, the world begins to feel responsive rather than indifferent.

Synchronicity does not make life predictable.
It makes life **conversational**.

And in that conversation, destiny is no longer a distant script waiting to be revealed. It becomes an unfolding dialogue—one that responds as you do, adjusts as you do, and guides not through control, but through **coherence**.

This chapter invites you to reclaim an ancient skill with modern discernment: the ability to recognize when life is speaking—and to listen without fear, fixation, or fantasy.

Because when awareness sharpens, the universe does not need to be loud.
Its patterns are already speaking—quietly, precisely, and right on time.

Synchronicity as Meaningful Pattern

The term **synchronicity** was formally articulated by **Carl Jung**, who described it as an *acausal connecting principle*—a phenomenon in which events are meaningfully related without a direct cause-and-effect link. In other words, two events occur together not because one *caused* the other, but because they share **meaning within a specific context**.

This distinction is crucial. Synchronicity does not deny causality; it simply asserts that causality is not the only organizing principle of reality. Some events align not through mechanical force, but through **semantic resonance**—they "fit" together in a way that communicates something to the observer. Meaning itself becomes the connective tissue.

Synchronicity challenges the assumption that reality is governed solely by linear chains of action and reaction. It suggests that **meaning can organize experience**, just as force and probability do. Where physics explains *how* things happen, synchronicity speaks to *why* certain moments matter—especially at thresholds of change, decision, or identity shift.

This is why synchronicity often appears at moments of heightened relevance:

- You think of someone you haven't spoken to in years—and they call.

- You ask for clarity—and the same message appears repeatedly through unrelated channels.

- You reach a decision point—and a pattern emerges that confirms, complicates, or redirects your choice.

What makes these moments striking is not their rarity, but their **timing**. They arrive when attention is already engaged, when the psyche is receptive, when meaning is being actively sought or negotiated. The outer event mirrors the inner state with uncanny precision.

Importantly, these moments are not instructions handed down from an external authority. They do not remove agency or dictate outcomes. **They are feedback**—signals that reflect alignment, misalignment, readiness, or resistance. They invite reflection rather than obedience.

Synchronicity does not say, *"Do this."*
It asks, *"What does this mean **now**?"*

When approached with discernment, synchronicity becomes a navigational aid rather than a belief system. It helps you sense when you are moving in coherence with your values, intentions, and timing—and when adjustment may be needed. It refines perception without overriding choice.

Seen this way, synchronicity is not mystical spectacle. It is **context-aware patterning**—a dialogue between consciousness and circumstance. And when you learn to recognize it without projection or fixation, it becomes one of the most elegant ways destiny communicates: not loudly, not forcefully, but precisely—right when meaning is ready to be noticed.

The Universe as a Communicating System

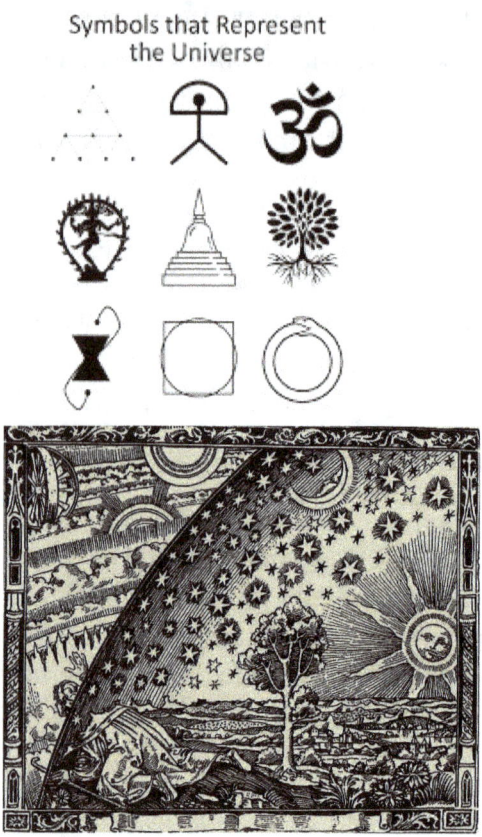

Symbols that Represent the Universe

From this lens, the universe is not silent. It is **responsive**. Not in the sense of issuing commands or orchestrating outcomes, but in the way any complex system responds to coherence. When intention, attention, and action align, feedback becomes noticeable. The environment reflects that alignment through timing, pattern, and convergence.

Patterns, signs, and timing function as a **form of dialogue**—especially when an individual is in heightened awareness. Numbers repeat not because they are magical, but because attention has synchronized with pattern. Encounters cluster because trajectories intersect. Opportunities and endings synchronize because readiness meets timing. These moments feel alive because they are relational—inner orientation meeting outer circumstance.

In this dialogue, **ease and resistance are signals**. When alignment is honored, effort often decreases while momentum increases. Things move with fewer obstacles, not because difficulty disappears, but because energy is no longer being spent fighting the current. When alignment is missed or ignored, resistance tends to increase. Friction multiplies. Timing slips. What once felt fluid becomes effortful. This is not punishment; it is information.

Importantly, this does not mean that everything is a sign. Not every coincidence carries meaning. Randomness exists. Noise exists. Projection exists. Discernment is what separates **signal from static**. Some moments matter because they intersect with intention, transition, or choice. Others pass without consequence. The difference lies not in the event itself, but in its **context and relevance**.

Learning the language of synchronicity is not about obsession or outsourcing authority to the external world. It is not about waiting for permission or searching for reassurance. It is about **attentive participation**—noticing when probability organizes itself in a way that mirrors your inner state and current direction.

This kind of listening is quiet and grounded. It does not inflate meaning where none exists, nor does it dismiss meaning when it appears. It recognizes that complex systems communicate through pattern long before they communicate through words.

When discernment sharpens, synchronicity becomes less mysterious and more practical. It helps you sense when you are in dialogue with life rather than in opposition to it. And in that dialogue, destiny does not feel imposed. It feels **responsive**—adjusting, reflecting, and refining as you do.

The universe does not need to shout.

When coherence is present, the message is already clear.

The Bridge Between Intuition and Probability

Modern science offers an unexpected ally in understanding synchronicity—not by validating superstition, but by **complicating the story of causality**. In quantum physics, probability replaces certainty at the most fundamental level of reality. Events do not exist as fixed outcomes waiting to occur; they exist as **ranges of possibility** until conditions allow one potential to take form.

Within this framework, observation matters. The observer is not a passive witness but a participant whose attention, measurement, and interaction influence which probabilities become relevant. This does not mean thoughts magically create reality, nor does it imply personal control over outcomes. It means that **consciousness participates in selection**, shaping how possibility organizes itself into experience.

This is where intuition enters—not as mystical guesswork, but as a **pattern-detecting faculty**. Intuition operates below conscious reasoning, integrating vast amounts of information—emotional cues, environmental signals, memory, timing—faster than deliberate thought. It senses coherence before logic can articulate it. When intuition "knows," it is often detecting **probability alignment**, not inventing meaning.

Synchronicity lives precisely in this overlap:

- Where **intuition detects pattern** before explanation arrives

- Where **probability clusters around meaning**, creating unlikely convergence

- Where **timing becomes statistically improbable but experientially exact**

These moments feel striking because they sit at the intersection of chance and relevance. Any single event could be coincidence. What makes synchronicity distinct is **patterned recurrence in meaningful context**—the same theme appearing across different channels at a moment when awareness is primed to receive it.

The mind does not invent these moments.
It **recognizes** them.

Recognition is different from projection. Projection imposes meaning. Recognition perceives it. Recognition happens when the inner state and outer event align with such precision that dismissal feels less rational than attention. The experience carries a felt sense of rightness—not certainty about outcome, but clarity about relevance.

This is why synchronicity often accompanies thresholds: decisions, transitions, endings, beginnings. At these moments, the field of possibility is already in flux. Attention sharpens. Sensitivity increases. Probability organizes more visibly around choice.

Seen this way, synchronicity is not a violation of scientific understanding—it is an **emergent property of complex systems interacting with conscious awareness**. It is where intuition and probability meet, where meaning rides the wave of chance without overriding it.

The universe does not suspend randomness to communicate.
It **uses probability itself** as a medium.

And when you learn to trust recognition without forcing interpretation, intuition becomes a bridge—not away from reason, but **into deeper coherence with how reality actually unfolds**.

When You're in Alignment

One of the clearest markers of alignment is not constant ease or the absence of challenge, but an **increase in synchronicity that feels coherent rather than chaotic**. When you are aligned, life does not necessarily become simple—but it becomes *responsive*. There is a sense that events are meeting you halfway, that timing is cooperating, and that effort is being translated into movement rather than resistance.

In alignment, **decisions are often affirmed through unexpected confirmation**. You make a choice internally—quietly, without needing validation—and shortly after, something external reflects that choice back to you. A conversation echoes your conclusion. An article appears addressing the exact question you were holding. An opportunity opens in the direction you just committed to. These confirmations do not tell you what to do; they signal that your internal orientation and external conditions are synchronized.

Alignment also shows up as **obstacles dissolving without force**. This does not mean challenges disappear, but that you stop pushing against what was never meant to move. Resistance gives way to redirection. What once required constant effort loosens when you stop fighting the current and begin working with it. Energy that was spent managing friction becomes available for creativity and execution.

You may notice that **encounters arrive at precisely the right moment**. People appear who carry missing information, perspective, or support. Meetings that once seemed unlikely happen naturally. Connections feel timely rather than strained. These moments are not random—they occur because trajectories intersect when timing aligns.

Another hallmark of alignment is when **the same message appears across unrelated contexts**. A theme repeats through different channels—conversation, media, dreams, numbers, or symbols—without being sought out. The repetition is not dramatic; it is consistent. The message feels less like persuasion and more like reinforcement.

This is not luck.
It is **feedback from a system responding to coherence**.

Conversely, when you are misaligned, the pattern often reverses. You may experience **repetition without progress**—the same situations looping without new insight or resolution. Effort increases, but results stagnate. Friction escalates. What once felt fluid becomes dense.

Missed timing becomes common. Opportunities arrive too late or too early. Conversations happen after decisions are made. Momentum stalls. Signals may become increasingly loud or uncomfortable—not to punish, but to interrupt. The system is attempting to redirect attention.

Synchronicity, in this sense, is neutral.
It does not flatter or reassure for comfort's sake.
It **informs**.

It tells you when you are moving with coherence and when recalibration is needed. It does not remove agency; it sharpens it. The information is only useful if received with humility and discernment rather than attachment.

Alignment is not about perfection or permanent ease. It is about **responsiveness**—your ability to listen, adjust, and engage consciously with what life is reflecting back to you. When that responsiveness is present, synchronicity increases not as spectacle, but as guidance.

And when guidance is received—not followed blindly, but integrated thoughtfully—destiny stops feeling imposed. It begins to feel **participatory**, unfolding through a dialogue between intention and timing, awareness and response.

Signs, Numbers, and Sequences

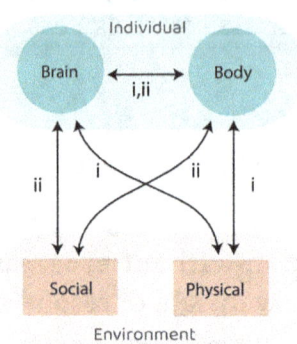
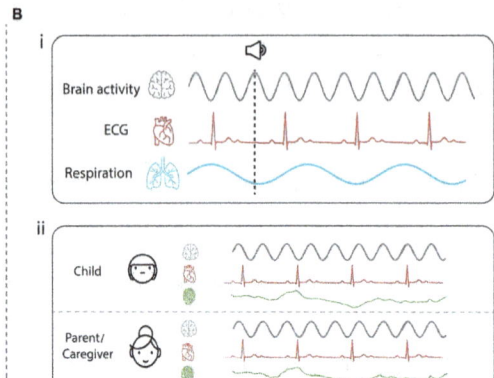

NUMBER SYNCHRONICITIES & THEIR MEANINGS

111 REMINDER THAT THOUGHTS CREATE REALITY. REASSURANCE OR WARNING.

222 GOOD OMEN FOR RELATIONSHIPS. SEEK BALANCE AND PEACE.

333 SIGN OF ENCOURAGEMENT. ANTICIPATE GOOD NEWS.

444 SIGN YOU'RE ON RIGHT PATH. FOLLOW YOUR INTUITION/KEEP GOING.

555 CHANGE IS COMING. GOOD OMEN FOR MANIFESTING. MAKE ROOM.

666 WARNING OF NEGATIVE THINKING. REFOCUS AND RETURN TO PURPOSE.

777 NEED FOR SOLITUDE AND REST. TAKE TIME OUT AND TURN INWARDS.

888 POWERFUL MANIFESTATION NUMBER. SUCCESS AND PROGRESS.

999 SOMETHING NEEDS TO END. RELEASE AND LET GO OF PAST.

911 STAY POSITIVE. REINVENT AFTER HARDSHIP. NEW DOORS OPENING.

1010 SOMETHING NEAR COMPLETION. KEEP WORKING TOWARDS YOUR GOALS.

1111 HIGHLY SPIRITUAL NUMBER. LEVELING UP. SIGN OF MANIFESTATION.

1212 ANGELS AND GUIDES SUPPORTING YOU. DREAM BIG AND TRUST THE UNIVERSE.

1234 REMINDER OF YOUR POTENTIAL. BELIEVE IN YOURSELF. LET GO.

2222 FIND BALANCE. REMINDER OF KARMA. KEEP FAITH IN THE UNIVERSE.

Repeating numbers, symbolic animals, recurring themes, and sequences of events are not mystical commands or external instructions demanding obedience. They are **pattern markers**—signals that emerge when the psyche and environment are synchronized around a moment of relevance. Their power does not come from superstition, but from **contextual resonance**.

These markers appear when attention is already engaged. They surface at moments of transition, questioning, or decision—when the mind is searching for coherence and the nervous system is alert. The repetition itself is not the message; it is the **signal that a message is present**. It invites reflection rather than compliance.

Crucially, the meaning of these signs is **not universal**. No number, animal, or symbol carries a fixed interpretation that applies to everyone at all times. Meaning is relational. It arises from the intersection between the symbol and the individual's internal state, history, and current threshold. A symbol that feels charged to one person may be irrelevant to another—not because one is more "spiritual," but because relevance differs.

A repeating number does not matter because of what it is numerically. It matters because of **when it appears** and what you were considering in that moment. A symbolic animal crossing your path is not significant because of its archetypal mythology alone, but because of what it evokes within you—memory, emotion, curiosity, or recognition. A sequence of events gains meaning not because it is rare, but because it aligns with an internal question seeking resolution.

These moments function as **mirrors**. They reflect back to you what is already moving within your awareness. They highlight themes that are ready to be noticed or integrated. They do not tell you what to do; they ask you to **pay attention**.

This is why over-interpretation dulls the signal. When every coincidence is treated as a directive, discernment collapses. When signs are approached with grounded curiosity rather than urgency, clarity emerges naturally. The symbol does not need to be decoded through rigid systems—it needs to be **felt, contextualized, and understood in relation to your lived experience**.

Signs, numbers, and sequences are not about control. They are about **orientation**. They help you notice when life is reflecting something back to you—inviting awareness, adjustment, or confirmation. They are subtle because they respect agency. They point without pushing.

In this way, synchronicity becomes less about chasing meaning and more about **recognizing when meaning is already present**. The world does not shout instructions. It whispers relevance.

And when you learn to listen without projecting, the patterns that emerge stop feeling mysterious. They begin to feel familiar—like reminders arriving at exactly the moment you are ready to understand them.

Why This Matters for Destiny

Destiny is not a static script written at birth and followed without deviation. It is **dynamic, responsive, and relational**. While your birth moment encodes potential—temperament, inclination, and learning style—how that potential unfolds is continuously shaped through interaction with experience, environment, and choice.

Synchronicity is one of the primary mechanisms through which destiny **updates itself in real time**.

Rather than dictating outcomes, synchronicity functions as a feedback system. It reflects how well your internal orientation—values, intentions, readiness—is matching the conditions you are engaging with. When alignment is present, momentum is reinforced. When misalignment emerges, timing shifts, friction increases, or signals repeat. These adjustments are not punitive. They are **informational**.

In this way, synchronicity does not override agency.
It **refines** it.

A chance encounter may nudge you toward a conversation you have been avoiding. A repeating message may confirm a decision already made internally. A sudden delay may slow momentum long enough for insight to catch up with action. These are not instructions imposed from outside, but **calibrations**—subtle adjustments that help choice become more accurate rather than more constrained.

This matters because destiny is not fulfilled through force. It unfolds through **responsiveness**. When individuals ignore feedback, life often escalates signals until attention is gained. When feedback is noticed and integrated, course correction becomes gentle rather than disruptive.

Understanding synchronicity equips you with discernment. It helps you:

- **Distinguish signal from coincidence**, recognizing when probability carries relevance and when it does not

- **Read patterns without projecting meaning**, avoiding both superstition and dismissal

- **Understand when intuition is guiding probability**, rather than replacing it

- **Recognize alignment through external reflection**, sensing when inner and outer realities are in dialogue

This skill set transforms destiny from something that happens *to* you into something that unfolds *with* you. You stop searching for signs as validation and start receiving patterns as information. You become less reactive and more responsive.

Ultimately, synchronicity matters because it restores **conversation** between consciousness and circumstance. It reminds you that life is not indifferent, nor is it controlling. It is adaptive—responding to clarity with movement and to confusion with pause.

When you learn to listen without surrendering agency, destiny stops feeling like a mystery waiting to be solved. It becomes a living process—one that adjusts, reflects, and refines as you do.

Not because your path is fixed.
But because your awareness is finally participating in how it unfolds.

A Shift in How You Listen

Synchronicity invites a different quality of attention—one that is **relaxed, curious, and grounded**, rather than anxious or hypervigilant. It does not ask you to scan the world for hidden messages or to assign meaning to every coincidence. Instead, it asks you to be present enough to notice when patterns naturally organize themselves around moments of relevance.

The posture shifts from seeking to **listening**.

The question is no longer, *"Is the universe sending me signs?"*—a question often rooted in uncertainty or the desire for reassurance. Instead, it becomes, *"Am I paying attention to the patterns already responding to me?"* This subtle change moves authority inward. Meaning is no longer something you wait to receive; it is something you recognize through engagement.

When awareness sharpens, communication becomes clearer—not because the universe suddenly starts speaking louder, but because **noise decreases**. Attention becomes less scattered. Timing becomes easier to sense. Patterns stand out without effort. What once felt ambiguous begins to feel precise, not through certainty of outcome, but through clarity of direction.

This way of listening is neither passive nor controlling. It is participatory. You remain responsible for interpretation, choice, and action. Synchronicity offers context, not instruction. It refines perception without replacing discernment.

Learning to read the language of the universe requires emotional regulation as much as intuition. Fear distorts signal. Obsession amplifies projection. Curiosity, by contrast, keeps perception open without attachment. It allows meaning to emerge without forcing conclusion.

When approached this way, destiny stops feeling distant, cryptic, or withheld. It no longer appears as a hidden code waiting to be cracked. It feels **interactive**—a responsive exchange between your inner orientation and the conditions you are moving through.

You notice when life meets you halfway.
You sense when timing opens or closes.
You adjust not because you are told to, but because awareness makes the next step obvious.

In this mode of listening, synchronicity becomes less dramatic and more dependable. It is not a spectacle—it is a **navigation system**, quietly updating as you move.

And when you trust your capacity to listen with discernment rather than fear, destiny stops feeling like something you are chasing.

It becomes something you are **in conversation with**—moment by moment, pattern by pattern, choice by choice.

CHAPTER 9

The Frequency of Fulfillment: Living Your Design

This chapter brings everything home.

Up to this point, you have explored destiny as blueprint, pattern, frequency, and inheritance. You have learned how purpose is encoded at birth, shaped by place, refined through experience, and echoed through lineage. Now the question becomes practical and embodied:

How do you live this knowledge—daily, relationally, and sustainably?

Fulfillment is not achieved by understanding your design intellectually. It emerges when your **daily choices resonate with your encoded frequency**. When astrology, numerology, Human Design, and ancestral insight stop being concepts you study—and become principles you apply.

This chapter reframes fulfillment not as a future achievement, but as a **state of coherence**.

Fulfillment arises when:

- Your work aligns with how your energy naturally moves

- Your relationships honor your nervous system and decision-making style

- Your health practices support your biological and energetic rhythms

- Your goals are set from resonance, not comparison or pressure

In other words, fulfillment is not about doing more.
It is about **doing what is correct for you—consistently**.

Here, manifestation is no longer framed as wishful thinking or forced positivity. It is understood as **vibrational alignment** —the natural outcome of coherent thought, emotion, behavior, and physiology moving in the same direction. Research in vibrational medicine, heart-brain coherence, and neuroplasticity supports this truth: systems that are synchronized function more efficiently, recover faster, and sustain momentum with less effort.

Living your design means:

- Making decisions from your correct authority

- Structuring your days in a way your nervous system can support

- Choosing environments that regulate rather than drain you

- Creating rituals that reinforce coherence instead of chasing motivation

This is where destiny becomes embodied.

You stop asking, *"What am I meant to do?"*
And begin asking, *"What state am I meant to live from?"*

Because when state changes, outcomes follow.

This chapter will guide you through:

- **Integrating your blueprint into daily life** without rigidity or overwhelm

- **Alignment tools** that support consistency rather than burnout

- **Rituals and reflective practices** tailored to your energetic design

- **Affirmations and coherence practices** grounded in neuroscience, not fantasy

Fulfillment, as you will see, is not the reward at the end of the path.

It is the **frequency you generate when you stop resisting who you are**.

And when you live from that frequency—career, relationships, health, and purpose begin to organize themselves around coherence rather than struggle.

This is not about becoming someone new.
It is about **finally living as who you already are—on purpose**.

Applying Your Blueprint to Daily Life

ENCODED IN THE STARS | 353

Living your design begins with **translation**—the movement from knowing to doing, from insight to habit, from concept to embodiment. A blueprint is only potential until it shapes behavior. It becomes real when it informs how you wake, how you make decisions, how you pace your work, how you relate to others, how you rest, and how you reset after stress. Alignment is not a single moment of clarity or a dramatic life overhaul; it is a **pattern of choices** repeated often enough for the nervous system to trust them.

This is why alignment must be sustainable. The body does not respond well to extremes or sudden reinvention. It responds to **consistency**. Small, repeatable choices—made in the same direction—create safety. Safety creates regulation. Regulation creates capacity. And capacity is what allows purpose to be lived rather than merely imagined.

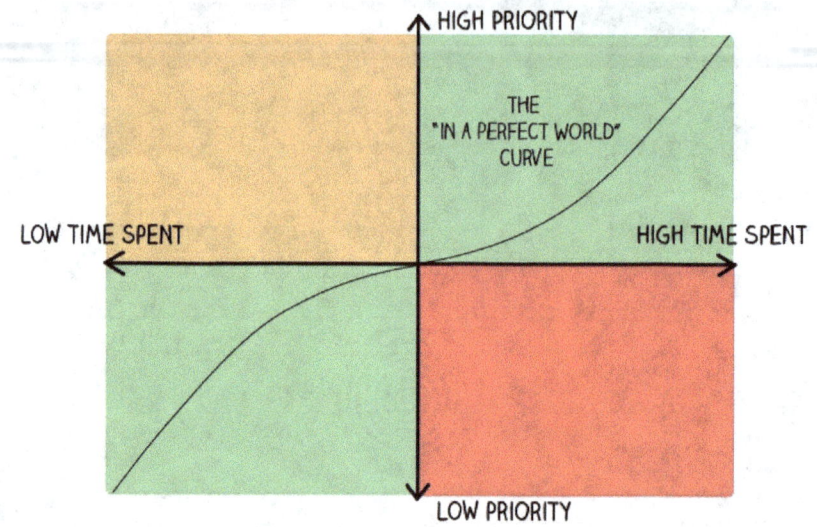

Start by identifying your **non-negotiables for coherence**. These are the conditions your system requires to function optimally—not ideally, but reliably. Sleep timing that respects your circadian rhythm is foundational; without it, cognition, mood, and decision-making degrade. Work blocks that match your natural energy output protect against burnout and inefficiency. Boundaries that safeguard recovery prevent chronic depletion. Environments that regulate—through light, sound, pace, and relational tone—allow your nervous system to remain responsive rather than defensive.

These elements are often mislabeled as indulgences. They are not.

They are **infrastructure**.

Just as a building requires a stable foundation before it can rise, fulfillment requires structural support before it can sustain momentum. When these supports are in place, effort decreases. You stop spending energy compensating for misalignment and start investing energy in expression.

When daily structure supports your frequency, **motivation becomes unnecessary**. You no longer rely on willpower to push yourself forward, because the path itself carries you. Momentum replaces force. Action feels less like self-discipline and more like natural continuation. You do not have to convince yourself to show up; your system is already oriented toward engagement.

This is the quiet power of living your design. It does not announce itself through constant excitement or intensity. It reveals itself through **ease that persists**, clarity that compounds, and progress that no longer requires self-negotiation.

Alignment, lived this way, is not a performance.

It is a relationship—with your body, your rhythm, and your capacity to grow without breaking.

And when that relationship is honored daily, fulfillment stops feeling like something you have to chase.

It becomes the **byproduct of coherence**, built one accurate choice at a time.

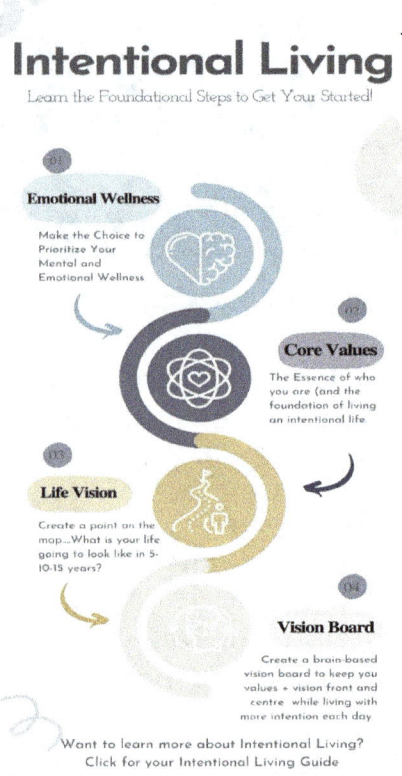

Aligning Career with Your Encoded Path

Career alignment is not about climbing higher or moving faster—it is about **placing your energy where it performs naturally**. Titles, prestige, and external validation often distract from the deeper question: *Does this role match the way my system is designed to work?* When role and rhythm are mismatched, even success feels draining. When they align, effort converts cleanly into impact.

Your blueprint offers a multidimensional lens for this placement. **Astrology** reveals vocational themes and the arenas where your contribution is meant to be visible —leadership, service, creativity, analysis, stewardship, or innovation. **Numerology** clarifies how you learn, adapt, and extract meaning—your cadence for growth, change, responsibility, or mastery. **Human Design** shows how your energy engages work—whether you are built to initiate, respond, guide, or sample—and how decisions should be made to preserve vitality. **Lineage** highlights inherited talents and responsibilities—capacities shaped by history that often point toward purpose rather than preference.

Together, these systems answer a practical question: *What kind of work environment allows my best energy to emerge without constant self-correction?*

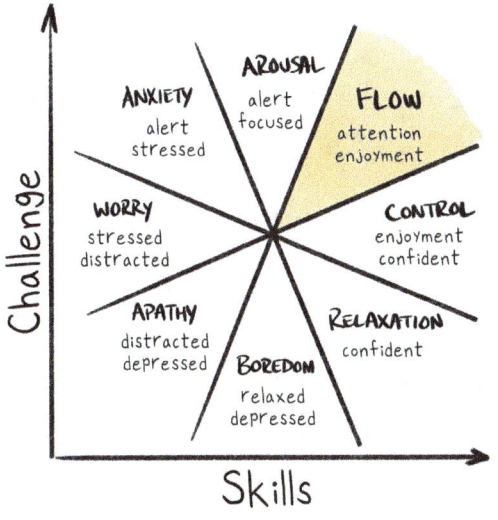

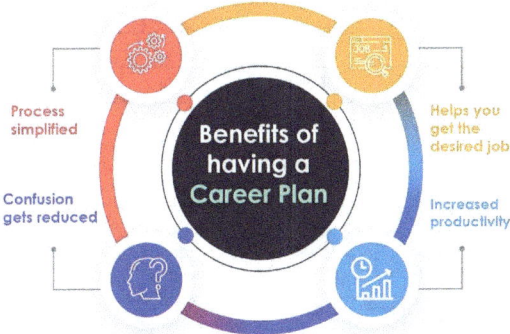

This is why accurate alignment begins with honest inquiry. Ask questions that cut through noise and status:

- **Does this role require constant initiation when my design thrives on response?**
  If your energy is meant to respond, roles demanding perpetual self-starting will exhaust you—even if you're capable. Conversely, if you are designed to initiate, waiting for permission will feel like suffocation.

- **Does my schedule honor my natural peaks—or fight**

them?

Some systems thrive in focused bursts; others in steady output; others in spacious cycles. A schedule that ignores your peaks forces compensation—through caffeine, stress, or self-criticism.

- **Am I rewarded for the kind of value I'm built to deliver?**
If your strength is synthesis, guidance, or depth, environments that only reward speed or volume will undervalue you. When reward structures match contribution, motivation stabilizes.

Fulfillment at work emerges when **output is correctly placed** —when what you naturally offer is what the role actually needs. In this state, productivity feels cleaner. Feedback feels relevant. Growth feels cumulative rather than depleting.

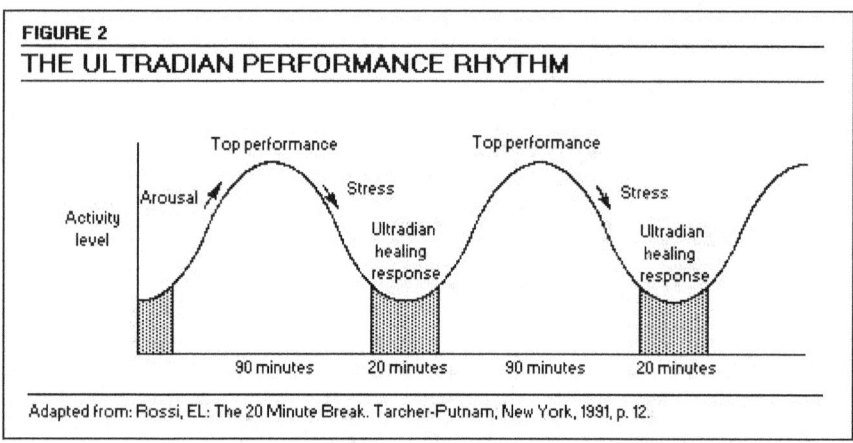

FIGURE 2
THE ULTRADIAN PERFORMANCE RHYTHM

Adapted from: Rossi, EL: The 20 Minute Break. Tarcher-Putnam, New York, 1991, p. 12.

This reframes career development entirely. You don't need more hustle. Hustle is often a sign of misplacement. You need **accurate placement**—roles, teams, timelines, and metrics that recognize your true value. When placement is correct, ambition becomes sustainable, contribution becomes visible, and work becomes a channel for expression rather than extraction.

Alignment doesn't lower standards.

It **raises efficiency**.

And when efficiency is rooted in design, fulfillment stops being something you chase after hours. It becomes the natural outcome of doing work that fits—day after day, decision by decision, with energy left to live the rest of your life.

Relational Coherence: Choosing Compatibility Over Chemistry

5 TRAUMA RESPONSES

Fight — To face any perceived threat aggressively

Flight — To run away from danger or threat

Freeze — Inability to move or act against a threat

Fawn — To please someone to avoid conflict

Flop — To collapse, become unreponsive, faint

Relationships flourish not through intensity alone, but through **regulation**. While chemistry can ignite attraction, it does not sustain connection. What sustains connection is **relational coherence**—the capacity for two nervous systems to settle, communicate, and adapt together over time. When coherence is present, intimacy deepens without depletion. When it is absent, even strong attraction can become exhausting.

WHAT IS CO-REGULATION?
A Guide to Nervous System Harmony

The Role of Co-regulation

Co-regulation is a supportive process where one person helps another manage their emotions, behavior, and physical responses through warm, connected interactions.

This shared experience helps individuals gradually develop self-regulation skills, **making it easier to handle life's challenges on their own.**

The Science of Co-regulation

The autonomic nervous system is key in regulating our emotional responses.

Co-regulation helps balance our *sympathetic* ("fight or flight") and *parasympathetic* ("rest and digest") systems.

This helps us achieve a state of safety and calm.

Why It Matters

Co-regulation fosters a sense of **safety**, especially for people with attachment challenges or trauma backgrounds.

It provides tools to help us understand and regulate our emotions, which supports overall **emotional resilience**.

A regulated client is **better able to engage** in therapeutic activities and learning, and participate in daily life tasks.

Barriers to Co-regulation
and How to Avoid Them

Provider Dysregulation
Use grounding techniques to stay calm when a client is highly dysregulated.

Sensory Overload
Simplify the environment or use soothing sensory tools to ease co-regulation.

Emotional Escalation
Respond to aggressive behavior with empathy and clear boundaries to encourage calm.

Your blueprint offers clarity here. It reveals **how you bond, how you decide, and how you recover** after emotional activation. Some designs need space before clarity arrives; reflection is not withdrawal—it is regulation. Others need dialogue to process; silence feels destabilizing rather than soothing. Some life paths thrive when partners share a mission or direction; others flourish through emotional attunement and relational safety. None of these needs are flaws. They are **design requirements**.

This is why compatibility matters more than chemistry. Compatibility is not sameness—it is **complementary**

regulation. Two people can be very different and still be compatible if their rhythms allow for mutual settling. Likewise, two people can be very similar and still be incompatible if their stress responses amplify rather than soothe one another.

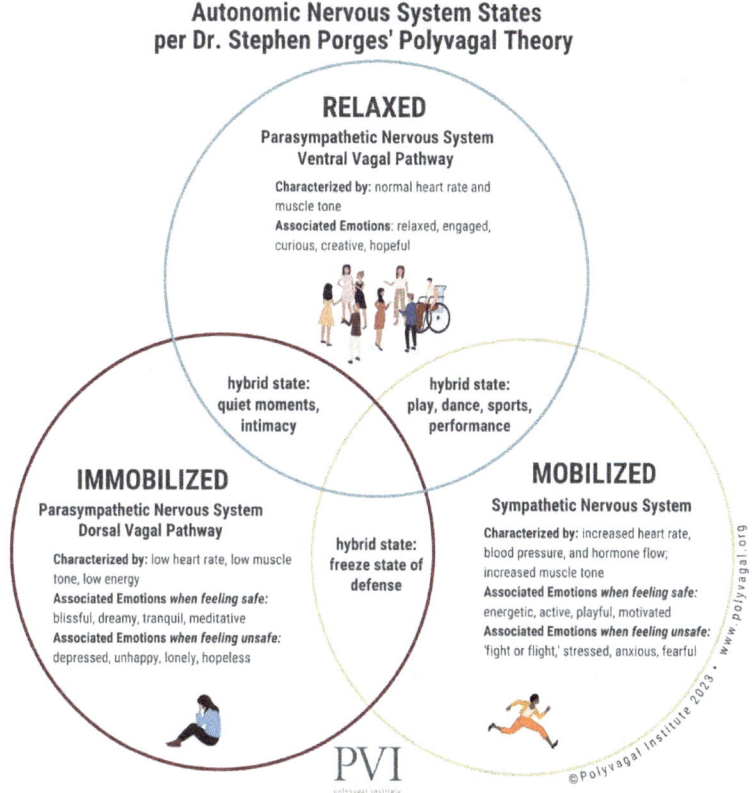

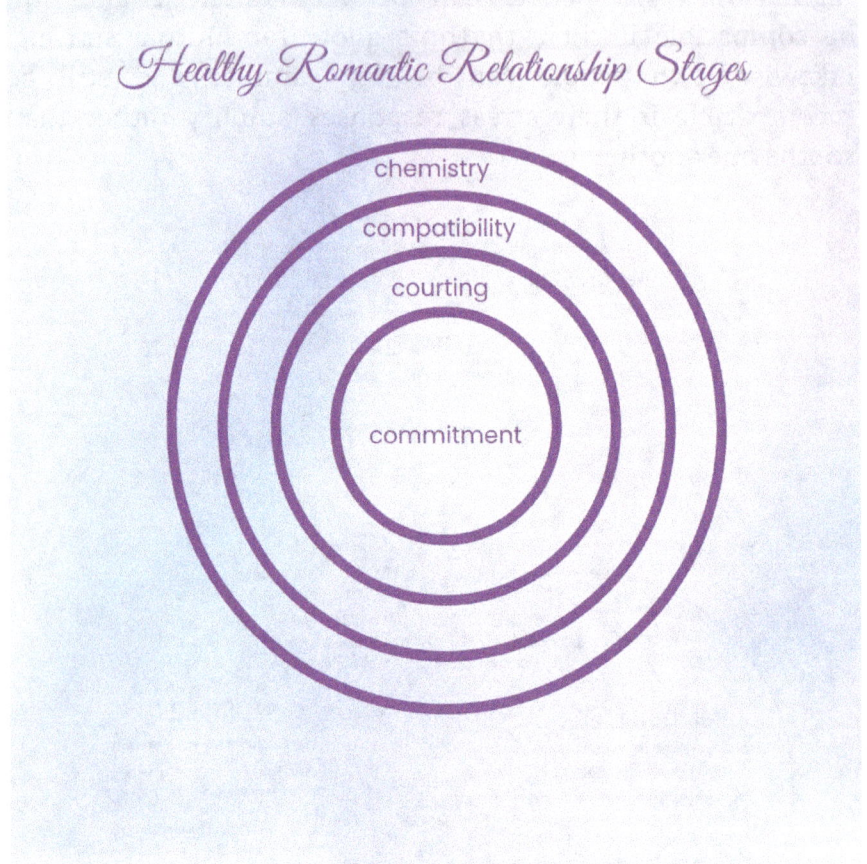

Choosing compatibility means honoring:

- **Timing** — how quickly or slowly clarity and commitment emerge

- **Communication style** — how information is processed and shared

- **Energetic limits** — how much stimulation, closeness, or independence is sustainable

When these elements are respected, relationships become **supportive containers for growth**. Conflict becomes navigable rather than destabilizing. Repair happens faster. Differences become informative rather than threatening. Growth feels encouraged—not extracted at the expense of well-being.

Relational coherence also reframes boundaries. Boundaries are not walls; they are **regulatory agreements** that protect connection by preventing overwhelm. When boundaries are aligned with design, they feel natural rather than defensive. They allow intimacy to deepen without triggering chronic stress responses.

In coherent relationships, growth feels resourced. You expand because there is safety to do so. You take risks because there is regulation to return to. You evolve not by self-abandonment, but by **mutual attunement**.

Chemistry may spark the beginning.
Compatibility determines whether the connection can **last, mature, and nourish**.

When you choose relationships that respect your nervous system and energetic limits, love stops feeling like labor. It becomes a place where purpose, healing, and joy are supported—rather than something you have to recover from.

Health as Frequency Management

Health is not best understood as the absence of symptoms or the relentless pursuit of optimization. It is the **presence of regulation**—the body's ability to respond, recover, and return to balance across changing conditions. When regulation is intact, resilience follows. When it is chronically disrupted, symptoms become the body's language of protest.

Seen through the lens of frequency, health is about **matching inputs to capacity**. Nourishment, movement, and recovery are not universal prescriptions; they are modulators of rhythm. What restores one nervous system may overwhelm another. What energizes one body may dysregulate another. Alignment begins by honoring how your system processes stimulation, effort, and rest.

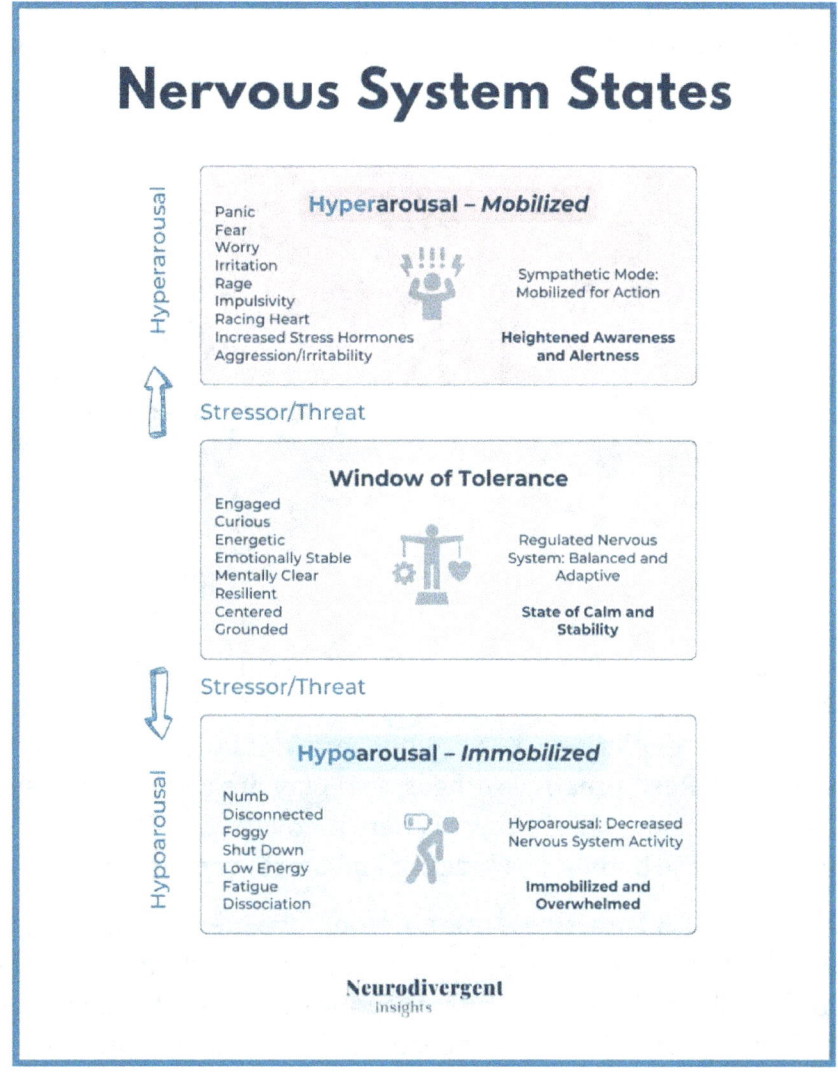

This is why **gentle consistency outperforms extremes**. Short bursts of intensity followed by collapse do not build health; they tax it. Small, repeatable practices—walks, stretching, steady meals, consistent sleep—signal safety to the nervous system. Safety allows repair. Repair builds capacity. Capacity supports growth.

Likewise, **rhythm matters more than rigidity**. Bodies thrive on predictable cycles, not inflexible rules. Eating at regular times, moving in ways that feel supportive rather than punishing, and sleeping in alignment with circadian cues all reinforce coherence. Rigidity often masks mistrust of the body; rhythm rebuilds trust.

Perhaps most transformative is reframing **recovery as a strategy, not a reward**. Recovery is not something you earn after depletion; it is what prevents depletion from occurring. Rest, breath, stillness, and play are active processes that recalibrate physiology. When recovery is planned and protected, the body stops bracing and starts cooperating.

When health practices match your frequency, resistance dissolves. You no longer have to force compliance or rely on discipline alone. The body responds because it recognizes itself in the practice. Signals become clearer. Energy stabilizes.

Symptoms soften not because they were silenced, but because the conditions that produced them have changed.

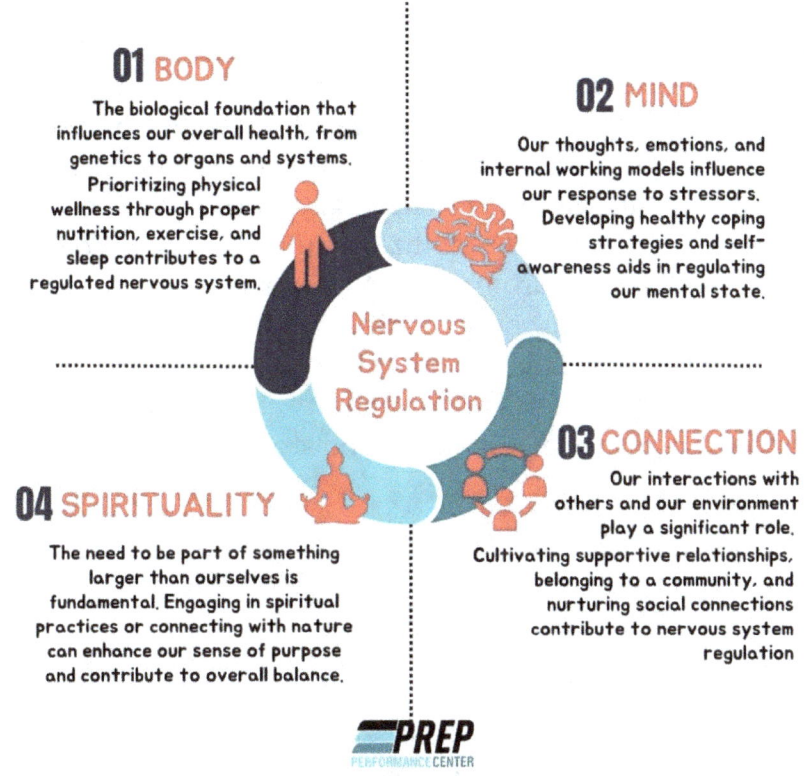

In this model, health is not something you chase.
It is something you **manage through coherence**.

And when coherence becomes the priority, the body shifts from survival to collaboration—working with you rather than against you, supporting the life you are designed to live rather than constantly asking for repair.

Tools for Energetic Coherence & Manifestation

Energetic coherence is the foundation upon which manifestation becomes reliable rather than erratic. Coherence means your physiological systems—heart, brain, breath, and nervous system—are synchronized and communicating efficiently. When coherence is present, decisions sharpen, emotional regulation stabilizes, and effort translates into impact. When it is absent, even the best intentions scatter.

Coherence Training is the most direct way to restore this alignment. Breath, posture, and emotion are the primary levers. Slow, rhythmic breathing signals safety to the nervous system; upright, relaxed posture supports efficient circulation and neural signaling; and intentionally cultivating a felt sense of appreciation or care stabilizes emotional tone. Together, these elements synchronize heart and brain rhythms, a state associated with improved clarity, resilience, and adaptive decision-making. This is not abstract—coherence can be measured through heart rate variability and has been linked to improved cognitive performance and stress recovery.

Coherent Breathing: Uses, Benefits, & How to PracticeSymptoms, Causes, and Treatment

How to Practice Coherent Breathing

1. Find a comfortable position
2. Remove any distractions
3. Begin to notice your breath
4. Place your hands on your belly
5. Start to lengthen your inhalations and exhalations, so that they last three seconds, continue this for one minute
6. Gradually increase your inhalations and exhalations to six seconds
7. Practice this for five minutes and work your way up to twenty minutes
8. If you find your mind wandering at any time, it's ok! Just bring your attention back to your breath
9. Record your thoughts in a journal

Neuroplastic Affirmations work when they are *embodied*, not aspirational. Words alone do little if the body does not agree. Effective affirmations are believable statements paired with breath and sensation—spoken slowly while feeling steadiness in the chest or ease in the body. Repetition matters because the brain wires what it repeats. Coherence matters because the nervous system decides whether that wiring will hold. When affirmations are practiced in a regulated state, they integrate as updated neural patterns rather than bouncing off resistance.

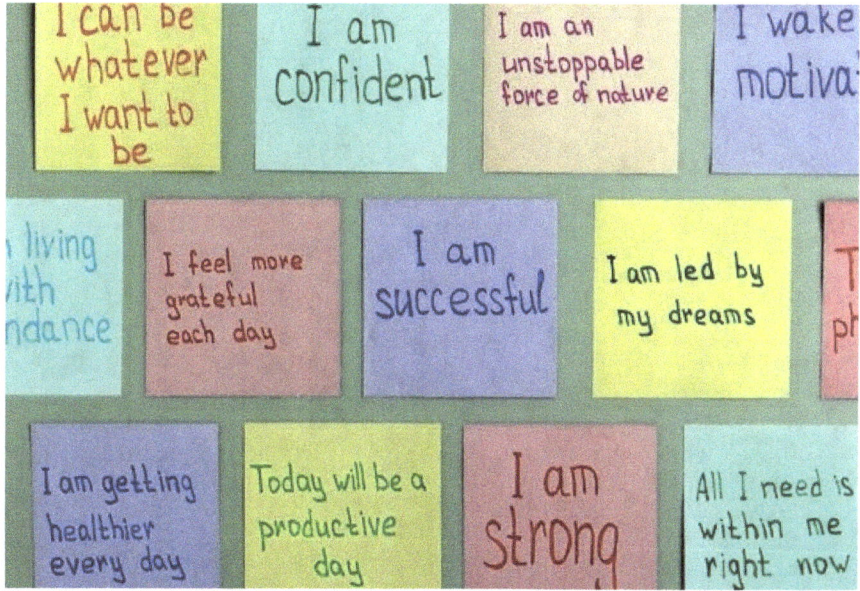

Vibrational Entrainment recognizes that the nervous system synchronizes to what it is exposed to. Music, light, movement, and even ambient sound shape internal rhythm. Fast, chaotic inputs push arousal; slow, steady inputs invite regulation. Choose inputs that match the *state you are cultivating*, not the state you are escaping. Gentle music to support focus, natural light to stabilize circadian rhythm, and rhythmic movement to discharge stress all entrain the system toward coherence.

This reframes manifestation entirely. Manifestation is not

wishing, visualizing harder, or forcing belief. It is **entrainment** —bringing your physiology, emotion, and attention into the same rhythm as the outcome you are moving toward. When your internal state matches your intention, action becomes cleaner, timing improves, and opportunities are recognized rather than missed.

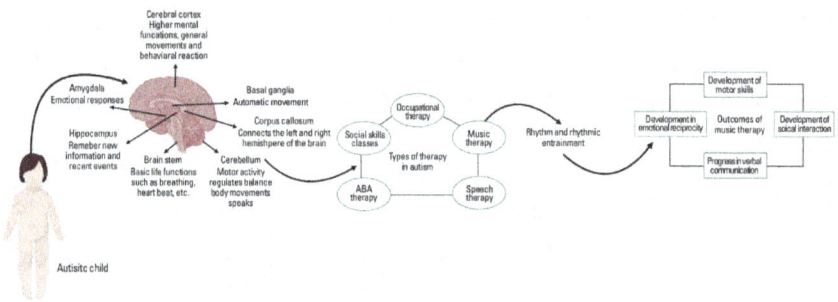

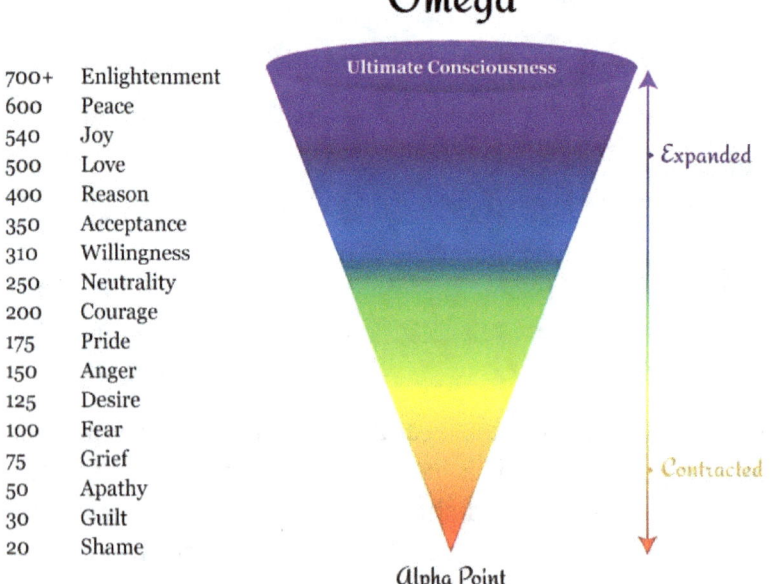

In coherent states, you do not chase results.
You **become compatible with them**.

These tools are not about control; they are about calibration. Used consistently, they create a stable internal environment where purpose can express itself without resistance. And when coherence becomes your baseline, manifestation stops feeling mysterious and starts feeling practical—an outcome of alignment practiced daily, breath by breath, choice by choice.

The Daily Alignment Ritual: Turning Awareness into Coherence

Check State (2 minutes):

Begin by noticing—not correcting—your current state. Bring gentle attention to your breath, the presence of tension in the body, and the emotional tone you're carrying. This is an audit, not an intervention. Noticing without fixing signals safety to the nervous system and establishes honesty as the foundation of alignment. When the body feels seen rather than managed, it relaxes its defenses. Awareness is the first regulator.

SIX WAYS TO PRACTICE GROUNDING
with anxiety & intense emotions

body
lay on the ground, press your toes into the floor, squeeze playdough

5 senses
wear your favorite sweatshirt, use essential oils, make a cup of tea

self-soothe
take a shower or bath, find a grounding object, light a candle

observe
describe an object in detail: color, texture, shadow, light, shapes

breathe
practice 4-7-8 breathing: inhale to 4, hold for 7, exhale to 8

distract
find all the square or green objects in the room, count by 7s, say the date

THE GROWLERY

Coherence Breath (4 minutes):

Shift into slow, rhythmic breathing—steady inhales and exhales that feel natural rather than forced. As breath settles, cultivate a felt sense of appreciation or care. This is not about positivity; it's about coherence. Appreciation stabilizes emotional tone and synchronizes heart and brain rhythms, creating a physiological state where clarity can emerge. In coherence, signals sharpen and noise quiets.

Authority Prompt (3 minutes):
Ask one decision-relevant question—something real and current. Then listen *somatically*. Notice sensations: expansion or contraction, ease or tension, warmth or heaviness. Do not analyze. Let the body answer first. This practice trains trust in embodied intelligence and reduces overthinking. Over time, accuracy improves as the system learns it will be listened to.

Intention (3 minutes):
Name the *state* you'll prioritize today—clarity, steadiness, courage, patience, focus. Choose a state, not an outcome. States are actionable and controllable; outcomes are not. By prioritizing a state, you orient behavior, perception, and decision-making toward coherence throughout the day.

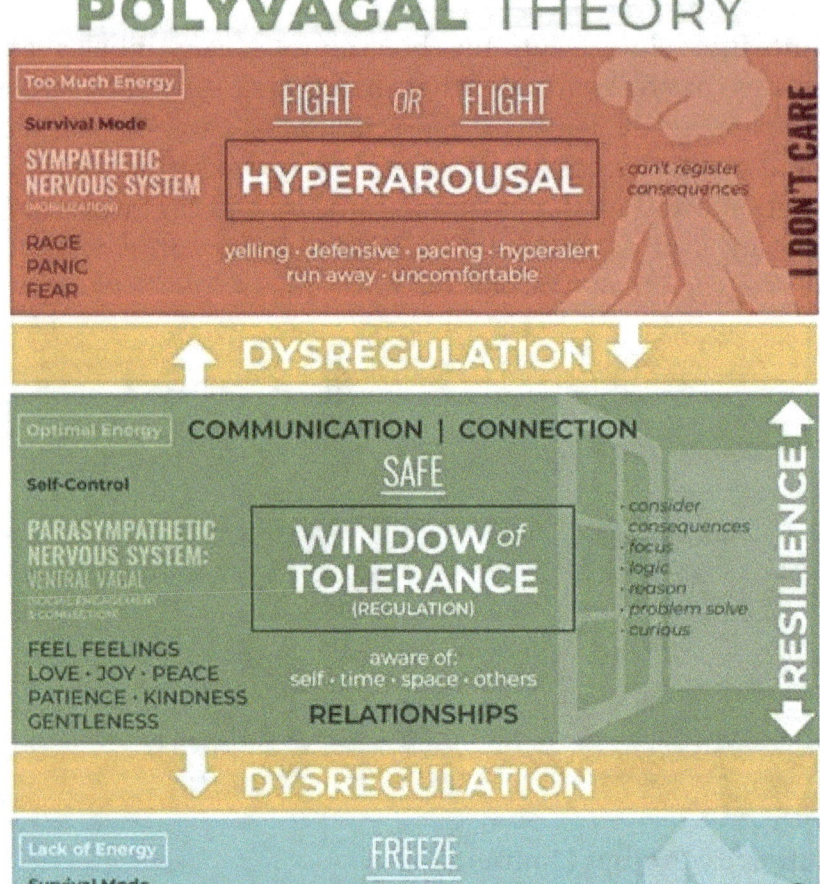

Seal (1 minute):

Complete the ritual with one small action that embodies the chosen state. It might be a posture adjustment, a boundary set, a message sent with intention, or a deliberate pause before beginning work. This anchors insight into behavior. The body learns through action; sealing the practice ensures integration.

The power of this ritual lies in **consistency, not intensity**. Ten to fifteen minutes done daily recalibrates far more effectively than occasional, elaborate practices. Over time, coherence becomes familiar, decision-making becomes cleaner, and alignment becomes the default rather than the exception.

This is how design becomes lived—quietly, reliably, and in ways your nervous system can sustain.

Energy Mapping Chart

An energy mapping chart turns intuition into **data you can work with**. Rather than guessing why certain days flow and others feel heavy, you begin observing patterns across time. This practice is not about self-critique; it is about **pattern literacy**—learning how your system actually functions in the real world.

	Energy Inflow	Energy Outflow	Review Priority
MENTAL			
Does your work and lifestyle, give you mental stimulus or exhaustion?			
Do your family, friends, time with groups give you mental stimulus or exhaustion?			
Does the team/organisation you work in give you mental stimulus or exhaustion?			
Is your habitual way of thinking positive and creative, or do you tend to worry and fret and focus on the negatives?			
Do you use both logical and intuitive skills in your work, and integrate them?			
Do uncertainty and conflicting data stimulate or dissipate your mental energy?			
Do you have leisure activities that give you mental energy or depletion?			
Other:			
SUBTOTAL			

Peak Energy Windows

Track when your energy naturally rises and stabilizes. Note the times of day when focus feels clean, creativity emerges easily, or communication flows. These windows are prime for cognitively demanding tasks, decisions, and visibility. Over time, you'll see reliable peaks—evidence that productivity is rhythmic, not random. Scheduling important work here is alignment in action.

Decision Accuracy Moments

Record decisions that felt clear and later proved accurate. What state were you in? What time of day? What conditions supported clarity—rest, coherence breathing, space, dialogue? This reveals **how and when your authority speaks most reliably**. You're not tracking outcomes to judge yourself; you're identifying the conditions that support good decisions so you can recreate them.

Friction Points

Notice where resistance clusters: recurring misunderstandings, procrastination, irritability, or stalled progress. Friction is information. It often signals misplacement (wrong timing, wrong environment, wrong role) rather than lack of discipline. Mapping friction helps you distinguish between challenges that grow you and misalignments that drain you.

Recovery Quality

Track how well you recover—not just how much you rest. Do breaks actually restore you, or do you return depleted? Which activities replenish versus numb? Quality recovery restores coherence and prepares the system for engagement. Poor recovery predicts burnout long before symptoms appear.

As you review your chart weekly, **patterns emerge**. You'll see where alignment is working—where energy, clarity, and ease coincide—and where recalibration is needed. This shifts self-improvement from effort to accuracy. Instead of pushing harder, you adjust placement, timing, or inputs.

Energy mapping reframes fulfillment as a **feedback-informed practice**. The chart becomes a mirror that teaches you how to live your design with precision—so alignment is not an abstract ideal, but a measurable, repeatable reality.

Affirmations by Design & Path: Speaking to the Body, Not the Ego

Morning Affirmations with Heart Coherence Meditation

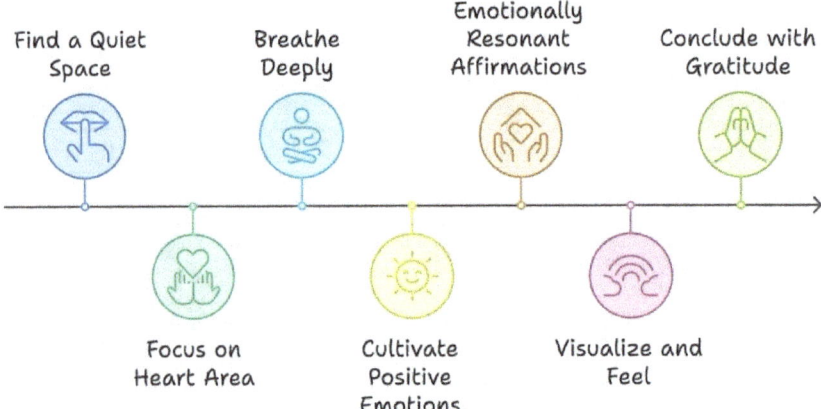

Affirmations are often misunderstood as motivational slogans meant to overpower doubt through repetition. When used this way, they frequently fail—because the nervous system does not respond to force. It responds to **coherence**. Affirmations work not because they are repeated loudly, but because they are **received somatically**.

Affirmations by design and path are not generic statements of aspiration. They are **frequency reminders**—language chosen to resonate with how your system actually learns, decides, and stabilizes. Their purpose is not to convince the mind of something new, but to **reorient the body toward what is already correct**.

> ## Why Choose Personalized Affirmations?
> - **Tailored to You:** Each affirmation is specifically crafted to resonate with your personal experiences, challenges, and aspirations.
> - **Empowering:** Boost your confidence and motivation with affirmations that speak directly to your soul.
> - **Manifest Your Goals:** Strengthen your manifestation practice with affirmations designed to align your mindset with your desires.
> - **Positive Mindset:** Overcome limiting beliefs and negative thoughts with targeted positive statements.
> - **Empowering:** Boost your confidence and motivation with affirmations that speak directly to your soul.

Consider the affirmations:

"I honor my rhythm; clarity meets me when I listen."
This affirmation reinforces patience and attunement. It reminds the system that clarity is not produced by urgency, but by listening to timing. It is especially regulating for individuals whose design requires response, reflection, or emotional processing before decision.

"I choose environments that support my nervous system."
This statement centers self-responsibility without self-blame. It affirms that well-being is shaped by context, not willpower alone. Repeating this affirmation helps the body recognize that safety and regulation are priorities, not indulgences.

"My decisions arise from coherence, not urgency."
This affirmation interrupts the stress-based habit of rushed decision-making. It trains the system to associate clarity with

calm and to trust somatic signals over pressure. Over time, it reshapes how choice is approached.

"What is correct for me unfolds with ease."

Ease here does not mean effortlessness—it means *lack of resistance*. This affirmation reassures the nervous system that alignment does not require struggle. It reduces the impulse to force outcomes and increases receptivity to timing.

TRADITIONAL YOGA (Hatha, Vinyasa, Ashtanga)	**EMBODIED YOGA**
Strengthens and stretches the physical body, strives to tame the mind with the goal of achieving a state of otherworldly enlightenment (*samadhi*).	Strives to turn off the "thinking" mind by activating your innate, primal healing capacity with the goal of healing yourself and amplifying your authentic energetic frequency.
Uses common physical shapes (*asana*) and alignment rules in repeated patterns or flows.	Uses the shapes of nature (circles, shaking and waves), in non-linear and non-habitual movements.
Uses the mind (in *asana*) or strives to tame the mind (in meditation.)	Bypasses the mind by turning up the volume on felt sensation.
Feel into *asana* in preparation for seated meditation to transcend the body.	*Feel* in order to heal and become more embodied.

How these affirmations are spoken matters more than what they say.

Speak slowly.
Speed activates urgency. Slowness invites regulation.

Feel first.
Before speaking, notice your breath, posture, and emotional tone. Let the body settle enough to receive the words.

Let the words land in the body.
After each phrase, pause. Notice sensation—warmth, softening, expansion, or even resistance. Resistance is not failure; it is information. Over time, repetition paired with coherence reduces resistance and builds trust.

Affirmations practiced this way become **neuroplastic interventions**. They rewire expectation, not by fantasy, but by repetition in a regulated state. The body learns that these statements are safe, accurate, and reliable.

In this context, affirmations are not about becoming someone else.
They are about **remembering how you function best**.

When spoken with presence, they stop being words you say—and become signals your system responds to.

The Practice of Fulfillment

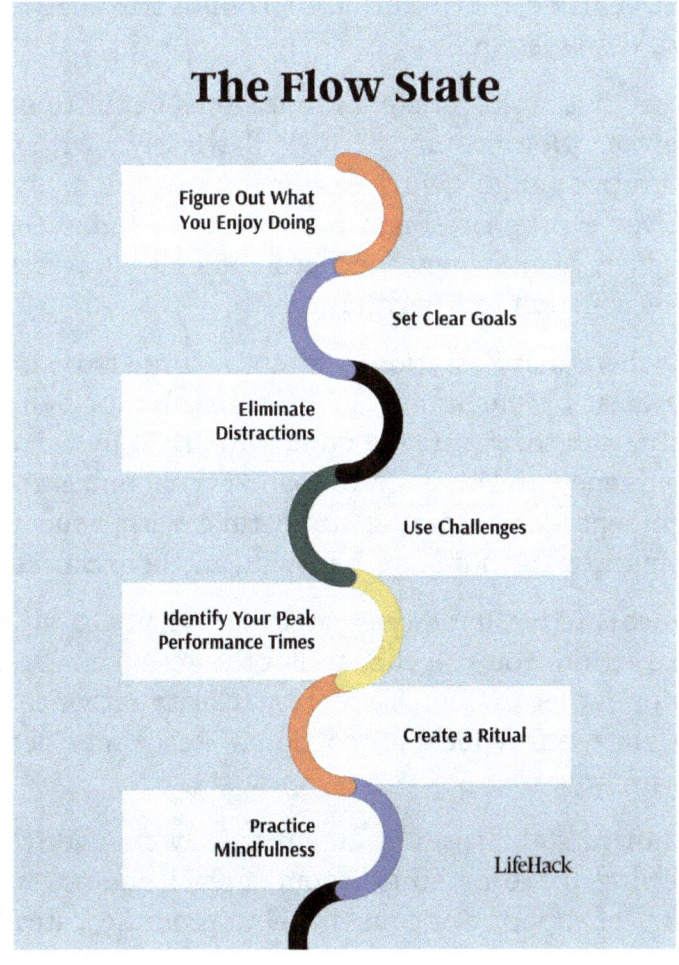

Fulfillment is not a destination you arrive at once everything is finally perfect. It is not a reward granted after enough effort, sacrifice, or achievement. Fulfillment is a **practice of accuracy**—the ongoing act of choosing what matches your design *today*, in this season, with the capacity you actually have. It is lived in increments, not declarations.

Accuracy means honesty with your energy. It means recognizing when something fits and when it doesn't—without judgment, self-criticism, or the need to justify misalignment. Each accurate choice stabilizes coherence a little more. Each inaccurate choice provides information, not failure. Over time, this feedback loop builds trust between you and your own system.

When you live from coherence, **outcomes begin to organize themselves**. Not instantly. Not flawlessly. But reliably. Opportunities align with readiness. Relationships sort themselves through resonance rather than force. Decisions feel cleaner, even when they are difficult. Progress stops requiring constant self-negotiation.

This is where manifestation is often misunderstood. You do not manifest by pushing, visualizing harder, or demanding certainty from the future. **You don't manifest by force.** Force signals urgency, and urgency destabilizes coherence. You allow by alignment—by becoming compatible with what you are calling in through your state, behavior, and boundaries.

Allowance is active. It requires participation, not passivity. You still take action. You still choose. But the action emerges from regulation rather than pressure, from clarity rather than fear. In that state, effort feels proportional. Resistance decreases. Timing improves.

As alignment stabilizes, fulfillment quietly changes shape. It stops feeling like something just out of reach and starts feeling **present**. Not euphoric or constant—but grounded, steady, and trustworthy. You recognize fulfillment not by excitement, but by the absence of internal friction.

Fulfillment becomes the frequency you live from.

It is expressed in how you pace your day, how you say yes and no, how you recover, how you choose environments, and how you respect your rhythm. It is built one accurate choice at a time—choices that may look small individually, but compound into a life that feels congruent.

This is the deepest promise of living your design:
Not that life becomes effortless,
but that it becomes **coherent**.

And coherence—practiced consistently—creates a form of fulfillment that does not need to be chased, proven, or protected.

It simply lives with you.

CHAPTER 10

The Return to Source: Purpose as Sacred Responsibility

This final chapter is not an ending—it is a **return**.

Throughout this book, you have explored destiny as blueprint, frequency, pattern, inheritance, activation, and lived coherence. You have learned that purpose is not something you chase, earn, or discover outside yourself. It is something you **remember, embody, and take responsibility for**. Here, the journey comes full circle—back to source, back to intention, back to conscious participation with life itself.

Purpose, at its deepest level, is not self-serving. It is **relational**. It lives at the intersection of soul design, human choice, and collective need. When you become aware of your blueprint, you are not given a badge of specialness—you are given a **charge**. Awareness expands responsibility, not burden, but stewardship.

This chapter reframes destiny as **co-creation**. Your life is not pre-written, nor is it random. It is a living timeline shaped by how you respond to what you are encoded to carry. Free will does not oppose destiny—it animates it. Each choice you make either harmonizes with your design or distorts it. Neither is punished. Both teach.

To live with conscious awareness of your divine blueprint is to understand that your existence has impact beyond personal fulfillment. Your regulation affects your relationships. Your healing alters lineage. Your coherence influences community. Your purpose naturally expresses itself through **service, love,**

and legacy, not obligation, but overflow.

This is where destiny matures.

You stop asking, *"What am I meant to do?"*
And begin asking, *"How am I meant to serve through who I am?"*

Service here does not mean sacrifice or self-erasure. It means alignment so accurate that your presence itself becomes beneficial. When you live correctly, contribution happens organically. You teach by example. You heal by regulation. You lead by coherence. You leave a legacy not just of accomplishments, but of **impact on the field you touched**.

This chapter will guide you to:

- Integrate soul purpose with service, community, and love

- Understand destiny and free will as collaborative forces

- Reflect on the legacy your frequency is already shaping

- Anchor your journey through guided reflection and journaling

The return to source is not ascension away from life.
It is **deeper embodiment within it**.

You do not dissolve into the universe.
You become a conscious expression of it.

And as you close this book, you are invited to carry one final truth forward:

You are not here to fulfill destiny alone.
You are here to **live it in relationship**—with others, with the world, and with the intelligence that encoded you into being.

Affirmation

I am encoded with divine intelligence,

and my life is the expression of universal order made manifest.

Destiny as Co-Creation: Where Blueprint Meets Choice

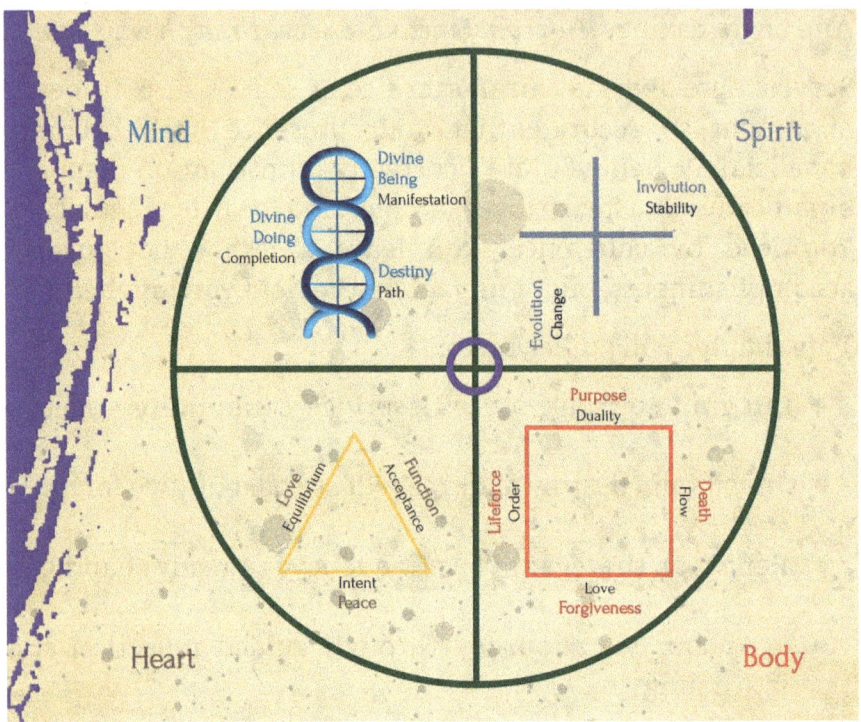

Destiny is not a script you obey; it is a **field you participate in**. A script implies inevitability and compliance. A field implies responsiveness, relationship, and movement. Your blueprint establishes the parameters of this field—your rhythm, inclinations, sensitivities, strengths, and learning style. It defines *how* energy wants to move through you, not *what* must happen to you. Choice is what animates that design. Without choice, destiny remains latent. With choice, it becomes lived.

Free will is often framed as the opposite of destiny, as if one negates the other. In truth, free will is the **instrument** through which destiny expresses itself. Each decision you make—large or small—tunes the frequency of your timeline. Choices do not simply determine outcomes; they shape *how* outcomes unfold, how much resistance or coherence accompanies them, and what lessons integrate along the way. In this sense, probability is not fixed. It is **responsive**. Your attention, regulation, and intention nudge probability toward alignment or recalibration.

This is why destiny feels different when you are present. Presence refines choice. When you choose from awareness, the field organizes with you. When you choose from urgency or fear, the field provides friction—not as punishment, but as feedback. Coherence increases when listening is accurate; correction increases when listening is bypassed. Both are part of the conversation.

Co-creation asks for **responsibility without rigidity**. Responsibility here does not mean blame or pressure to get it right. It means acknowledging that your state matters—that how you listen, pace, and respond shapes what unfolds. Rigidity collapses learning; presence expands it. You are not required to be perfect—only **attentive**. When awareness is engaged, even missteps become instructional rather than derailing. Errors refine discernment. Detours reveal preference. Resistance clarifies boundaries.

The timeline adapts because **you adapt**. This is the quiet power of co-creation. Life is not waiting to judge your performance; it is responding to your accuracy. When you listen carefully—to your body, to timing, to pattern—and choose with courage, the field meets you. Doors open with less force. Endings complete with less drama. Momentum builds not from control, but from congruence.

In co-creation, destiny is neither imposed nor invented. It is **participated**. You bring awareness. The field brings feedback. Together, they shape a path that feels less like compliance and more like collaboration—where meaning emerges not from certainty, but from the ongoing dialogue between blueprint and choice.

Purpose in Service: When Alignment Becomes Contribution

Purpose matures into service not through obligation, but through **stability**. When your nervous system is regulated and your choices are accurate, your presence naturally becomes beneficial to others. This is not because you are trying to help, fix, or save—but because coherence is contagious. Regulated systems support regulation around them. Clear decisions create clarity in shared spaces. Integrity invites trust.

Service, in this sense, is not martyrdom or self-erasure. It is **overflow**. You give what you have stabilized. When your energy is not spent compensating for misalignment, it becomes available for contribution. When your boundaries are intact, your generosity is sustainable. When your purpose is embodied, service stops feeling like sacrifice and starts feeling like expression.

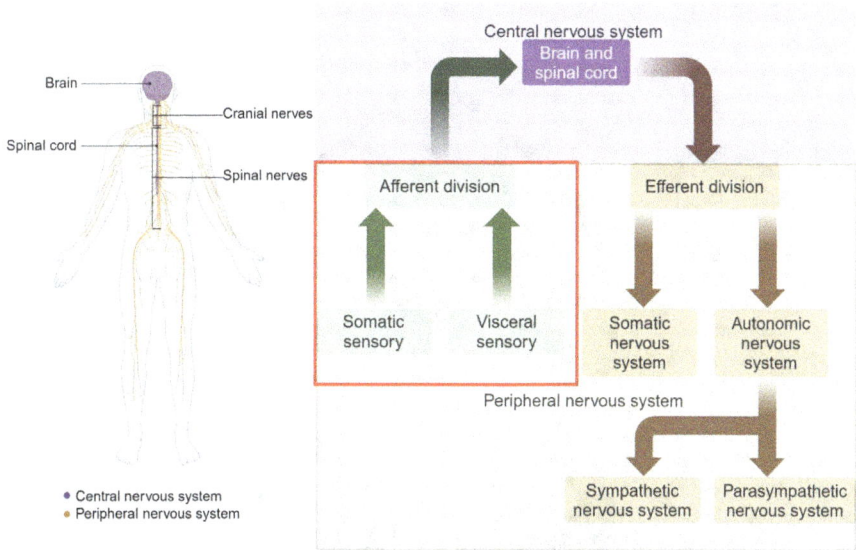

Importantly, service does not look the same for everyone. Alignment reveals *how* contribution wants to move through you. For some designs, service expresses as **guidance**—seeing systems clearly, offering perspective, optimizing pathways for others. For others, it emerges as **creation**—bringing ideas, beauty, or solutions into form. For others still, service lives in **restoration or protection**—holding safety, continuity, or care in spaces that need steadiness. And for many, it shows up as **synthesis**—connecting ideas, people, or disciplines into coherent wholes.

What unites these expressions is not role or scale, but **utility born of alignment**. You help because you are positioned to help. You contribute because your presence fits the need—not because you are seeking validation or trying to prove worth. In aligned service, effort feels proportional. Impact feels real. Recognition, when it comes, is a byproduct rather than a requirement.

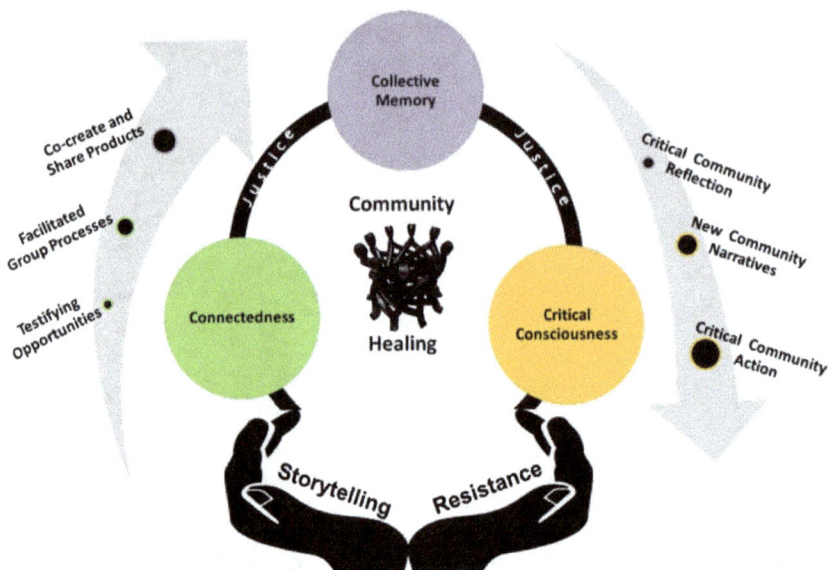

Figure 1. C-HeARTS Framework

This reframes contribution entirely. Service is no longer something you *do* to earn purpose. It is something that **emerges** when purpose is lived accurately. The more coherent you become, the more naturally your life intersects with the needs around you.

In this way, purpose and service are not separate paths.
They are the same movement—**alignment expressed outward**.

When alignment becomes contribution, you stop asking how to be useful.
Your usefulness becomes evident—quietly, consistently, and in ways that last.

Legacy as Frequency: What You Leave in the Field

Legacy is often mistaken for what is accumulated—titles earned, assets gathered, milestones recorded. But accumulation fades. **Frequency persists**. What truly lasts is the quality of presence you brought into spaces and the patterns your life stabilized for others. Legacy is not what you leave *behind*; it is what you leave *within* the field you touched.

Your regulation teaches others how to settle—often without a word spoken. When you pause instead of react, you demonstrate a new option for response. When you remain grounded under pressure, you model safety in uncertainty. Nervous systems learn from proximity. Coherence transmits. This is legacy as lived instruction.

Your boundaries model self-respect. Each time you honor your limits without guilt, you quietly normalize integrity. Others learn that care does not require collapse, and contribution does not require self-erasure. Over time, these modeled boundaries recalibrate what is considered acceptable, possible, and healthy within families, teams, and communities.

Your courage widens what feels possible. Courage is not loud—it is consistent. When you choose accuracy over approval, truth over convenience, and coherence over urgency, you expand the horizon for those watching and those who will come after you. In lineage terms, this is how ceilings lift. In community terms, this is how culture evolves.

This is **legacy as frequency**—the ripple your coherence leaves behind. It does not require recognition to be real. It does not depend on scale to be significant. Small, regulated actions compound into enduring impact because they alter the baseline of what feels safe, doable, and true.

When you live correctly, you don't need to manage legacy.
You don't curate it, protect it, or perform it.
It happens.

The field remembers—not as a story told, but as a pattern stabilized. Long after actions are forgotten, the frequency remains: in how others breathe under stress, how they choose under pressure, how they treat themselves and one another.

That is the quiet permanence of legacy.
Not what you owned.
Not what you achieved.
But **how you made coherence possible—by living it**.

Bridging Destiny and Free Will: Choosing the Next Right Step

Bridging destiny and free will is not a philosophical exercise—it is a **practical discipline**. Destiny does not require you to see the entire path at once. In fact, insisting on certainty about the future often pulls you out of alignment with the present. Free will functions best when it operates at a human scale: one choice, one adjustment, one accurate step at a time.

This is why the most powerful question is rarely *"What is my ultimate purpose?"*
It is *"What is the next right step from where I am now?"*

Smaller questions keep you grounded in reality. They invite responsiveness rather than fantasy. Instead of demanding a perfect outcome, they ask for **accurate engagement**. Accuracy is something your nervous system can support. Perfection is not.

Choosing the next right step honors both destiny and free will. Destiny provides direction—the general arc shaped by your design, values, and lineage. Free will supplies movement—the willingness to act, pause, or redirect based on real-time feedback. When these work together, life becomes navigable rather than overwhelming.

Let timing teach you. Timing is not passive waiting; it is **attentive patience**. Some insights arrive only after the body settles. Some doors open only after readiness matures. When coherence is prioritized—through regulation, clarity, and honest self-assessment—information becomes accessible. You begin to sense when to move and when to wait, not through fear, but through felt readiness.

Clarity, in this model, is **incremental**. It rarely arrives all at once. It sharpens through action taken in alignment, then refined through feedback. Each accurate step builds trust—trust in your perception, your body, and the dialogue you are in with life. From that trust, momentum grows naturally.

Momentum follows accuracy.
Not urgency.
Not pressure.
Not force.

When steps are chosen correctly—even if they are small—energy compounds. Resistance lessens. Options expand. You find yourself moving forward without needing constant reassurance.

This is how destiny and free will cooperate:
Destiny sets the tone.
Free will chooses the step.
Coherence keeps them in conversation.

And in that conversation, the future does not need to be perfectly known.
It only needs to be **met—accurately, one step at a time**.

Integration Practices: Embodying What You Now Know

Integration is where insight becomes lived wisdom. Without integration, understanding stays intellectual—interesting, but unstable. These practices are designed to be brief, repeatable, and **nervous-system friendly**, so what you've learned can settle into the body rather than remain in the mind. Think of them as invitations, not obligations. Their power lies in presence, not perfection.

Guided Reflection (5–7 minutes)

Begin by turning attention inward with curiosity rather than critique. Reflection is not analysis; it is listening.

What feels most settled in me right now?
This question orients you toward coherence instead of deficit. Noticing what is already stable builds trust in your internal compass and reduces the impulse to fix what isn't broken.

Where am I forcing—and what happens if I soften?
Forcing is often subtle: over-efforting, over-explaining, rushing clarity. This question invites an experiment in gentleness. Softening does not mean giving up; it means allowing regulation to lead.

What choice today would increase coherence by 10%?
Small adjustments compound. A ten-percent shift is realistic and actionable—changing tone, pacing, timing, or boundary. Coherence grows through increments.

Journaling Prompts

Journaling externalizes pattern so it can be seen clearly. Write without editing; let honesty lead.

Where has alignment already changed my life this year?
This grounds your journey in evidence. Recognizing progress reinforces trust in alignment as a reliable strategy.

What form of service emerges naturally from who I am?
Notice what you give without depletion—what feels obvious, easy, or meaningful when you're regulated. That's where service lives.

What legacy do I feel responsible to steward—not perform?
Stewardship is care over time. This question separates genuine responsibility from performative pressure.

Which choices bring my body relief rather than tension?
The body keeps accurate records. Relief is information. Let it guide you toward decisions that sustain rather than drain.

Short Integration Meditation (2 minutes)

Sit comfortably. Allow your spine to lengthen without effort. Slow your breath—no counting, just easing the pace. Place one hand on your chest and feel the warmth and contact.

Recall a recent moment of clarity—however small. Let the body recognize that state. Notice any softening, steadiness, or ease. Gently whisper to yourself: **"I choose accuracy."**

Sit for one minute. Don't force anything. Simply notice what settles.

These practices are not meant to be done once and forgotten. They are **anchors**—ways to return to coherence when life accelerates. Over time, they train your system to recognize alignment quickly and respond with confidence.

Integration is not about doing more.
It is about **letting what you know live through you**.

And when knowledge becomes embodied, destiny stops feeling abstract.
It becomes something you practice—quietly, accurately, and every day.

Affirmation

I am encoded with divine intelligence.
I choose coherence.
I serve through alignment.
My life is universal order—made manifest.

BONUS CHAPTER

Medical Astrology: The Body as a Celestial Map

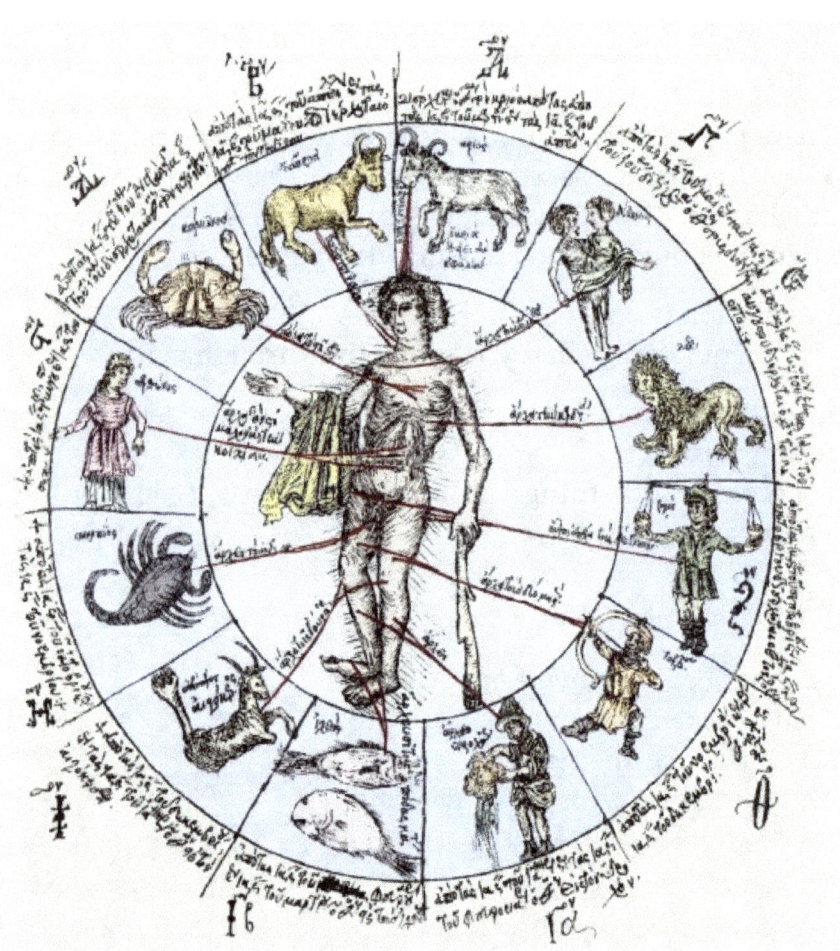

Listening to the Body Through Pattern

Medical Astrology is one of the oldest integrative healing frameworks known to humanity. Long before laboratory tests, imaging, and pharmaceuticals, ancient physicians observed the body through **relationship**—relationship to the seasons, to planetary cycles, to elemental balance, and to the rhythms of daily life. They understood the human being as a **microcosm of the cosmos**, where each organ system resonated with specific qualities of heat and cold, movement and stillness, expansion and contraction. Health, in this worldview, was not an isolated bodily event; it was a state of harmony between the individual and the larger rhythms of nature.

This perspective did not arise from superstition. It emerged from **long-term pattern observation**. Physicians noticed that certain conditions flared at predictable times, that emotional states influenced digestion and immunity, that sleep, light, and seasonal change altered vitality. Planetary symbolism provided a language to organize these observations—linking function to rhythm, and symptom to imbalance—long before physiology had names for hormones, neurotransmitters, or circadian genes.

This chapter does not replace medical care. It does not diagnose, prescribe, or treat disease. Instead, it **adds context** —a symbolic and rhythmic lens that helps you listen to the body with greater precision and compassion. Where modern medicine excels at identifying mechanisms and interventions, Medical Astrology excels at highlighting **where attention is needed**, **when support is most effective**, and **how stress and imbalance may be organizing themselves somatically**.

At its core, Medical Astrology teaches a simple but profound truth: **the body speaks in patterns**. Symptoms are not random failures or betrayals. They are communications—signals about balance, timing, stress load, adaptation, and unmet needs. Pain, fatigue, inflammation, and dysregulation are not moral judgments; they are feedback loops asking for recalibration.

When read alongside modern science, astrology becomes less about belief and more about **orientation**. It does not claim that planets cause illness. Rather, it offers a **map for where**

to listen. Just as a weather map does not cause a storm but helps you prepare for it, Medical Astrology helps you notice vulnerable systems, cyclical sensitivities, and the impact of stress on physiology—so interventions can be chosen with greater accuracy.

This integrative view aligns seamlessly with contemporary research. Chronobiology confirms that organs function on timing cycles. Psychoneuroimmunology demonstrates that emotional stress alters immune response. Neuroscience shows that perception, safety, and regulation directly affect bodily repair. Medical Astrology simply provides a **symbolic framework** that organizes these truths into an accessible language—one that honors the body as intelligent, adaptive, and responsive.

In this light, health is not about fixing a broken machine. It is about **restoring dialogue** with a living system. Medical Astrology invites you to shift from fighting symptoms to **interpreting signals**, from overriding the body to collaborating with it.

When you listen through rhythm instead of judgment, the body becomes not an obstacle to purpose—but a guide toward deeper alignment, resilience, and care.

The Zodiac and the Body: Archetypal Correspondence

In Medical Astrology, each zodiac sign governs both a **region of the body** and a **style of physiological expression**. These correspondences are not arbitrary. They reflect energetic principles—initiation, stabilization, circulation, digestion, regulation—that are mirrored in anatomy, endocrine function, neural signaling, and immune response. In this framework, the zodiac describes *how energy organizes itself in the body*, especially under stress, growth, or adaptation.

These associations do not claim causation. They describe **patterns of sensitivity and resilience**—areas where the body may speak more clearly when imbalance arises, and areas that respond powerfully when supported correctly.

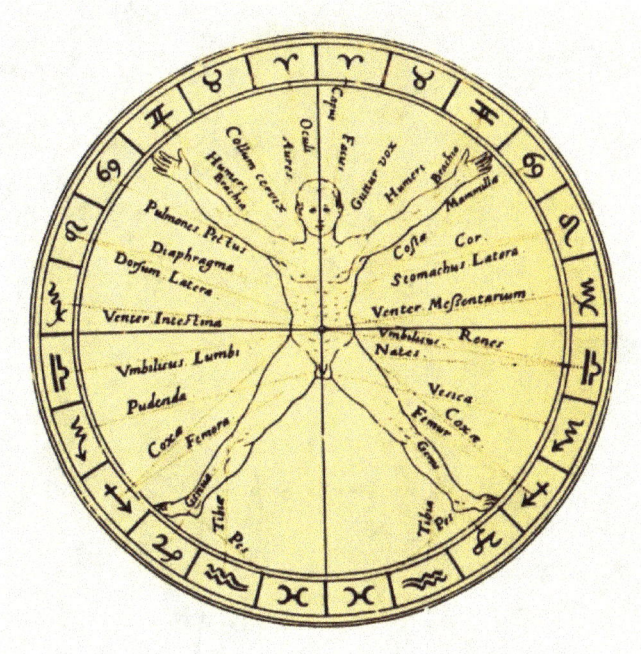

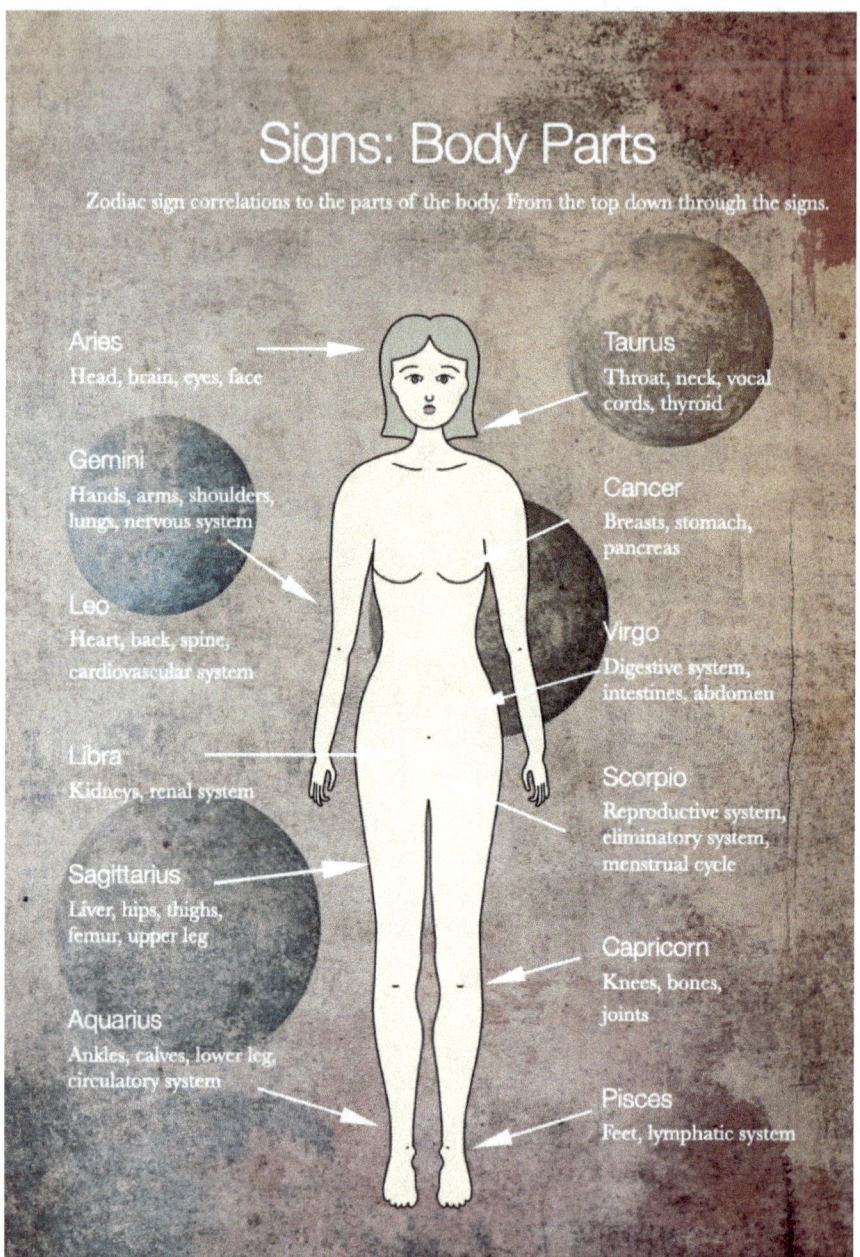

Aries — Head, brain, adrenal response (initiation, inflammation)

Aries governs initiation and rapid response. In the body,

this corresponds to the head, brain, and adrenal system—structures responsible for alertness, fight-or-flight activation, and decisiveness. Under stress, Aries energy may show up as headaches, tension, or inflammatory responses. When supported, it offers courage, vitality, and the capacity to act decisively without burnout.

Taurus — Throat, neck, thyroid (metabolism, voice, regulation)
Taurus governs stabilization and sustainability. Physiologically, this maps to the throat, neck, and thyroid—key regulators of metabolism, energy use, and expression. Stress here may manifest as throat tightness, voice suppression, or metabolic imbalance. When balanced, Taurus energy supports steady energy levels, grounded presence, and embodied self-expression.

Gemini — Lungs, arms, nervous system (communication, oxygenation)
Gemini rules movement, exchange, and information flow. This is reflected in the lungs, arms, and nervous system—systems responsible for oxygen delivery, signaling, and coordination. Dysregulation may appear as anxiety, shallow breathing, or nervous overstimulation. When supported, Gemini energy enhances adaptability, learning, and clear communication.

Cancer — Stomach, breasts, lymph (nourishment, immunity)
Cancer governs nourishment, protection, and emotional safety. In the body, this corresponds to the stomach, breasts, and lymphatic system—structures tied to digestion, immunity, and fluid balance. Stress can show up as digestive sensitivity or immune fluctuation. Balanced Cancer energy supports deep nourishment, emotional regulation, and immune resilience.

Leo — Heart, spine, circulation (vitality, coherence)
Leo represents vitality and self-expression. Its bodily correspondence—the heart, spine, and circulatory system

—reflects this central organizing force. Dysregulation may appear as fatigue, circulatory strain, or issues with posture and confidence. When supported, Leo energy promotes coherence, strong circulation, and embodied leadership.

Virgo — Intestines, digestion, assimilation (processing, absorption)
Virgo governs refinement, discernment, and integration. This maps to the intestines and digestive processes responsible for absorption and elimination. Under stress, Virgo energy may manifest as gut imbalance or over-analysis impacting digestion. When balanced, it supports efficient assimilation—nutritionally, emotionally, and cognitively.

Libra — Kidneys, lower back, balance systems (equilibrium)
Libra governs balance and reciprocity. In the body, this corresponds to the kidneys and lower back—systems regulating fluid balance, electrolytes, and structural symmetry. Stress may show up as lower back pain or issues with balance and boundaries. Supported Libra energy fosters equilibrium, relational harmony, and physiological balance.

Scorpio — Reproductive organs, elimination (detox, regeneration)
Scorpio governs transformation and renewal. Its correspondence with reproductive organs and elimination systems reflects detoxification, regeneration, and deep cellular processes. Dysregulation may present as hormonal imbalance or stagnation. When supported, Scorpio energy enables profound healing, resilience, and regenerative capacity.

Sagittarius — Hips, liver, mobility (expansion, metabolism)
Sagittarius represents expansion and exploration. In the body, this maps to the hips and liver—structures associated with movement, detoxification, and metabolic processing. Stress may appear as restlessness, hip tension, or liver overload. Balanced Sagittarius energy supports mobility, optimism, and metabolic efficiency.

Capricorn — Bones, joints, skin (structure, endurance)
Capricorn governs structure and longevity. Its bodily correspondence includes bones, joints, and skin—the framework and boundaries of the body. Under strain, this may show up as stiffness, joint pain, or chronic conditions. When supported, Capricorn energy provides endurance, stability, and long-term resilience.

Aquarius — Ankles, circulation, nervous regulation (flow, innovation)
Aquarius governs innovation and systemic flow. This corresponds to the ankles, circulation, and nervous regulation—areas related to distribution and connectivity. Dysregulation may appear as circulatory issues or nervous system sensitivity. Supported Aquarius energy enhances adaptability, circulation, and progressive regulation.

Pisces — Feet, immune/lymphatic sensitivity (integration, boundaries)
Pisces governs integration and permeability. In the body, this maps to the feet and immune/lymphatic systems—areas sensitive to boundaries and overall systemic load. Stress may manifest as fatigue or immune sensitivity. Balanced Pisces energy supports compassion, integration, and restorative healing.

These correspondences are **not diagnoses**. They are **zones of sensitivity and strength**—areas that may ask for extra care during stress, transition, or overload, and areas that can become sources of resilience when rhythm, nourishment, and regulation are honored. Used consciously, Medical Astrology helps you listen to the body as an intelligent system—one that communicates through pattern long before pathology appears.

Planets as Physiological Teachers

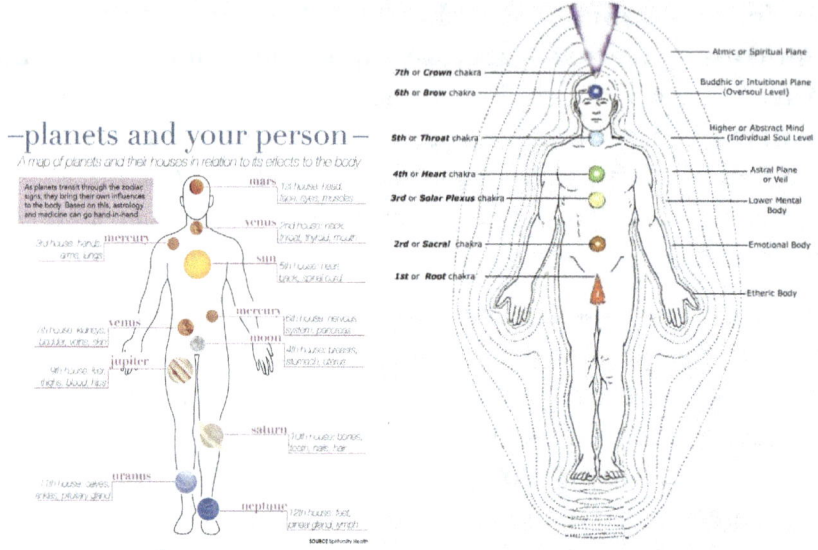

In Medical Astrology, planets are understood not as distant forces acting upon the body, but as **archetypal teachers** that describe *how energy moves through physiological systems*. Each planet corresponds to a specific mode of regulation—activation, nourishment, communication, repair—mirrored in anatomy, hormones, neural signaling, and immune response. Together, they form a symbolic language for understanding *patterns of function*, especially under stress or transition.

Sun — Vitality, circadian rhythm, life force
The Sun represents central vitality and coherence. Physiologically, it reflects circadian regulation, mitochondrial energy production, and overall life force. When solar energy is balanced, energy feels steady and purpose-driven. When stressed—through sleep disruption, burnout, or loss of meaning—the body may express fatigue, weakened immunity, or diminished resilience.

Moon — Fluids, digestion, emotional-somatic memory
The Moon governs rhythm, fluids, and memory. In the body, this shows up in digestion, lymphatic flow, hormonal tides, and emotional-somatic imprinting. Lunar stress can manifest

as digestive sensitivity, fluid retention, sleep disturbances, or mood-linked symptoms. When supported, lunar balance enhances nourishment, emotional regulation, and restorative rest.

Mercury — Nervous system, cognition, signaling
Mercury describes communication and processing. Physiologically, it maps to the nervous system, breath, and cognitive signaling. Under strain, Mercury-related imbalance may appear as anxiety, racing thoughts, shallow breathing, or sensory overload. When regulated, Mercury supports clarity, adaptability, and efficient information flow.

Venus — Hormones, glucose balance, pleasure–recovery axis
Venus governs attraction, balance, and pleasure. In the body, this corresponds to hormonal harmony, glucose regulation, and the ability to receive rest and enjoyment. Venus stress may show up as hormonal imbalance, sugar dysregulation, or difficulty relaxing. Balanced Venus energy supports recovery, sweetness in life, and metabolic ease.

Mars — Inflammation, muscle tone, immune activation
Mars represents action and defense. Physiologically, it aligns with muscle tone, inflammation, and immune activation. When Mars is overactivated—through chronic stress or overexertion—the body may show inflammation, tension, or irritability. When underexpressed, vitality can feel low. Balanced Mars supports healthy boundaries, strength, and responsive immunity.

Jupiter — Growth, liver, nutrient processing
Jupiter governs expansion and assimilation. In the body, this reflects liver function, nutrient processing, and growth cycles. Excessive Jupiter energy may manifest as overindulgence or metabolic strain; deficiency may show as stagnation or lack of optimism. Balanced Jupiter supports robust digestion, detox support, and healthy expansion.

Saturn — Structure, bones, chronic patterns
Saturn represents structure and endurance. Physiologically, it corresponds to bones, joints, skin, and long-term patterns. Saturn stress often appears as stiffness, chronic conditions, or fatigue linked to over-responsibility. When supported, Saturn provides stability, integrity, and sustainable strength.

Uranus — Electrical signaling, sudden shifts
Uranus governs innovation and disruption. In the body, it maps to electrical signaling, sudden neurological shifts, and stress reactivity. Uranian imbalance may present as nervous system sensitivity, insomnia, or sudden symptom changes. Balanced Uranus supports adaptability, insight, and flexible regulation.

Neptune — Sensitivity, immunity, permeability
Neptune governs dissolution and permeability. Physiologically, it aligns with immune sensitivity, boundaries, and detox pathways. Stress here may show up as fatigue, immune vulnerability, or difficulty distinguishing internal from external stressors. When supported, Neptune enhances compassion, integration, and restorative healing.

Pluto — Detoxification, cellular regeneration
Pluto represents deep transformation. In the body, it corresponds to detoxification, elimination, and cellular regeneration. Plutonian stress may surface as issues requiring deep healing or long-term transformation. Balanced Pluto supports renewal, resilience, and profound regenerative capacity.

When planetary energies are **stressed—by transits, environment, lifestyle, or emotional load—the body often expresses it symbolically**. Fatigue, tension, inflammation, or dysregulation are not random failures; they are signals indicating which *mode of regulation* needs attention. Medical Astrology offers a compassionate framework for listening to these signals early—so support can be applied through rhythm, recovery, and care—before imbalance becomes entrenched.

In this way, planets become teachers not of fate, but of **physiological wisdom**—guiding you toward alignment through the body's own language of pattern and response.

Houses and Health: Where Stress Manifests

In Medical Astrology, **houses describe where life energy expresses—and where stress tends to accumulate**. While every house has physiological relevance, the **6th and 12th houses** are central to understanding health, resilience, and breakdown. Together, they form a feedback loop between *daily function* and *deep restoration*.

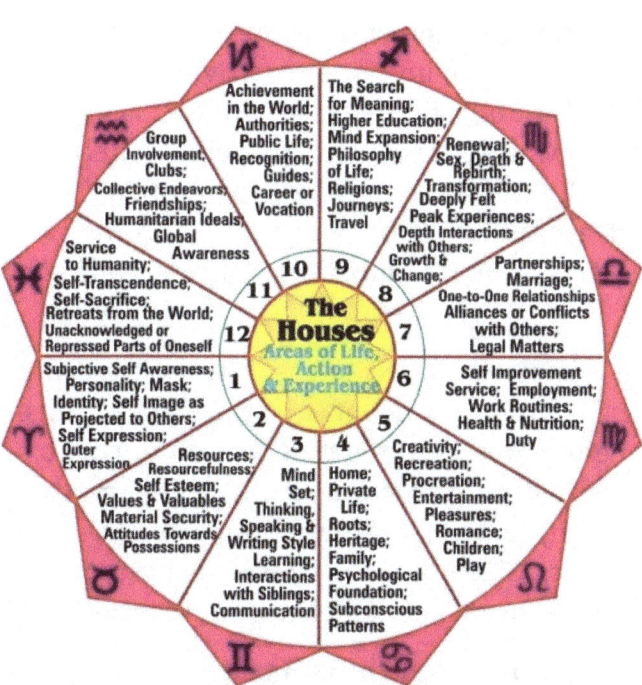

The 6th House: Daily Rhythms, Work, and Health Routines

The 6th house governs the mechanics of everyday life—sleep

timing, nutrition, movement, work habits, and the small choices repeated until they become physiology. It reflects how the body manages stress on a day-to-day basis. When this house is emphasized, the individual is often **highly sensitive to routine**. Small disruptions—irregular meals, inconsistent sleep, misaligned workloads—can have outsized effects on energy, digestion, mood, and immunity.

Health challenges connected to the 6th house rarely respond to dramatic interventions alone. They improve through **precision and consistency**: refining schedules, simplifying inputs, and matching effort to energy capacity. The body here asks for *maintenance*, not heroics. When rhythm is honored, symptoms often soften without force.

The 12th House: The Unconscious, Immunity, and Chronic Stress

The 12th house governs what operates beneath awareness—long-term stress load, immune sensitivity, emotional residue, and the cost of unprocessed experience. It is associated with rest, withdrawal, dreams, and the body's need to dissolve accumulated tension. Heavy activity here often points to **hidden stress**: patterns of overgiving, chronic vigilance, or suppressed emotion that quietly tax the nervous and immune systems.

Health manifestations tied to the 12th house can feel vague or cyclical—fatigue without a clear cause, sensitivity to environments, or symptoms that worsen during overwhelm. Healing here does not come from doing more. It comes from **allowing less**—less stimulation, less pressure, less self-abandonment. Sleep quality, nervous system safety, and periods of true disengagement become essential medicine.

Refining Rhythm, Not Pushing Harder

When the 6th and 12th houses are emphasized, the body is asking for a specific lesson: **health is restored through rhythm, not resistance**. Stress accumulates when daily demands exceed recovery capacity. Balance returns when effort and rest are recalibrated with honesty.

Rather than overriding symptoms, Medical Astrology invites a different approach:

- Adjust routines before pathology forms

- Protect sleep and recovery as non-negotiables

- Treat sensitivity as information, not weakness

In this framework, improvement comes not from intensity, but from *attunement*. The body is not asking to be conquered. It is asking to be listened to—at the level of timing, pace, and care.

When rhythm is refined, stress loses its grip. And when stress releases, the body remembers how to heal itself.

Elements, Temperament, and Regulation

Medical Astrology approaches health through **elemental balance**—a dynamic conversation between temperament, environment, and regulation. The four elements are not abstractions; they describe **how energy moves through physiology**. Each element carries strengths and vulnerabilities, and each requires specific forms of support to remain coherent. Imbalance does not mean something is wrong—it means inputs no longer match needs.

The Four Elements of Western Herbalism
- traditional interpretation -

△	**Fire** is hot & dry. It transforms energy. Most active during summer & childhood.
△	**Air** is hot & moist. It adapts energy. Most active during spring & youth.
▽	**Water** is moist & cold. It receives energy. Most active during winter & old age.
▽	**Earth** is cold & dry. It condenses energy. Most active during autumn & middle age.

Fire: Heat, Inflammation, Adrenal Drive

Fire governs initiation, metabolism, and mobilization. In the body, excess Fire can show up as inflammation, tension, irritability, insomnia, or adrenal exhaustion from constant activation. Fire-dominant temperaments often thrive on purpose and momentum, but they burn out when pacing is ignored.

Regulation for Fire is not suppression—it is **cooling and containment**. Slower rhythms, adequate sleep, mineral support, anti-inflammatory nourishment, and intentional rest allow Fire to express as vitality rather than volatility. When Fire is regulated, energy becomes sustainable instead of explosive.

Earth: Density, Structure, and Stagnation

Earth governs stability, structure, and assimilation. When Earth is excessive or under-supported, the body may experience heaviness, sluggish digestion, fluid retention, or resistance to change. Earth-dominant systems can become stuck—not because they are broken, but because movement has slowed too much.

Earth thrives with **gentle activation**: regular movement, hydration, fiber-rich nourishment, and routine circulation. Consistency is medicine here—but rigidity is not. When Earth flows, endurance becomes resilience rather than burden.

Air: Nervous Activity and Cognitive Load

Air governs communication, signaling, and exchange—especially within the nervous system. Excess Air often presents as anxiety, restlessness, shallow breathing, overthinking, or sleep disruption. Air-dominant temperaments are highly perceptive, but can become dysregulated by overstimulation.

Regulation for Air comes through **grounding and breath regulation**. Slow, extended exhales, body-based practices, reduced sensory input, and stable routines help settle neural overactivity. When Air is balanced, clarity replaces agitation and insight replaces overwhelm.

Water: Fluidity, Emotion, and Absorption

Water governs fluids, immunity, and emotional processing. Excess Water can appear as fluid retention, lethargy, mood saturation, or difficulty with boundaries—taking on more than the system can process. Water-dominant bodies are deeply intuitive, but can become overwhelmed without containment.

Water requires **structure and drainage**. Clear boundaries, rhythmic routines, lymphatic support, movement that encourages flow, and emotional expression prevent stagnation. When Water is regulated, empathy becomes wisdom rather than exhaustion.

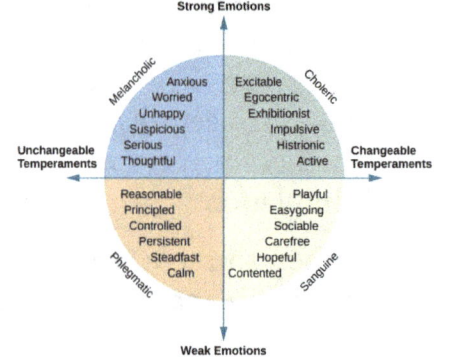

Dynamic Balance, Not Perfection

Elemental balance is not static. Needs shift with stress, seasons, age, and life events. Health emerges when **inputs match elemental needs in real time**—when cooling meets heat, movement meets density, grounding meets stimulation, and structure meets fluidity.

Medical Astrology does not ask you to eliminate any element. Each one is necessary. The goal is **coherence**, not dominance.

When temperament is honored and regulation is responsive, the body stops compensating—and starts collaborating.

Timing Matters: Lunar & Transit Awareness

One of the most practical contributions of Medical Astrology is its emphasis on **timing**. Health is not only about *what* you do, but *when* you do it. The body operates in cycles—daily, monthly, seasonal—and when actions align with those cycles, regulation requires less effort. When timing is ignored, even well-intentioned practices can feel exhausting or ineffective.

The Moon as a Regulator of the Body
The Moon exerts a measurable influence on fluids, circadian rhythm, and emotional processing. Given that the human body is largely water, it is unsurprising that lunar phases

correlate with shifts in sleep quality, appetite, digestion, and mood. Many people notice increased sensitivity, vivid dreams, or emotional intensity during certain phases—not because the Moon causes imbalance, but because it **amplifies what is already present**.

From a Medical Astrology lens, the Moon reflects the body's *immediate state*. It highlights how well you are adapting, digesting, and recovering in real time. Paying attention to lunar rhythms can therefore improve self-regulation without adding complexity.

Lunar Phases as Supportive Rhythms
Rather than rigid rules, lunar awareness offers **guiding rhythms**:

- **New Moon** often coincides with lower energy and inward focus. This can be a supportive time for rest, intention-setting, gentle resets, or beginning low-demand practices.

- **Waxing Moon** tends to support building energy —learning, strengthening habits, gradual increases in activity.

- **Full Moon** frequently amplifies emotion, stimulation, and fluid movement. For some, this is a time of insight or expression; for others, it calls for extra grounding and sleep protection.

- **Waning Moon** supports release—simplifying, detoxifying, completing cycles, and letting go of what is no longer needed.

These patterns are not prescriptive. They are **invitations**—ways to work *with* physiology rather than overriding it.

Transit Awareness: Context, Not Control
Beyond the Moon, broader planetary transits can correlate

with periods of increased stress, fatigue, or recovery needs. In Medical Astrology, this awareness is used not to predict illness, but to **adjust expectations**. During demanding transits, the body may require more rest, slower pacing, or additional support. During supportive ones, resilience and recovery may come more easily.

This reframes health challenges. Instead of asking, "What is wrong with me?" the question becomes, "What season am I in—and what does my body need right now?"

Health Through Rhythm, Not Rigidity

Medical Astrology does not ask you to schedule life around the sky. It invites you to notice **when effort is met with ease and when it meets resistance**. Over time, this awareness cultivates trust in your internal timing—knowing when to push, when to pause, and when to restore.

When actions respect rhythm, the nervous system relaxes. Healing becomes more efficient. And health stops feeling like a battle against the body—and starts feeling like a partnership with time itself.

Scientific Bridge: Why This Works Symbolically

Medical Astrology endures not because it competes with science, but because it **anticipates it symbolically**. Long before laboratories could measure hormones, neural firing, or immune signaling, physicians tracked patterns—when symptoms appeared, how seasons altered vitality, why stress disrupted digestion or sleep. Modern research now provides the mechanisms that explain why rhythm-based care works.

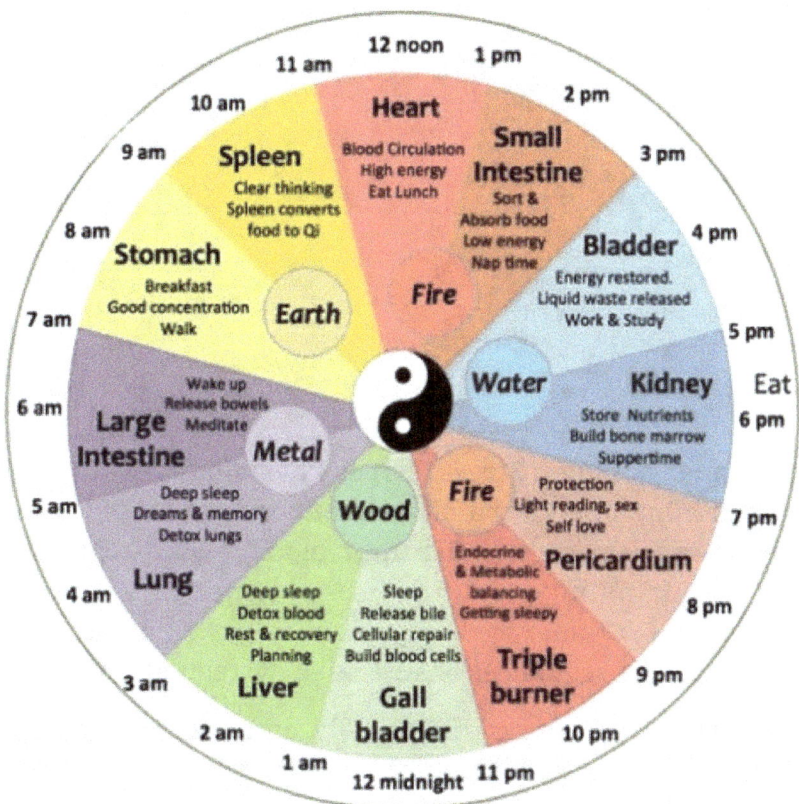

Chronobiology: The Body Runs on Time

Chronobiology demonstrates that organs and systems operate on internal clocks. Digestion, detoxification, hormone release, immune activity, and tissue repair all follow predictable timing preferences. When behaviors—sleep, meals, work, recovery—align with these rhythms, physiological efficiency improves. When timing is disrupted, inflammation, metabolic dysregulation, and fatigue increase.

Astrology mirrors this insight symbolically by emphasizing cycles and timing. It offers a language for *when* support is most effective, without claiming causation. The map is symbolic;

the biology is real.

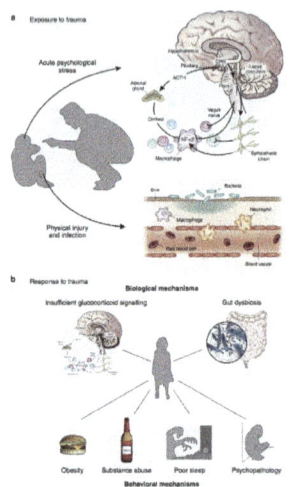

Neuroendocrinology: Stress Shapes Physiology

Research in neuroendocrinology confirms that chronic stress alters cortisol patterns, disrupts blood sugar regulation, suppresses immunity, and increases systemic inflammation. These effects are not psychological in origin alone—they are biochemical consequences of sustained dysregulation.

Astrological frameworks historically associated stress with imbalance, excess heat, depletion, or stagnation—descriptions that align closely with modern understandings of inflammatory load and hormonal strain. The symbolism points toward regulation; the science explains how it occurs.

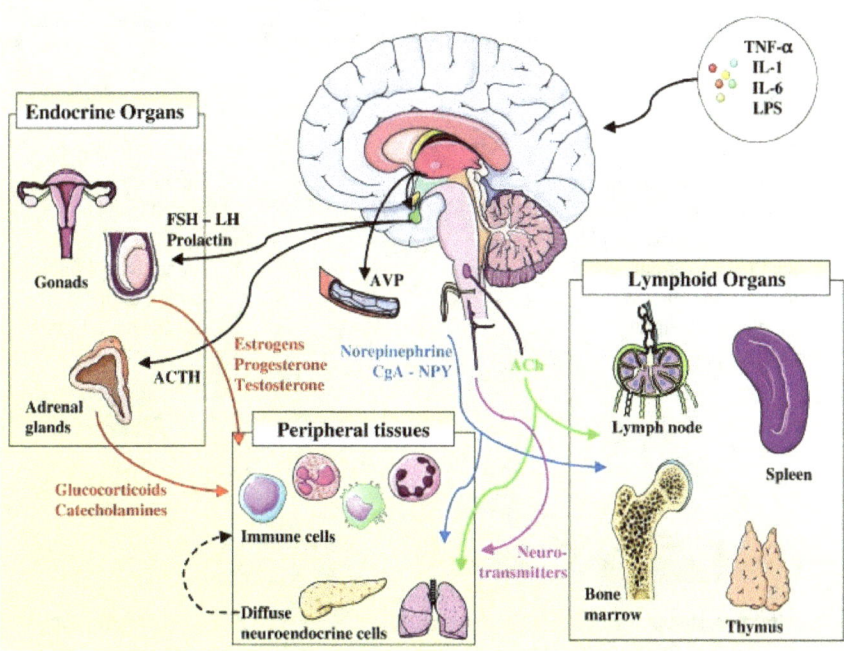

Psychoneuroimmunology: Emotion and Immunity Are Linked

Psychoneuroimmunology has firmly established that emotional states influence immune function. Grief, fear, and chronic vigilance suppress immune response, while safety, connection, and regulation enhance it. The body does not separate emotion from physiology; it integrates them continuously.

Medical Astrology reflects this integration by associating emotional states with specific systems and rhythms. Again, astrology does not claim that symbols cause outcomes. It **maps correspondence**, helping individuals recognize when emotional load may be translating into physical stress.

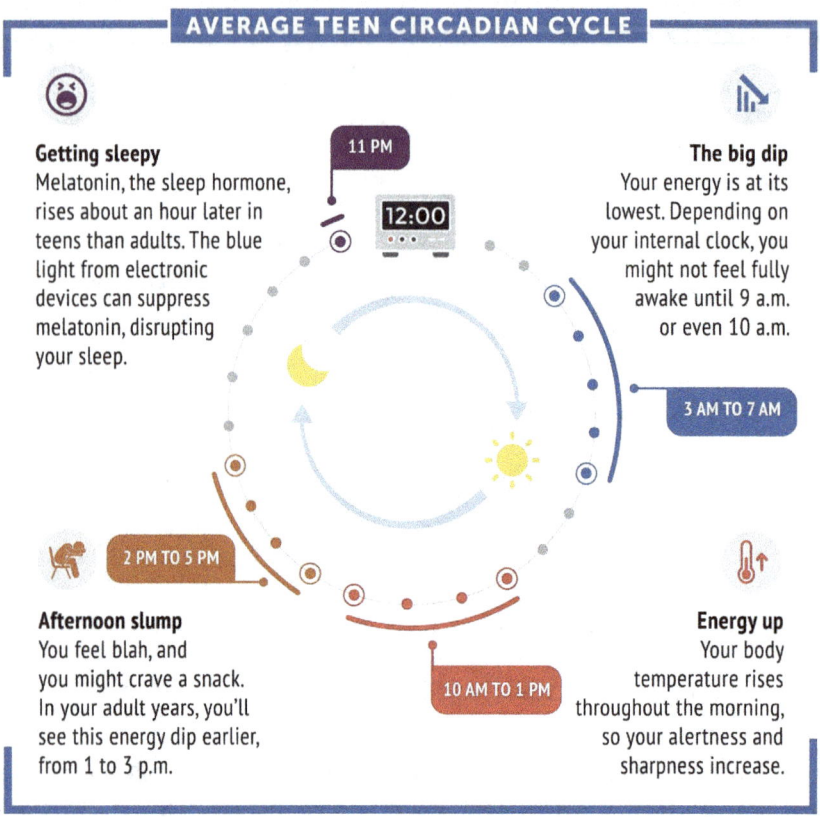

Symbolic Mirrors, Biological Truths

Astrology functions as a **pattern-recognition interface**—a way to translate complex, multi-system interactions into an accessible framework. It does not replace biology, diagnostics, or treatment. It mirrors biological reality symbolically, offering orientation rather than instruction.

When individuals align behavior with timing, capacity, and regulation—whether guided by chronobiology, neuroscience, or symbolic systems—the result is the same: reduced stress load, improved coherence, and more sustainable health.

The power of Medical Astrology lies not in prediction, but in **attunement**. It reminds us that healing is rhythmic, contextual, and relational. Science explains the mechanisms.

Astrology helps us remember to listen.

PRACTICAL TOOL: YOUR MEDICAL ASTROLOGY CHECK-IN

This check-in is designed to help you **translate insight into regulation**. It is not diagnostic, predictive, or prescriptive. It is observational—an invitation to notice patterns between stress, rhythm, and bodily response. The goal is not to fix the body, but to **listen to it more accurately**.

Step 1: Note Your Sun, Moon, And Rising Signs

These three placements describe how vitality, emotional processing, and daily interface with the world are expressed in the body.

- **Sun** reflects baseline vitality, energy distribution, and how life force is sustained.

- **Moon** reflects fluid balance, digestion, sleep quality, emotional-somatic memory, and stress sensitivity.

- **Rising (Ascendant)** reflects posture, physical interface with the environment, and how stress enters the system.

Write these three signs down before moving forward.

Step 2: Identify Their Corresponding Body Zones

Using the zodiac-to-body correspondences, identify the anatomical regions linked to each sign. These zones are **areas of sensitivity and strength**, not weakness.

For example:

- A strong lunar placement may show up in digestion, sleep, or lymphatic patterns.

- A stressed ascendant may appear as muscle tension, headaches, or postural fatigue.

- Sun-ruled areas often signal when vitality is being overdrawn or undernourished.

Notice patterns over time, not isolated symptoms.

Step 3: Observe What Happens During Stress

Instead of asking "What's wrong?", ask:

- Where does tension appear first?

- Which system becomes reactive when I'm overwhelmed?

- What sensations repeat when I push past my limits?

This step reframes symptoms as **feedback**, not failure. The body is showing you *where regulation breaks down first* under pressure.

Step 4: Adjust Rhythm Before Adding Intensity

Before adding supplements, workouts, or productivity strategies, adjust **rhythm**:

- Sleep timing and consistency

- Hydration and nourishment cadence

- Work/rest pacing

- Sensory input (noise, light, screens)

Often, symptoms soften when rhythm is restored—without force. Intensity can come later, if needed.

Reflection Prompt

> **Where is my body asking for rhythm rather than force?**

Sit with this question without rushing to solve it. Let the answer emerge through sensation, not analysis.

Why This Tool Matters

This check-in shifts the relationship with your body from adversarial to collaborative. It honors a truth both ancient and modern science agree on: **regulation precedes repair**.

Medical Astrology does not tell you what to do. It helps you notice *where to listen first*. And when rhythm is restored, the body often does the rest on its own.

Ethical Reminder

Medical Astrology is a **complementary, reflective framework**, not a diagnostic or treatment system. It does not replace clinical evaluation, medical testing, or evidence-based care. Physical symptoms, emotional distress, and chronic conditions deserve assessment and support from **qualified healthcare professionals** trained to diagnose and treat illness safely.

This lens is offered to **enhance awareness**, not to encourage self-diagnosis or self-treatment. Its purpose is to help you notice patterns of stress, timing, rhythm, and regulation—so you can communicate more clearly with your care team, make supportive lifestyle adjustments, and engage your health with greater compassion and responsibility.

Using Medical Astrology ethically means:

- Seeking medical evaluation when symptoms arise or persist

- Following professional guidance for treatment and medication

- Viewing astrological insights as contextual information, not medical conclusions

- Prioritizing safety, consent, and evidence-based care at all times

When used responsibly, Medical Astrology can support **better listening, earlier awareness, and more attuned self-care**—but it should never be used to replace medical advice, delay treatment, or override professional judgment.

In short:
Use this framework to **listen better**, not to self-treat.

CONCLUSION

Remembering What You've Always Been

You have now traveled two paths that were never separate.

Through *Awakened Science*, you were shown that modern physics, neuroscience, and biology do not dismantle spirituality—they **confirm it**. Through *Encoded in the Stars*, you were shown that your life is not an accident moving blindly through time, but a **patterned intelligence unfolding with intention**. Together, these works illuminate a single truth:

The universe has always been with you—because you have always been of it.

From the birth of the cosmos to the moment you took your first breath, everything has been intertwined. Divinely entangled. Guiding, leading, healing, and expanding through relationship rather than separation. You are not a visitor in this universe—you are an expression of it.

When you choose to navigate life from a higher mind—one that sees beyond fear, scarcity, and randomness—you begin to recognize that **nothing is wasted**. Every road taken, every delay, every disruption, every relationship, every ending becomes legible. Each experience serves a purpose:
a lesson,
an initiation,
an activation,
a chance to complete a cycle,
or an invitation to revisit something once missed—but now

ready to be integrated.

This understanding echoes across traditions. Scripture reminds us, in **1 Corinthians 10:13**, that no trial arrives without provision—that endurance is paired with a way through. Spiritual wisdom echoes the same truth in a different language: **those entrusted with the heaviest work are also entrusted with the greatest capacity to survive it**.

Across cultures, it is understood that the cycle breakers, the healers, the truth-tellers, the so-called black sheep of family lines are not anomalies—they are *assignments*. They are often given the hardest roads not because they are being punished, but because **they are equipped**. Equipped with resilience. With perception. With the capacity to thrive where others could not, and to build lives that previous generations were never permitted to imagine.

These are the ones who endure what broke those before them—and then go on to transform it. They are blessed not with ease, but with **gifts**: insight, intuition, strength, and the courage to choose differently. Their lives become bridges between what was endured and what is now possible.

When you move in alignment—with the universe, with your ancestors, with your higher self, and with the Most High—you are never left without support. Guidance appears. Endurance rises. Pathways open. Not always comfortably, but **reliably**.

This is not blind faith.
It is conscious relationship.

Destiny, as you have learned, is not something that happens *to* you. It is something that moves *through* you—responsive to your awareness, your choices, and your willingness to listen. When you live in coherence with your design, your lineage, and your inner knowing, life does not become effortless—but it becomes **meaningful**.

And meaning changes everything.

You are not here to escape your story.
You are here to **complete it**.
Not by erasing the past, but by carrying it forward with wisdom, regulation, and love.

May you walk forward knowing this:
You are encoded with divine intelligence.
Your life is not random—it is relational.
And every step you take in awareness becomes an act of creation.

The universe is not waiting for you to become something else.
It has been waiting for you to **remember who you already are**.

ENCODED IN THE STARS | 431

APPENDIX A — Glossary of Cosmic Sciences

This glossary offers clear, grounded definitions for key concepts used throughout *Encoded in the Stars*. These terms are presented as **descriptive frameworks**, not dogma—languages for understanding pattern, rhythm, and relationship.

Astrocartography
A branch of astrology that maps planetary positions from a natal chart onto geographic locations, highlighting regions where specific life themes are energetically emphasized.

Astrology (Psychological / Archetypal)
A symbolic system that interprets planetary movements and placements as reflections of psychological patterns, developmental themes, and cycles of experience—not deterministic prediction.

Biofield
The electromagnetic and energetic field generated by the human body, interacting continuously with internal physiology and external environmental fields.

Chronobiology
The scientific study of biological rhythms, including circadian, ultradian, and infradian cycles that regulate sleep, hormones, metabolism, and immunity.

Coherence
A state in which physiological systems—particularly heart, brain, and nervous system—are synchronized, resulting in improved regulation, clarity, and resilience.

Epigenetics
The study of how environmental factors, stress, nutrition, and emotional experience influence gene expression without altering DNA sequence.

Human Design
An integrative system synthesizing astrology, the I Ching,

Kabbalah, chakra theory, and genetics to describe energy mechanics, decision-making strategies, and alignment.

Karma (Evolutionary Context)
Momentum created by past actions, experiences, and adaptations—biological, psychological, and energetic—seeking integration rather than punishment.

Life Path Number
In numerology, the primary vibrational frequency derived from one's birth date, describing how learning, growth, and purpose unfold.

Medical Astrology
A symbolic framework linking zodiac signs, planets, elements, and houses to physiological systems and rhythms, used for awareness—not diagnosis.

Morphic Resonance
A hypothesis proposed by Rupert Sheldrake suggesting that systems inherit collective memory through resonance across time.

Neuroplasticity
The brain's ability to reorganize neural pathways in response to experience, learning, and environment.

Synchronicity
A concept introduced by Carl Jung describing meaningful coincidence—events linked by meaning rather than linear causation.

APPENDIX B — Recommended Tools & Platforms

The following tools support self-study, reflection, and integration. Inclusion does not imply endorsement of interpretation style—use discernment and personal resonance.

Astrology & Astrocartography

- **Astro.com (Astrodienst)** — natal charts, transits, astrocartography maps

- **Astro-Seek.com** — chart calculation and house/system comparisons

Human Design

- **MyHumanDesign.com** — foundational charts and type descriptions

- **Genetic Matrix** — advanced Human Design analytics

Numerology

- **World Numerology** — Life Path, Expression, and Soul Urge calculations

- **Cafe Astrology (Numerology section)** — accessible breakdowns

Health, Rhythm & Coherence

- **HeartMath Institute** — coherence training and heart-brain research

- **Oura / WHOOP / Garmin (HRV tools)** — rhythm and recovery tracking

These tools are most effective when used as **mirrors**, not authorities.

APPENDIX C — Scientific & Metaphysical Research Citations

This book draws from interdisciplinary research across science, psychology, and spirituality. Below is a representative foundation for further study.

Scientific Foundations

- Lipton, B. — *The Biology of Belief* (Epigenetics)
- Yehuda, R. et al. — Epigenetic transmission of trauma
- McCraty, R. et al. — Heart-brain coherence (HeartMath Institute)
- Sapolsky, R. — Stress physiology and cortisol research
- Porges, S. — Polyvagal Theory
- Siegel, D. — Interpersonal neurobiology

Psychology & Consciousness

- Jung, C.G. — *Synchronicity: An Acausal Connecting Principle*
- Kahneman, D. — Cognitive processing and intuition
- van der Kolk, B. — Trauma and somatic memory

Physics & Systems Theory

- Bohm, D. — Implicate order and wholeness
- Prigogine, I. — Chaos theory and self-organizing systems

- Penrose, R. — Consciousness and quantum theory

Metaphysical & Cross-Cultural Sources

- I Ching (Book of Changes)

- Kabbalistic Tree of Life

- African and Indigenous ancestral cosmologies

- Eastern philosophies of karma and cyclic time

Closing Note on the Appendices

These appendices are not meant to overwhelm—they are meant to **anchor**. They exist so that insight does not dissolve once the final page is turned.

Knowledge becomes wisdom when it is **lived**.
Destiny becomes embodied when awareness becomes practice.

Return to these pages whenever alignment feels unclear.
They are not answers.
They are reminders.

www.ingramcontent.com/pod-product-compliance
Lightning Source LLC
Chambersburg PA
CBHW070306230426
43664CB00015B/2647